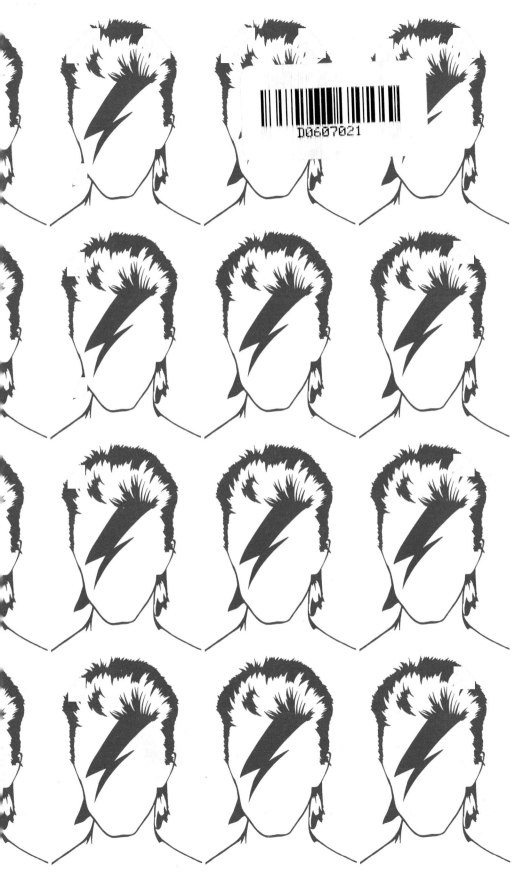

D0607021

Ziggyology

For Spike Reeve-Daniels.

A Starman is born.

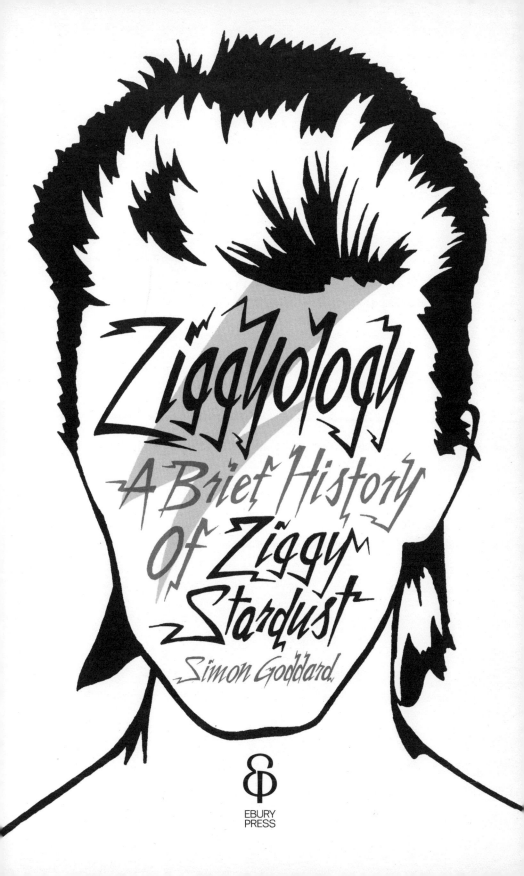

Ziggyology

A Brief History Of Ziggy Stardust

Simon Goddard

EBURY
PRESS

1 3 5 7 9 10 8 6 4 2

First published in 2013 by Ebury Press, an imprint of Ebury Publishing
A Random House Group company

Copyright © Simon Goddard 2013

Simon Goddard has asserted his right to be identified as the author of this Work
in accordance with the Copyright, Designs and Patents Act 1988

The Random House Group Limited Reg. No. 954009

Addresses for companies within the Random House Group can be found at
www.randomhouse.co.uk

A CIP catalogue record for this book is available from the British Library

The Random House Group Limited supports the Forest Stewardship Council® (FSC®),
the leading international forest-certification organisation. Our books carrying the
FSC label are printed on FSC®-certified paper. FSC is the only forest-certification
scheme supported by the leading environmental organisations, including Greenpeace.
Our paper procurement policy can be found at www.randomhouse.co.uk/environment

Designed and set by seagulls.net

Printed and bound in Great Britain by Clays Ltd, St Ives PLC

ISBN 9780091948887

To buy books by your favourite authors and register for offers visit
www.randomhouse.co.uk

CONTENTS

BOOK II: THE EARTH UNDER THE STARMAN

PREFACE

This is a book about Ziggy Stardust, the alien pop star who inhabited the mind, voice and trousers of David Bowie from, roughly, late 1971 until his death on stage at the Hammersmith Odeon on 3 July 1973.

It is the story of how Ziggy entered Bowie's head and what happened once he got there.

It is the story of how long it took human civilisation to arrive at the concept of Ziggy Stardust and how short it took for one human to do his bidding before resorting to suicide.

This book is mostly the story of Ziggy Stardust but only sometimes the story of David Bowie.

All events, places and characters in this book are based on factual documentary evidence and eyewitness testimony.

This book was written out of love –

For Ziggy, Ronno, Weird and Gilly.

For art and outer space.

For glamour and rock 'n' roll.

For youth and hope.

For glitter and nail paint.

And for all those who, like its author, choose to live looking up at the stars.

Simon Goddard
Telephone kiosk 0207 734 8719
London

'If you really want to make an apple pie from scratch, you must first invent the universe.'

CARL SAGAN

PROLOGUE

THE EVE OF NO MORE

'Since the dawn of time over 100 billion human beings have walked on this planet.

Now, 100 billion is about the number of stars in our Milky Way galaxy. This means that for everyone who's ever lived there could be a star.

Stars are suns with planets circling around them. So isn't it an interesting thought that there's enough land in the sky for everyone to have a whole world?

We don't know how many of those worlds are inhabited, or by what kinds of creatures, but one day we should know. Perhaps by radio. Perhaps by other means. Perhaps by contact.

The impact of that on the human race will be profound.'

ARTHUR C. CLARKE

To any eyes of any creatures on any worlds that might be peering across the gulf of space to the planet Earth, it is a Tuesday just like any other Tuesday. So named by England's Nordic ancestors after their god of war, Tiw. Or as the Romans called him, Mars.

Just another day of Mars in the city of London. Mankind swarming to and fro in its infinite complacency. Sweetly oblivious to any remote yet penetrating interstellar gaze. Blissfully unaware that anyone or anything out there in the endless outreach of space might be tuning in, trying to decipher and decode the strange signals of human life. That their words, phrases, songs, sounds, wild halloo and brutal noise could be echoing through the cosmos towards alien ears in a random transmission of exotic gibberish. Of work-to-rule, IRA, strip-kings, picket lines, Double Diamond, Nimble, Mark Phillips and Princess Anne. Of upstairs, downstairs, Watergate, Follyfoot, Fenn Street, Colditz and 'Honey, can the can'. Of Hawkeye, Hot Lips, Bobby Crush, Elephant Boy, Edward Heath, Idi Amin and Dave Allen At Large. Of 'Skweeze me!', 'It's frothy, man', 'Stay on the bus, forget about us', 'Wombling free', 'Nice one, Cyril' and 'Is there life on Mars?'

As the planet spins the sun shines high and bright over London, hitting 25 degrees as the clock tightly ticks towards noon. Our focus drifts south, to the edge of the city in the suburb of Bromley, through the streets where H. G. Wells once scampered with youthful dreams of mankind's annihilation. On the lawn outside Princes Plain School for Girls there is a deathly hush of anxiety. Detective Superintendent Alan Jones and his 'softly, softly' squad are gently prodding their fingers of suspicion at the teenage pupils. Jones believes one of them may be responsible for the kidnap of a seven-week-old baby girl from her mother's pram; the child was later discovered alive, just, covered in flies and maggots at the foot of an oak tree in nearby woodland and is now fighting for her life in hospital. Such is the cruel nature of crime on this day of Mars: of headless torsos found half buried in mudbanks; of car bombs and hunger strikes; of babies freely snatched from unattended prams to be found in clumps like unpicked daisies on every high street.

A jolt north to Catford, home of the baby girl's mother, where an all elbows and Instamatic-camera rabble gather around the entrance of a new supermarket to see a 45-year-old TV star cut the ribbon. 'It's the biggest crowd I've ever seen!' declares Bruce Forsyth, tossing apples and comic books at boggle-eyed children as the Band of Life Guards skirl into activity encouraged by the baton twirls of comic mascot 'Major Saver'. Those who don't immediately encircle Forsyth in a jig of waving pens soon set the tills ringing with Koo marmalade, Chiltonian biscuits and the impulsive extravagance of some Hirondelle table wine; praying the latter's reward of a fuzzy head and double Green Shield stamps will justify the havoc wreaked upon that week's housekeeping. Others peruse the home-furnishings department with childish wonder, staring with impoverished sadness at their moping convex reflection in a Swan Regal kettle or stroking covetous paws across the scientific miracle that is the Goblin Teasmade. Such is the substance of material dreams on this day of Mars: of Servis Supertwins, of Vymura wallpaper, of Wyclox Moonbeams.

Our attention is grabbed by fresh hysteria now echoing from the grassy courts of Wimbledon's All England Lawn Tennis & Croquet Club. Today, in what is being billed as the 'Battle of the Heartthrobs', quarter-final war is being raged with ball and racket between national pride Roger Taylor and a formidable 17-year-old string-bean Viking named Bjorn Borg. Taylor is this year's number-three favourite; formerly sixteenth until a mass boycott by players in support of controversially suspended Yugoslavian Niki Pilić greatly exaggerated his odds. Taylor sweats and puffs to match victory but is unable to prevent the stands quaking with the contagious aftershock of his opponent's oestrogen-boiling beauty. A girl from Bromley is canvassed for her opinion by a reporter outside the grounds. 'When I see Borg,' she sighs, wilting in the afternoon heat, 'I think, WOW!' Such are the simply stirred loins on this day of Mars: by shining knights of Cassidy and Osmond, by fair maid Susans Lloyd and Stranks.

Evening approaches. A scorched scent hangs in the air over Battersea Pleasure Gardens, still smouldering after this morning's inferno when dolphins Flipper and Bubbles only just avoided being poached alive in their pool. Across the river, in the heart of the city, work-weary drones snatch the evening paper from peachy-cheeked vendors before scampering underground, squishing their fraying tempers together in smoky cylinders to digest it in silent contortion, grateful for whatever mental diversion from bodily discomfort it can bring. Actress Betty Grable, cultivator of a pair of legs magnificent enough to be insured for $1 million by Lloyd's of London, has died of cancer, aged 56. And in Oxford, a teenage boy has been jailed indefinitely for an unprovoked attack on a meths-drinking Irish tramp whom he robbed of 1½ pence after beating to death with a brick. The boy's defence blames the influence of the recent film *A Clockwork Orange*. In sentencing, the judge agrees the film has 'produced a canker among the impressionable young which all reasonable people desire to see stamped out at once'.

Like trapped nerves the commuters flinch and shudder over the gory particulars of the 'Clockwork Killer' while above their heads in Leicester Square queues form to see the same source of youthful canker at the Cinecenta. On the other side of the square at the Empire they're drawn by the equally dystopic lure of *Soylent Green*, mankind's vision of an over-populated future fifty years hence where the best available solution is state-rationed cannibalism. It is the last film to star Hollywood veteran Edward G. Robinson who died in January and whose renowned art collection has been auctioned today a few hundred yards away in Sotheby's. One particular dealer from New York leaves the sale £270,000 lighter in the pocket after paying a record sum for Robinson's most treasured 'blue period' work by Pablo Picasso, himself buried in the grounds of his French chateau only weeks ago. Catalogued as '*La Mort (La Mise Au Tombeau)*', it is one of the Spaniard's many tributes to his best friend, the poet Carlos Casagemas, who committed suicide by shooting himself in the head in a Montmartre café, here immortalised as the swaddled Jesus-like centrepiece of a crowd of mourners. The tragic lyricist who ended his life so publicly. 'La Mort', 'My Death', waiting like a Bible truth and a beggar blind. So the gavel strikes and the stars align with perfect poignancy on this day of Mars.

Westwards now, past parks, parliament and palace, beyond hospital and harbour, over sauntering pedestrian and squashed passenger, on bus and train, on foot and bicycle; above the squeaking handpumps and chiming cash registers of Arms, Dukes, Lords, Oaks and Princesses, the sound of lips smacking on Courage and Watneys Red, sucking on Rothmans and Dunhill, glasses chinking the midweek merry melodies of Pernod and Cutty Sark. Until, finally, our appointed place. Where the river Thames bends in coquettish horseshoe, as if carving so unmistakable a shape to guide all roving eyes ashore. Hear its murky waters softly lapping, beckoning us upon the northern bank to Hammersmith. Past the low rafters of Riverside Studios, once haunted by the cries of Bernard Quatermass, sidling through the byways and balconies of Queen Caroline and Peabody estates – 'no cycling, roller skating, cricket, football, ball games, hawkers, canvassers or street musicians here', if you please.

Almost there, now stretching before us the elevated concrete serpent of the Westway, just three years young, trembling with the thunder of Austin Allegro, Vauxhall Viva and Hillman Imp, a tuneless hum robust enough to vibrate the bones in St Paul's churchyard below it; the rotting femurs and fibulas of forgotten Barbaras, Esthers, Williams, Johns and Georges who perished centuries ago never knowing the sweet perfume of petroleum exhaust nor the thrill of putting a tiger in one's tank.

The hour and place upon us on this day of Mars, the scent of fate hangs heavy, fogging the summer air opposite St Paul's outside the Odeon cinema. Not merely because this week's feature presentation is a comedy about funeral arrangements, Billy Wilder's *Avanti!* starring Jack Lemmon. Death knows this building only too well. Just two days ago, on Sunday afternoon, its flip-up felt seats were warmed by the bony buttocks of pensioners paying five pence apiece for the promise of tapping their toes to a tunesome recital by organist Laurence James. They instead endured the unexpected trauma of witnessing said Mr James, a mere 53 years-old, flop upon the keyboard and croak his life's last chorus before he'd so much as chirruped 'Any requests?' The reaper has wet his scythe once here this week. Tonight he returns for an encore.

There will be no *Avanti!* at the Odeon this evening. The projector stands silent, Lemmon's wisest cracks restrained in their film canister until tomorrow when normal service is resumed. It is for fleshly, rather than flickering, spectacle that glorious commotion now stirs upon its steps in the dusky shadow of the Westway. Policemen without coats boil with bewilderment at the swarm of little monsters encircling them. A hurricane of fabric and facial fancy: pinks, purples and scarlets; gauchos, Crusoes and Johnny Halfmast; high waistbands, deep cuffs and daggered lapels; denim, gingham and rayon; loonpants, tubetops and slingbacks; leopard print, polyester and lycra; the caped, the tight-buttoned and the bare-navelled; in mauve bangles, button badges and faceted necklaces; hair sprayed, spiked and coppery red, Wood Nymph blonde and flowing free, streaked with timid shocks of blues gone wrong, even-winged and centre-parted; nails murky gold, liquorice black and lichen green; eyelids turquoise and Tic-Tac orange, boy and girl; faces gashed in lipstick zigzags, black-mouthed, silver-eyelashed, Pierrot-cheeked, a Miners' panstick parade of stars, symbols and reptilian scales on every other jowl, neck and forehead.

On the hoarding above the entrance: 'From 8 p.m., We're All Working Together With David Bowie.' Yet on every available pillar, it is the sacred image of their saviour.

Their Starman.

For this is no ordinary day of Mars. This is judgement day for its Spiders and crucifixion for its cosmic messiah. The man who fell to Earth to rip a rainbow in an oblivion of grey. The file in the sponge cake beckoning the wretched to hack through the bars of their Green Shield stamp prison. The embellisher of the drab. The twister of teenage necks from the gutter to the stars. The liberator of the slaves to duty and conformity. The nail-varnished hand outstretching to the lonesome and unloved. The greatest pop star of all time. The greatest pop star of all space. Who tonight will commit rock 'n' roll suicide live on stage at the Hammersmith Odeon.

Today is Tuesday, the third of July, 1973.

The day of the death of Ziggy Stardust.

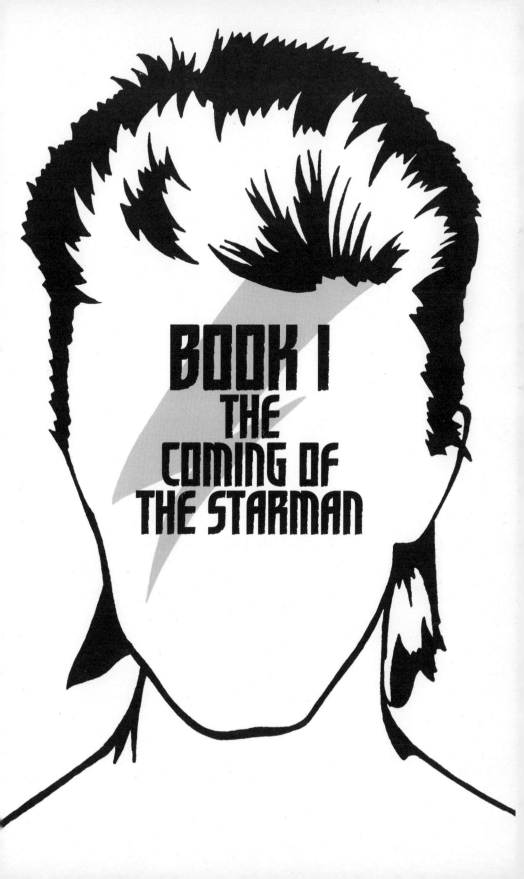

BOOK I
THE
COMING OF
THE STARMAN

ONE
THE DREAM

The history of Ziggy Stardust is the history of a thought. A wild and beautiful thought. A dwelling on the infinite mystique of a bewitching otherness. A dream, a fear, a fantasy, a wonder which humanity would knead, sculpt, chisel, clothe, polish, adorn and bejewel for hundreds and thousands of years until it maximised and crystallised as flesh, bone, fabric and song in the mind and trousers of David Bowie.

It is a story as old as time. It is a story as old as the stars that sent him. It is a story which begins, as it will end, somewhere in the vicinity of Yorkshire.

Yorkshire. Land of suicide crags and boggy moors the dun colour of dismay. Where half the genes of the boy who would be Ziggy were fashioned in Doncaster, birthplace of his father. Where the men blessed to become the Spiders From Mars were incubated in the East Riding. And where westwards near Bingley the story of all cosmic origin found its voice in the village of Gilstead. There, in 1915, a different sort of Starman was born to local wool merchant Ben Hoyle and his Beethoven-loving pianist wife, Mabel. They christened him Frederick. Fred Hoyle of Gilstead. The man who taught the world that all the elements in the known universe were first created in the centres of stars like our own sun; that when stars spent their energy they exploded in a supernova dispersing those elements out into the cold infinity of space until the process began all over again, gas and dust clumping together to form new stars, new planets and new life-forms. Cosmologist, astrophysicist, author, radical. And the midwife of the actual birth of the universe.

The boy who would be Ziggy was just two years-old, crawling around a terrace in Brixton the day Hoyle unconsciously kissed history, on Monday 28 March 1949. Hoyle, then a 33-year-old maths tutor at Cambridge, had been invited by the BBC to present a radio lecture on new developments in cosmology. He began by announcing he'd 'reached the conclusion that the universe is in a state of continuous creation', a eureka moment he'd stumbled upon without spending years cricking his spine bent over a telescope, or agonised nights of algebraic insomnia, but by a chance visit to the cinema.

Three years earlier he'd been to see the Ealing studios' drama *Dead Of Night*, a collection of five horror stories told through the linking narrative of an architect's visit to a country farmhouse. In the opening scenes the architect drives to the house where the owner introduces him to a group of strangers, all of whom he believes to have already met in a previous dream. At the climax of the film the architect realises everything he and the audience have seen and heard for the last ninety minutes is also a dream when he is suddenly awoken at home in his bed by a ringing telephone. He answers and speaks to the owner of a farmhouse inviting him to visit for the weekend. He automatically accepts, slightly puzzled by a nagging sense of déjà vu. The closing credits roll over the same scenes of his arrival at the farmhouse seen at the start of the film, the doomed architect evidently trapped for eternity in an endless looping nightmare.

It was this simple cyclical plot of a horror film which inspired Hoyle and his Cambridge colleagues Hermann Bondi and Thomas Gold to propose an ageless universe with no beginning and no end, forever repeating on itself for infinity. Hoyle used his March 1949 BBC broadcast to promote this same 'steady state theory' while taking meticulous care to debunk rival ideas about cosmic origins. The most popular alternative was one supported by America's Edwin Hubble, whose study of light spectra from distant galaxies revealed convincing evidence of an expanding universe – one which must, if still expanding, have logically once started from a finite point of nothingness.

'These theories,' Hoyle scoffed, 'were based on the hypothesis that all matter in the universe was created in one big bang at a particular time in the remote past.'

Hoyle chose the childlike phrase 'big bang' to belittle the expanding universe argument as naïve. Except by doing so he coined a metaphor so simple and accessible it very quickly became the century's standard model of cosmology. One he'd detonated, by mistake, through nothing more than Yorkshire sarcasm.

So it was that Yorkshire gave the universe the genes of Ziggy, the Spiders From Mars and the big bang. And so it was that the big bang gave the universe Yorkshire, the Spiders From Mars, the genes of Ziggy and the universe itself.

Nearly 14 billion years ago an unfathomable void of nothingness erupted in an unstoppable spewing of light and heat. An edgeless maelstrom of fire and ash. A fullness as unimaginable as the emptiness that preceded it. A raging intergalactic blizzard which cooled for an eternity to form the first stars, living and dying billions of years before our sun existed. Stars which vanished in supernovas hurricaning more stardust back into space, taking new eternities to form new stars, new planets and, eventually, new life.

The same stardust that created the enveloping sphere of the world now surrounding you including the eyes you use to read this page and the tips of the fingers that turn them. The page itself, whether paper or liquid crystal. The fabric against your skin and the floor beneath you. The bricks and glass that house you and the streets, hillocks and estuaries beyond them, from the sands of Ibiza to the marshes of the Norfolk Broads. The atoms of everything and everyone that has ever existed or ever will exist. Beethoven's tuning fork. The spokes of H. G. Wells' bicycle. Gustav Holst's baton. The brylcreem in the hair of Elvis Presley and Vince Taylor. The black plastic shading Andy Warhol's eyes from the Manhattan daylight. The lens of Stanley Kubrick. The blood trickling from the slashed torso of Iggy Pop. The tree hacked down to make Ronno's white Les Paul. The coat of red paint on a model K2 phonebox in Mayfair. The first bass drum on 'Five Years' and the last violin on 'Rock 'N' Roll Suicide'. All of it. Every molecule. Made of stardust.

The word 'stardust' has been in our vocabulary for less than two hundred years. It appears neither in the Bible nor any of the works of Shakespeare. *The Oxford English Dictionary* records its entry into the language in the year 1844, meaning 'lots of small stars that look like dust through a telescope'. By 1879 the definition was added of 'dust that supposedly falls from outer space to the earth'. But even then, in the late Victorian age, as H. G. Wells wrote in *The War Of The Worlds* of 'an oblong profundity with the stardust streaked across it', humans remained largely oblivious to this wonder of their origins and that of the cosmos itself.

The history of Ziggy Stardust is the history of that stardust which became the human race. As soon as the first humans had dragged themselves upright to gaze at the night sky they started to wonder whether there might be some*thing* out *there*. Mystified by the heavens, early man succumbed to pagan impulses of gods and monsters, worship and sacrifice, mumbo and jumbo. Their primitive minds didn't see Starmen in the sky but apocalyptic space dragons which tried to gobble up the sun, plunging the world into permanent darkness; or, as we'd call the phenomenon today, a solar eclipse.

In what was once Mesopotamia they imagined the Earth to be a flat strip beneath a domed heaven, with hidden doorways either side to allow the sun to creep in at dawn and slither out at twilight. The Sumerians and Babylonians believed in the power of stars and the creatures within them, constructing humongous layered temples flanked by stairways climbing straight to heaven. From here they would survey the cosmos, chart its movements and convert their findings into a mathematical framework of the first known astronomical data. At the summit of these temples lay a dedicated shrine to the god of their city, placed there like a divine helicopter pad beckoning him to step from heaven and descend into their midst. Using sun-baked bricks made from the dust beneath their feet, the Babylonians were the first civilisation in human history to erect a welcome mat for the Starman. Such temples had a special name meaning 'the highest place'. Ziggurats.

The ancient Greeks also made gods of constellations, paying special attention to those non-twinkling bodies which roamed the sky of their own free will: these wandering stars they named the planets. In the vast cloudy streak dissecting the night sky they saw a shower of milk spurting from the breast of the goddess Hera; thousands of years later, because of the Greeks we still refer to that starry haze as the Milky Way. But like the Babylonians before them who invented writing, geometry, the seven-day week, the twelve-month calendar and the sixty-minute hour, the Greeks gave us infinitely more than urns and fables: the concept of atoms; the deduction that the sun must be a ball of hot rock; and that the Earth wasn't flat but a sphere. And, in minds as keen as the scholar Epicurus, the first idle daydreams of Ziggy. 'We must believe,' wrote Epicurus, around 400 BC, 'that in all worlds there are living creatures.'

The mathematician Pythagoras, an early Greek superstar who played a one-string guitar called a 'Cosmic Monocord' and cultivated his own simpering fan club, was the first to suggest there were tunes to be heard among the orbits of the planets – a 'music of the spheres'. Yet Pythagoras also typified the worst conceits of Greek intellectualism. He alone set about dismantling the stairways to heaven, as dreamed by the Babylonians, with an idealised geometric model of space. One where there could be no transit of life between the Earth, the planets and the stars, each contained in a conglomeration of sealed crystal spheres spinning in perfect harmony. Such was the 'cosmos', a word he'd invented, according to Pythagoras. Literally, a load of balls.

The influence of Pythagorean arrogance rattled in the bones of successors such as Aristotle and Ptolemy, who between them established a widespread faith in geocentricism: the belief that we, on Earth, must be the centre of the universe, with the sun spinning around us. When Greek and Roman myth and superstition were eventually devoured by the God-fearing terror of Christianity, the church upheld Aristotle's geocentric system as sacrosanct. It wasn't that an alien visitor like Ziggy Stardust had become unthinkable in the human brain. Worse, he'd become undiscussable. The Christians only had room in their pious imagination for one Starman, sent to Earth from the heavens to attract apostles and spread joy before being ritually crucified. To look for or even suggest there might be others was to invite disembowelment, death and eternal hellfire.

And so the stars, and its Starman, continued to shine for over another thousand years of human fear and holy ignorance. Unobserved and undisturbed.

The post-medieval dunce age lobotomising northern Europe was finally shattered by a handful of deliberating heroes, restless of mind, courageous of soul, who between them stripped the world of its geocentric blindfold and re-ignited the flames of cosmic fancy. The first murmur of truth came from Nicolaus Copernicus, author of the 1543 page-turner *On The Revolutions Of The Heavenly Spheres*, which dared to imply the Earth revolved around the sun and not vice versa. Tragically for its author, as the book's presses rolled Copernicus lay comatose on his deathbed, waking just the once to feel a first edition pressed into his hands before giving up the ghost. If the relief of seeing his life's work in print didn't finish him off it could have been the shock of discovering the anonymous preface inserted without his consent by its German publisher. Hoping to dodge any blasphemous controversy, it feebly informed the reader that the theories within 'need not be true'.

Of the brave papal cage-rattlers who followed Copernicus, none were more heedless of harm than late-sixteenth-century Neapolitan monk and occupational bother-magnet Giordano Bruno. A devout Copernican, he went one further by suggesting the sun was a star exactly like all other stars, and spoke openly of his belief that life existed somewhere among them. For which the Catholic Church dragged him into a market square in Rome, tied him to a stake, buried him up to his chin in kindling and barbecued him alive.

As Bruno's charred remains were being unceremoniously dumped in the river Tiber, some three hundred miles north in the University of Padua, a 36-year-old geometry teacher called Galileo was busy composing his own troublesome cosmic jive. *The Starry Messenger* was a jaw-clunking collection of scientific data about the night sky as he'd observed using a brand new invention, the telescope. But it took another book to fully baste Galileo in enough sacrilege to merit his own public roasting. Warned by the Pope not to promote the heretical opinions of Bruno and Copernicus before him, Galileo wrote *Dialogue Concerning The Two Chief World Systems*, convinced he'd found a cunning loophole. It took the form of a fictional conversation between two men: one defending the traditional geocentric view of the church, the other skilfully presenting its author's contrary evidence that Earth revolved around the sun. At the end a third character, intended as an independent observer, weighs up the arguments of both before choosing to agree with Galileo's man. Unfortunately, the book wasn't cunning enough to prevent Galileo's trial before the Roman Inquisition, who menaced him into renouncing his beliefs under pain of having his elderly limbs yanked from their sockets. While he avoided Bruno's martyr's pyre he spent the last eight years of his life under miserable house arrest, the last three of those blind. He died a broken man at the age of 77 on 8 January 1642. Three hundred and five years prior to the day the boy who would be Ziggy was born.

In his early years, long before he'd excited Catholic thumbscrews, the young Galileo received a book out of the blue from a fellow astronomer in Germany. The book was *The Cosmic Mystery*, a weird mix of space theory and geometric insanity which at its core proposed a Copernican model of the heavens. The author was Johannes Kepler, a luckless maths teacher who claimed to have taken a bath only once in his entire life and, possibly as a result, suffered from such severe haemorrhoids that he often wrote standing up. Kepler asked a friend travelling to Italy to deliver his book to Galileo, hoping to befriend him. Sadly, any camaraderie failed to blossom. Unwilling to indulge his German rival, the Italian ignored most of his letters repeatedly pleading to borrow a telescope, finally palming Kepler off with the weakest of excuses that he did have a spare but he'd 'lent it to someone else'.

Kepler would nevertheless brand his name upon history without Galileo's assistance. Like Pythagoras, he also heard melodies in space among the movements of the planets. As early as 1599 he described using musical notation a chord made by 'strumming' the solar system like the strings of a guitar. The notes roughly corresponded to a C major chord – the same key as 'Starman'. Where Galileo had stubbornly held to the classical sanctity of perfect circles and misjudged the planetary orbits along the same lines, Kepler was the genius who calculated that the planets moved in ellipses at a variable speed dependent on how close they were to the sun's gravity. And where Galileo had thought extraterrestrial life 'false and damnable', Kepler was already writing the script for first contact.

As a Protestant caught among Catholic religious upheaval and territorial war in Reformation Europe, Kepler shared Galileo's caution in writing a mandate for the Copernican model of the solar system. But whereas Galileo's *Dialogue* nudged fiction only so far as an imagined conversation, Kepler's *The Dream* shoved disbelief into new dimensions of literary wonder. It followed the adventures of Duracotus, the son of an Icelandic witch, who is spirited to the surface of the moon by demons. There he describes space as seen from a new non-terrestrial perspective and paints a vivid portrait of alien life: benign giant lunar inhabitants with legs like camels, those on the dark side confined to an icy life of misery and hardship, so sensitive to the sun that it blisters their frail skin. Kepler's intention was to present science fact in the guise of fiction. In doing so, this smelly seventeenth-century German romantic with chronic piles gave the world science-fiction.

Kepler's *The Dream* took over a decade to write and was never published in his lifetime, though it was circulated in private and copied, badly, with near-fatal consequences for his mother. Frau Kepler was a village gossip who brewed and sold mind-altering homeopathic drugs. Stories began circulating that her 'cures' caused blindness. Other witnesses came forward swearing she could walk through locked doors and had once cursed a pig, which cried itself to death. It didn't help that her own aunt had been burned as a witch years earlier. Second-hand copies of *The Dream*, with its alarming parallels with the hero's demon-summoning mother, only added to her woes. Frau Kepler was arrested and confined to a cell where the local witchfinder general spent many hours showing her his instruments of torture in laborious detail. She was eventually released, physically unharmed but mentally ruined, only thanks to her famous son's intervention.

The trial took its emotional toll on both. His mother died within the year and Kepler within the decade. He left behind his own self-penned epitaph – 'Skybound was the mind, earthbound the body rests' – and an assured place among the pioneering gods of modern astronomy. Among his last books was *Harmony Of The Worlds,* continuing his fascination with Pythagoras' 'music of the spheres'. In the closing pages Kepler allowed himself to slip into a rare cosmic stupor, so stoned on the harmonic beauty of the planets' song that his thoughts wandered to the existence of extraterrestrial life. What was the point, argued Kepler, of creating other worlds with their own moons if no creatures were there to admire them? Was God so limited in his creativity that he exhausted himself on the Earth and left the other planets bereft? There had to be something, or someone, up there tuning in to the same ecstatic interplanetary song.

TWO
THE STRANGE ONES

As Johannes Kepler stood at his writing desk near the Czech–Austrian border, buttocks smarting, head lost in a trance of music, space and extraterrestrials, five and a half thousand miles away on the other side of the world a very different band of dreamers began sewing the tentative threads of the Starman's wardrobe.

Early-seventeenth-century Japan was a land as alien to the West as the camel-legged lunar colony of Kepler's science fiction. The first European traders arrived there only decades earlier in 1543, the year Copernicus died, discovering an isolated island nation with its own design aesthetic, curious military codes and complex language system. In turn, these first Portuguese visitors were received by locals as 'southern barbarians', so named because they ate with their fingers rather than chopsticks and, much like Kepler, reeked to high heaven. Once the merchant sailors opened up trade routes the Christian missionaries followed, hoping to convert a country steeped in Buddhism and ancient Shinto creation myths based upon the belief that all matter originated in a giant egg which burst and separated, as heaven and Earth; a premise not so far away from the big bang.

This new foreign influence upon Japan coincided with the end of feudal war, which had bloodied the soil for centuries. Peace, of sorts, was finally established in the early 1600s by Tokugawa Ieyasu, a warlord who became the country's central dictator, establishing a new social order bound by strict class divides. Though technically ruled by an emperor, the real power in Japan lay in the hands of the samurai (warrior) class – ruled by the *shogun* (supreme military commander) and his *shogunate* (government), consisting of *daimyo* (local samurai chiefs) and their respective samurai officers.

Becoming a samurai wasn't a matter of ambition but of inheritance, their power and privilege passed down the family line from father to son. It carried a strict etiquette of conduct, haircut and dress (including the unique right to carry two swords), and a rank-dependent annual allowance of rice, the main measure of wealth. The samurai's authority was absolute, but only so long as their *daimyo* chiefs kept them in service. If for any reason they should disgrace their code of honour, or should their master's estate suddenly collapse, the samurai were immediately stripped of their status, becoming *ronin* – literally 'men adrift', wandering swords for hire.

Below the samurai class were the *chonin* – everybody else, each with their own caste name according to occupation. The samurai were forbidden to fraternise with the *chonin* who were denied the privileges of their elite society. This class hierarchy was rigid, leaving no gap for, or hope of, mobility. And it was out of that tense divide between rich and poor, warrior and peasant, that androgynous glamour first ruffled its sleeves.

Peacetime under the Tokugawa *shogunate* was bad news for a large samurai population. With too many warriors and nobody to battle, thousands became unemployed, swelling the number of destitute *ronin*. At the same time, with the increase in foreign trade, the merchant class rose in wealth, gaining new power. Inevitably, the merchants and *ronin* united to create the *otokodate*: gangs recruited from *ronin*, hired by merchants to supposedly protect towns from any samurai intimidation.

The ruling *shogunate* were less worried about the mafia-style *otokodate* than the emergence of another distinct social tribe around the same time: a new generation of flamboyant young ruffians flaunting all social norms of dress and hairstyle. Juvenile delinquents with outrageous beards, sideburns and skinheads, shaved temples and foreheads with taunting ponytails swishing down to their backsides. Street-loitering droogs who fought, bickered and sang boisterously in public, refusing allegiance to any local lord but finding rough brotherhood in the 'Thorny Group', the 'Chinese Dogs' and similar gangs of cosmic yobs. Brash pretty boys in women's clothing, scandalously short-hemmed kimonos with velvet collars, whose long scabbards were decorated with bombastic graffiti. 'I am 23 years-old! I have lived too long! I will never restrain myself!'

These post-feudal fashion freaks – almost exclusively male and openly gay – were feared and despised. In an uncanny premonition of what was to happen on the streets of Britain nearly three hundred years later, one artist of the period disparagingly labelled them 'punks'. Much like the punk rockers of the 1970s they found their few allies among the working classes, delighting in their flashy clothes as a joyous riposte to *shogunate* tyranny. And it was here also, among the peasants, that they earned their name. One derived from the word 'kabuki', meaning to deviate; to bend; to be different; to be strange.

Kabukimono. The deviators. Or, more accurately, the strange ones.

Sometime around 1604 – the year Kepler observed a supernova in the Milky Way with his naked eye (to date still the most recent explosion of stardust in our galaxy) – a young female priestess already under the influence of her *kabukimono* lover began dancing and singing on the dry bed of the Kamo River. Her name was Okuni, a former temple maiden who, as was common, had been sent out into the streets to busk for funds. Yet her act was unlike anything the country's peasants had previously seen. An oscillating sexual enigma between male and female, Okuni mixed erotica with religion, women's make-up with men's hats and trousers, dancing with prayer; singing of eastern Shintoism while around her neck swung chains of western crosses. A seventeenth-century Japanese Madonna.

Starved of theatre – an elite pleasure then taking the sombre, stylised form of *Noh* drama, reserved for the samurai alone – the peasants were beguiled by Okuni's antics, and demanded more. In response she formed her own female dance troupe, and with it the seed of a new *kabukimono* people's theatre. The audience christened it *onna kabuki* – women's strangeness – eventually clipped back to the short, simpler kabuki.

Forced to set up theatres in designated red-light areas beside sake houses and brothels, kabuki attracted a similar roughneck clientele. In its earliest form it was less like staged drama than cabaret. Female singers and dancers, many also working prostitutes, followed Okuni's lead, mixing shamanistic ritual with geisha burlesque; teasing their male audiences with exotic furs and fabrics or sensuously inhaling on suggestively curly pipes. The crackling sexual tension typically erupted in riots, becoming so widespread that by 1629 the *shogunate* intervened, banning kabuki as a 'national disturbance'. Or at least *onna* kabuki as performed by women.

It didn't stop the titillating parade of temptresses. If anything, kabuki sex and violence got worse. Now an all-male domain, female roles were given to specially trained teenage boys named *wakashu*; carefully schooled adolescent gender-benders whose impact upon the crowd's libido was even more volcanic. Bisexuality was rife in feudal Japanese society, even among the samurai who visited kabuki theatres disguised as peasants where they'd end up brawling over their favourite boys' favours; whole theatres were destroyed by lust-induced rampages between warring fans. It was only a matter of time before the corrupting thighs and slender shoulders of the *wakashu* boys were also banned by the *shogunate*.

The theatres stayed in business though the term 'kabuki', now tarred with too much controversy, was temporarily dropped for the ambiguous 'mimed theatrical show'. At the end of the century it made its slow, cautious return, still in the hands of male companies who now cultivated a new wave of adult female impersonators, *onnagata*.

These coquettish cross-dressers weren't part-time drag queens but occupational transvestites who took method acting to its 24/7 extreme, behaving as women off stage and on. Their dedication not only suspended the sexual illusion for male audiences but won them female admirers who copied their fashions; women dressing after men dressing as women. Fiercely loyal fan clubs were formed for the most popular *onnagata*, their rules ejecting any member caught paying to see a rival star; the most devout apostles even changed their name to that of their idol. On stage the *onnagata* drove audiences just as insane as the *wakashu* before them. Theatres hummed and hawed with men rocking and groaning, stabbing themselves in the leg to ease their desire, or exploding in screams of 'God! I'll die!' Respectable samurai were driven to bankruptcy, selling their swords to buy actors gifts and trinkets, while Buddhist monks risked prison by stealing temple treasures to woo their favourites. None of which could pass for very long unnoticed by the *shogunate* before more restrictions were applied.

The crux of kabuki's moral disorder seemed to be hair. Nothing agitated a randy late-seventeenth-century Japanese male quite like long forelocks. The *shogunate* decided that the threshold of 'too sexy' lay at half an inch, making regular inspections of theatres to ensure this wasn't breached. With mandatory shaved heads and blunt forelocks, the actors were likened to 'cats with their ears cut off'. Wigs were also banned. As a last resort the *onnagata* took to wearing purple-coloured headscarves. This the *shogunate* allowed, unprepared for the fetisishtic connotations the purple headscarf would quickly assume among kabuki-goers. Bald cats from Japan shrouded in purple silk, these weird, wonderful gender-defying shemales were now considered sexier than ever.

Kabuki continued to evolve much the same way, surviving all attempts to muffle, neuter or impair its sensual allure and visual extravagance. By the mid-nineteenth century, when Japan finally re-established links with the West after nearly two hundred years of wilful isolation, it was still the most popular entertainment of the masses. The free improvisations of its origins may have been replaced by its own set of dramatic conventions and performance codes but its inborn spirit of fantasy, glamour and spectacle remained intact. Men buried in heavy make-up, faces sinking beneath masks of jagged red and blue lines. Garish costumes with padded shoulders and flowing sleeves. The painted *onnagata* tugging the tightrope between the sexes. Graceful mime and grand gesture. And an audience who worshipped these players as supermen, if not gods from another world.

THREE
ROCK 'N' ROLL

By the late-eighteenth-century the slowly multiplying cells of the Starman twinkled across the planet like randomly scattered sequins on an otherwise bare bauble, sparkling in disconnected astronomers' dreams and kabuki silks but lacking any means to stitch together. Nor could they until the invigorating power of music was exploded in all its spastic ecstasy. Music which didn't merely please the ear and pivot the ankle, but engorged the heart and molested the senses. Music which plunged a white hot harpoon into the listener's forehead, a blissful agony conjuring answers to the greatest mysteries of our existence which couldn't otherwise be expressed in words. For the pulse of Ziggy Stardust to start throbbing the world needed to invent rock 'n' roll. The world needed Ludwig van Beethoven.

All jumps, all jives, all beats, all bumps, all grooves, all grinds, all whams, all bams, all wops, all bops begin with Beethoven. Without him Elvis could never have wandered down Lonely Street nor Lou Reed to the corner of Lexington, one-two-five. Alex the droog would never have slooshied with visions of birds of rarest-spun metal like silvery wine flowing in a spaceship. And there'd be no robot fanfare bubbling above wild, expectant teenage screams to introduce, in the flesh, Ziggy Stardust and The Spiders From Mars.

It may have taken Japanese kabuki to erect the Starman's stage, but it was Beethoven alone who ripped open its curtains. The early-twentieth-century science writer J. W. N. Sullivan summed up his music as possessing 'alien despair' and 'a remote and frozen anguish wailing over implacable destiny … like a memory from some ancient and starless night of the soul.' Beethoven himself agreed his melodies came to him unsummoned from another plane. 'I could seize them with my hands,' he's supposed to have said. 'Out in the open air, in the woods while walking, in the silence of the nights.'

As his first biographer put it, Ludwig was 'a boy from an ideal world tossed upon the earth', crashing in the German city of Bonn in 1770. His unpleasant alcoholic father practically lassoed him to a piano as soon as he could crawl, shoving him into his first public concert at the age of seven. A child prodigy, he was distant and moody, with small but piercing eyes, and tawny skin so coarsely pock-marked he was given the nickname 'the Spaniard'. On the cusp of his adolescent dream of studying music in Vienna (according to several sketchy accounts, as a pupil of Mozart) he was recalled to Bonn by his mother's death. With his dad too drunk to hold the family together, Ludwig had no choice but to remain there as head of the household. Four years of despair and frustration crept by before he was mercifully hauled back to Vienna as a pupil of the ageing 'father of the symphony', Joseph Haydn. The unspoken understanding was that when Beethoven finally came to publish his own music, in keeping with the etiquette of the day he would show due gratitude to his master and sign himself 'pupil of Haydn'. Except Beethoven bowed to nobody. 'Haydn taught me nothing,' he'd brag, adding he deliberately avoided listening to all other composers so as not to taint his own raw genius.

So began his punk rock odyssey through the salons and concert halls of the Austrian Habsburg Empire: young Ludwig Rotten, stomping along Stephansplatz, hair falling messily out from under his wig, clothes grubby and ill-matching, his scowling Spaniard face and his crude yokel accent which had raised many a powder-puffed Duchess's eyebrow. Yet in spite of being such a bad tempered scruff that the police once mistook him for a tramp, Viennese society welcomed him as a pianist of godlike proportions.

When encouraged to take part in virtuoso play-offs with rival musicians, Beethoven demolished them all. He relished displaying dextrous one-handed feats that his so-called 'mortal enemies' were biologically unable to mimic with less than two. If he didn't crush his opponents musically, he out-psyched them mentally. Challengers could pummel their clavichords for five minutes in a sweat of concentration only to be punctured by Ludwig's stony-faced yawn: 'So, when are you going to start?' At his most obstreperous, goaded by one countess into playing for sport, he begrudgingly took his place at the piano only to slam his forearms upon the keys in a tuneless din. 'That, madam,' he announced, standing up to leave, 'is my piece for the evening.'

Music was the one love of Beethoven's life, though he didn't have a lot of choice. Despite countless unrequited infatuations, he'd never marry. One singer he proposed to laughed him off as 'too ugly and half mad'. His later landlords and neighbours would have agreed. If Beethoven decided he needed more light he'd start knocking holes in the brickwork to create makeshift windows. In the summer months he'd keep cool by pouring buckets of water over his head, the water seeping through the floorboards soaking the tenants below. Among the most vivid reports of knocking uninvited *chez* Beethoven is having the door answered by a grimacing ogre in goat-hair jacket and trousers, pads of stained yellowing cotton wool poking out of his ears, and the drying crusts of shaving foam spattering his face; the visitor deducing that he must have half-prepared shaving that morning only to forget while he spent the rest of the day consumed by composing.

Beethoven spat and raged at the outside world, but with good reason. At the age of 27 the worst tragedy he could have ever conceived befell him. A sick joke from God, which would have monumental impact not merely on Beethoven's life and music but on the life and language of all music to come.

Over a hundred years before Brian Jones and Jimi Hendrix, the first casualty of the fabled 27 Club was Beethoven's hearing. He'd been keeping its steady deterioration a secret for years, privately suffering all sorts of humiliating quack treatments: pouring oils in his ears, stewing in cold baths, and once spending two days with his arms encased in poisonous bark from a shrub so toxic that in extreme cases it could induce a coma. All in vain. The cause of his gradual deafness is still a mystery – early suggestions of syphilis have since been ruled out – as is the original diagnosis, thanks to the doctor who upon his dying wishes destroyed all medical records. Whatever the reason, there was to be no cure in early-nineteenth-century Europe.

In the year 1802, still only aged 31, the partially deaf Beethoven suffered an epiphany of angst while resting in Heiligenstadt, a hamlet just outside Vienna. He compiled his emotions in a letter addressed to his brothers, the notorious 'Heiligenstadt Testament'. Part rock 'n' roll suicide note, part vow of spiritual defiance, he openly acknowledged his incurable deafness and its devastating psychological effect. 'I was compelled early to isolate myself, to live in loneliness,' he wrote. 'I would have put an end to my life – only art it was that withheld me … it seemed impossible to leave the world until I produced all that I felt called upon to produce. And so I endured this wretched existence.'

Prior to Beethoven, all composers, Mozart included, were resigned to the fact that their work was purely for the entertainment of their patrons. Conveying emotion and mood were never their objective: only a desire to create nice, occasionally clever, but always pleasing tunes. Isolated from the rest of the world by ever encroaching deafness, music became Beethoven's sole means of expression. In his first major piece after returning from Heiligenstadt, his Third Symphony, he drew a line in the sand between the functional crowd-pleasers of his youth and a new epoch in sound and meaning. Nicknamed the 'Eroica' ('Heroic') Symphony and originally inspired by Napoleon, its eponymous hero was really Beethoven himself, the gut-galloping orchestration articulating the courage and passion of a handicapped composer coming to terms with his fate: the triumph of art over illness. With the Eroica, Beethoven cracked the code. Music had only been about music until Beethoven showed the world music was about life itself, turning his own joy, sorrow, elation and agony into giant, glorious sound.

The weight of drama of his tunes was so intense it created apocryphal romantic myths which have whistled through the ages. In the opening of his Fifth Symphony, Beethoven unveiled the most famous riff in the history of Western music: 'Der-der-der DERRR!' The legend is he intended this to sound like the hand of death rapping his knuckles on the door. Another has it his equally famous 'Moonlight Sonata' was written for a blind girl so as to describe the eerie tranquillity of a moonlit night. Yet the sonata only earned its popular nickname after Beethoven's death. These fables nevertheless cement Beethoven's genius in the ears of his listeners. It doesn't matter whether Beethoven himself *wanted* his 'Piano Sonata No.14 In C Sharp Minor' to sound like moonlight. Its sad, starry gloom resonates in our ears anyway, just as the start of the Fifth remains a musical machine-gun of stuttering terror.

The world cursed Beethoven to become, as he put it, 'the unhappiest of God's creatures'. But in the intoxicating power of his psychological sound paintings, he ensured his immortality.

Of all Beethoven's greatest hits, none frothed with more cosmic bliss than the one Ziggy Stardust would rightly choose as his live entrance music. It was a tune, or rather an idea, which had preoccupied the composer since his desperate youth in Bonn. Its genesis was a German poem written in 1785 celebrating the ideals of freedom and universal brotherhood by

Friederich Schiller, 'An Die Freude', or 'Ode To Joy'. Its subject matter may have seemed strangely at odds with Beethoven's surface misanthropy, a euphoric hymn to freedom, universal brotherhood and the glory of God: 'Seek him above the starry vault, for he must dwell above the stars.' Yet the poem entranced Beethoven throughout his adult life, forever experimenting with rough drafts and works-in-progress, attempting to put Schiller's words to music.

Only in his last decade – as a sick man in his fifties, haunted by money worries, completely deaf and more mentally remote than ever – did he solve the problem. In 1822 he received an offer from the newly formed London Philharmonic Society. Huge fans of Beethoven, they'd been trying to coax him to visit England for years and were now willing to pay fifty pounds if he agreed to write them a brand new symphony. He accepted, needing the money, but in a last hurrah of creative brilliance used it as an opportunity to nail the Schiller idea.

Two years later, his Ninth Symphony was finished. Beethoven's monster. The longest symphony anyone had ever written: stretching over an hour, it broke with all orchestral tradition by adding a choir into its epic last movement. And within that movement was the tune Ziggy picked. The tune which, in the words of the late Beatle-loving classical critic William Mann, 'Beethoven must have intended to rock the world.'

The world first rocked to the Ninth in Vienna on 7 May 1824. Its debut was painfully underprepared. In rehearsals one of the main vocal soloists fell ill, spending a night vomiting fifteen times in succession after drinking some dodgy wine; ironically, a gift to Beethoven which he'd passed on in all innocence. The orchestra and choir complained about the score's superhuman demands, another soloist famously telling him to his face he was 'a tyrant over all vocal organs'. Come the day of the show Beethoven couldn't be bothered to hire a standard black tailcoat, so took to the podium in bright green. He spent the entire concert deaf to reality, lost in his own head music. After the final crescendo he continued conducting thin air, eyes shut, baton quivering, oblivious to the thundering applause behind him until one of the vocal soloists turned him round to see the reaction. Beethoven basked in five standing ovations. The Viennese claps seemed to type out the oozing disbelief of a contemporary German reviewer. His verdict on the Ninth: 'The colossal products of the son of the gods, who has just brought the holy, life-giving flame directly from heaven.'

His own life-giving flame was cruelly snuffed out in Vienna on 26 March 1827. Beethoven was 56. He'd spoken his last words on his deathbed three days earlier, when a shipment of wine arrived to ease his suffering: 'Pity, pity, too late.'

Shortly afterwards he slipped into a coma until stirred by a violent thunderstorm. It's said he opened his eyes, rose forward from his pillows and clenched a fist at the sky before flopping back dead. The last thing Beethoven saw was a flash of lightning, his room illuminated by a whip of electrical energy zigzagging across the heavens.

In 1977, four years after the death of Ziggy Stardust, NASA launched the two Voyager space probes. Their purpose was to send data back from the outer gas planets – Jupiter, Saturn, Uranus and Neptune – before continuing their journey beyond our solar system, out into the unknown of the Milky Way. Each Voyager carried aboard written messages, photos and a gold-coated copper phonograph record with its own playback equipment containing human greetings in nearly sixty languages, whale song, sound effects and a selection of music: 'A message to possible extraterrestrial civilisations that might encounter the spacecraft in some distant space and time.'

Choosing which music to send out beyond the stars excited great debate among the Voyager scientists. Among them was Bernard Oliver, founder of Hewlett-Packard, who suggested all it should contain was Beethoven's Ninth. In the end twenty-seven pieces of music were chosen from around the world. The Beatles didn't make the selection only because their record company were too stupid to give consent. But Chuck Berry did, alongside a diverse mix including Mozart, Louis Armstrong, Blind Willie Johnson, Stravinsky and three pieces by Bach.

Two pieces by Beethoven also made the final Voyager Golden Record playlist. The first movement of the Fifth Symphony ('Der-der-der DERRR!') and the Cavatina from 'String Quartet No.13 In B Flat', one of his celebrated Late Quartets written just before his death. Dismissed at the time as 'the work of a lunatic', the Late Quartets are now revered by scholars as the apex of his canon. Strange, sparse, challenging, they are a cosmic musical aurora unto themselves. The Voyager team's Ann Druyan, wife of cosmologist and fellow team member Carl Sagan, was so moved the first time she heard the Cavatina she wondered, 'How it would ever be possible to repay Beethoven for the experience?' Sagan ensuring its place on the Voyager Golden Record 'at least partly' repaid that debt.

The record is sequenced in such a way that whichever alien ears first encounter it, the very first thing they'll hear is the opening bars of Beethoven's Cavatina followed by the spoken greetings. The twenty-seven pieces of music follow, with the Cavatina in full as the last track. Of all the human beings who have ever lived, it is Ludwig van Beethoven who has the first and last word in contacting extraterrestrial life. It may take a hundred years, a thousand, ten thousand, a million or more. Voyager's Golden Record is built to survive over four and a half billion years. It may even be traversing distant galaxies long after the human race has ceased to exist; the obscure time capsule of an insignificant species.

The tyrant over all vocal organs, the son of the gods and the unhappiest of his creatures did more than help create Ziggy Stardust. Somewhere out there, right now, his music is soaring through deep space: the outstretched hand from an alien world on the far side of the cosmos ready to inform whoever finds it they are not alone. Encrypted for ever on Voyager's Golden Record, Beethoven *is* Ziggy Stardust.

FOUR
THE DIFFERENT BOY

No one would have believed, in the last years of the nineteenth-century, that this world was being keenly prepared for the coming of an extraterrestrial rock 'n' roll demigod. Not Queen Victoria, not Charles Darwin, not the Pre-Raphaelite Brotherhood. By the year 1872, one hundred years before the Starman landed, humanity had discovered astronomy, glamour and music but had yet to fully flinch with the panic and wonder of visitation. Not until an arch futurist, whose shoe leather warmed the same suburban streets as the boy who would be Ziggy, took his fearless pen and fearsome imagination to forever change our relationship with outer space. Future generations would call him 'the father of science fiction'. His mother called him 'Bertie'. As in Herbert George Wells.

In 1872, Wells was a six-year-old living above his family's ailing crockery shop at 47 High Street, Bromley. Once a market town in Kent, Bromley was undergoing a dramatic population boom thanks to recent rail links destined to transform it into a commuter suburb of the late-Victorian London sprawl. As the pseudonymous 'Bromstead', Wells described his childhood surroundings in one of his later novels as 'a dull useless boiling-up of human activities, an immense clustering of futilities'. To puncture the tedium young Bertie escaped in wicked daydreams of military assault over his humdrum townsfolk. 'I used to walk about Bromley, a small rather undernourished boy, meanly clad and whistling detestably between his teeth,' he recalled. Pictures of carnage and devastation raged in his head, of 'phantom orderlies' galloping at his command 'to shift the guns and concentrate fire on yonder houses below'. At the age of 13, the Martian heat ray hibernating deep in H. G. Wells' subconscious was already laying waste to Greater London.

Bertie spent much of his youth serving dismal apprenticeships as a draper and chemist, his schooling interrupted to boost the desperate finances of his parents' crockery business, which was doomed, much like their marriage. His eventual salvation was a love of writing, science and a free studentship scheme which accepted him as a trainee teacher in London. He'd recall the first morning he walked from his shabby Notting Hill lodging house across Kensington Gardens to what was then the Normal School of Science as 'one of the great days of my life'. Wells' teacher and mentor during his first year was 'Darwin's bulldog', the great evolutionary biologist Thomas Henry Huxley, grandfather of *Brave New World* author Aldous Huxley. When student poverty relented, the young Wells treated himself to the occasional concert at the school's neighbouring Albert Hall; in his semi-autobiographical masterpiece *Tono-Bungay* he recalls being there 'one night in a real rapture' transfixed by Beethoven's Ninth. He also fell under the spell of socialism and the budding Fabian Society, attending Sunday meetings at William Morris' house on the riverbank in Hammersmith, just a few hundred yards from the site where the Odeon cinema would one day stand flickering Technicolor tales he'd yet to write.

It took him seven years of redrafting before he published his debut novel, by then a twice married 28-year-old working from the kitchen table of a rented flat in Camden. Nobody had read anything quite like *The Time Machine*, a concept so familiar to us after over a century cemented in our thoughts that we can barely comprehend how outlandish and original it must have seemed in the year 1895, when late-Victorian readers were still mourning Sherlock Holmes' fatal tussle with Moriarty at Reichenbach Falls and otherwise outraged by that year's trial of Oscar Wilde. The older Wells would jokingly lampoon its story of a scientist who builds a contraption capable of rushing 'to and fro along the Time Dimension' as 'a tissue of absurdities'. But the core of the book was a political allegory, imagining a nightmare world eight hundred millennia into the future where the evolutionary consequences of the Victorian class divide lead to two violently contrasting human species: an ineffectual bourgeois elite and a savage, cannibalistic ape-like proletariat. This hierarchical conflict between *Homo sapiens* and *Homo superior* would prevail in much of Wells' work, provoking harsh criticism from his socialist peers with his morally ambiguous portrayals of Nietzschean-style 'Supermen'.

The Time Machine was the first of many groundbreaking science-fiction firsts that Wells rattled out of his Camden kitchen in a ferocious two-year burst of creativity. *The Wonderful Visit* was a proto-Ziggyish fable of the man who fell to Earth, an angel shot down in a country village by a vicar mistaking him for a rare species of bird. *The Island Of Dr Moreau* offered a grim genetic morality tale, the horror story of a shipwrecked man who stumbles upon a crazed vivisectionist whose cruel experiments transform wild animals into semi-human 'beast folk'. And the self-explanatory *The Invisible Man* was another genre-defining classic about the dangers of scientific miracle and its effect on the frail human ego predisposed to evil.

These alone ensured Wells a degree of literary immortality. But in 1897 he went one better with a story so simple yet fantastic it not only beckoned down the Starman but inspired the human race to launch itself beyond our atmosphere, commencing the countdown for the next century's space race. By the time he began writing it he'd retreated back to suburbia. To Woking, where he learned to master the bicycle, his blazing muse haunted afresh by the ghost of his meanly clad, detestable whistling genocidal boyhood. 'I wheeled about the district,' Wells recalled, 'marking down suitable places and people for destruction by my Martians.' From the vantage of his saddle trundling down the leafy byways of parochial Surrey, Wells' mind conceived the extraterrestrial carnage of *The War Of The Worlds*.

Wells credited his older brother, Frank, with the original idea – a funny 'what if?' scenario discussed while strolling around Woking – though the novel was as much an ingenious marriage of a new nineteenth-century literary genre and contemporary astronomy.

Twenty years earlier, British Lieutenant-Colonel George Tomkyns Chesney published *The Battle Of Dorking*, a prophetic warning of British invasion by a German army who score a decisive victory in the Surrey market town of its title. Written as military propaganda after the end of the Franco–Prussian War and escalating concern over the future of Europe, its plot provided Wells with a readymade 'invasion fiction' template of provincial pandemonium. Dorking itself was only fourteen miles from Woking.

The second influence on Wells was recent press speculation bringing an ancient human concern zapping into the modern world. 'Is there life on Mars?' The claims stemmed from an Italian astronomer, Giovanni Schiaparelli, whose careful observations by telescope led him to believe the Martian surface was crisscrossed with a series of channels – *canali* in Italian. Schiaparelli's use of the word *canali* was taken literally by America's Percival Lowell who went further by proposing these aquatic byways had been specifically engineered by an intelligent species to syphon ice water away from the polar caps to irrigate Mars' arid terrain. Lowell argued that the difference in gravity between their planet and ours would mean the Martian navvies could build their canals three times more efficiently. 'Quite possibly, such Martian folk are possessed of inventions of which we have not dreamed,' wrote Lowell. 'Certainly, what we see hints at the existence of beings who are in advance of, not behind us, in the journey of life.' The Martian debate and Lowell's excited hullaballoo made front pages around the world, including London's *Evening Standard* which remarked with typical Victorian caution, 'The possibility of the presence of inhabitants on Mars, differing, of course, from human beings, cannot be denied.'

It was against this backdrop of paranoia about homeland security, European unrest, the dying days of Victorian England and fierce debate about life on Mars that Wells first took to his bicycle, returning home to dash off *The War Of The Worlds* on a steady diet of little more than tea and toast.

Like so many of Wells' heroes, the book's anonymous narrator is a thinly-disguised self-portrait of a science journalist living with his wife in late-Victorian Woking. After early astronomical warning of strange flares springing from Mars' surface, an interplanetary missile crash-lands on the outskirts of town at Horsell Common. Locals first mistake it for a meteorite only to watch in horror as slimy, bear-sized ovoid monsters with tentacle limbs and V-shaped mouths emerge from its crater. Wells' Martians, 'cool and unsympathetic', incinerate the gathering army with their heat ray before assembling an armada of fighting tripod machines and embarking on a campaign of total annihilation. The narrator narrowly escapes capture as he makes his slow journey on foot to London. When he finally arrives the city is mysteriously deserted. The sound of weird distress signals leads him through Regent's Park to Primrose Hill (favourite strolling grounds for Wells and his second wife) where he discovers the aliens defeated. Not by human military strength but by the microscopic germs in Earth's atmosphere. 'The Martians – *dead!* – slain by the putrefactive and disease bacteria against which their systems were unprepared.'

First serialised in magazine form, *The War Of The Worlds* was published as a six-shilling novel to immediate acclaim in January 1898. It has never been out of print. Less than three hundred years earlier Kepler had first felt tremors of the Starman in his peculiar lunar fantasy *The Dream* only to land his mother in the dock for 'witchcraft'. The reception to Wells' Martian nightmare was proof enough of the progressive shift in humanity's readiness to dwell upon the unknown awaiting us in space. In its frontispiece, Wells set a subtly paraphrased quote from his 'favourite book', seventeenth-century scholar Robert Burton's epic compendium *The Anatomy Of Melancholy*. 'But who shall dwell in these worlds if they be inhabited? … Are we or they Lords of the World … And how are all things made for man?' Poignantly, the words were those of Johannes Kepler.

The book's rapid international fame owed much to pirate versions in foreign newspapers deliberately breaching Wells' copyright. As *Fighters From Mars* it was serialised in *The Boston Post*, all mention of Surrey locations swapped for those in and around Massachusetts. Wells' unofficial Boston remix gripped the imagination of one particular bronchial teenage boy in Worcester. Robert Goddard wasn't so much scared of the alien heat rays obliterating the townsfolk forty miles away in Lexington as he was fascinated with the technical ingenuity of the Martian vessels travelling through millions of miles of interplanetary space to land on Earth. On an October evening in 1899, the 17-year-old Goddard experienced an epiphany sat among the branches of a cherry tree, lost in hallucinations of a manmade spacecraft hurtling towards Mars. Before going to bed he wrote in his diary. 'I was a different boy when I descended from the tree.'

Inspired by Wells, Goddard became the pioneer of twentieth-century rocket science, designing the first fuel rocket which ultimately put man in outer space. Remove Goddard from the equation of history and we remove Neil Armstrong's giant leap for mankind from the Apollo 11 lander to the surface of the moon, and with it the commemorative ballad of orbital isolation called 'Space Oddity'. So the cosmic baton slips through the fingers of H. G. Wells to Robert Goddard and to Ziggy Stardust. From one different boy to another.

Forty years after *The War Of The Worlds*, Wells returned to the theme of Martian invasion in one of his last sci-fi novels, 1937's *Star-Begotten*, which he dedicated to a lifelong admirer of his work, 'my friend Winston

Spencer Churchill'. In stark contrast to the tentacled aliens and three-legged fighting machines of his previous book, here the Martians adopt a covert cold war-style offensive, sending unseen cosmic rays through space which will transform all new-born children into superbeings until the human race has been entirely replaced. 'This is the story of an idea,' wrote Wells. 'Maybe we have not heard the last of this idea.'

At the time of his death on 13 August 1946, six weeks shy of his eightieth birthday, Wells had authored over one hundred and fifty books, pamphlets and collections. Among them was a short story first published in *The Strand* magazine in 1902 called 'The Inexperienced Ghost', about a man who meets a sorry spectre unable to return to the spirit world until he remembers the special series of hand gestures allowing him to pass between the dimensions. The year before Wells died the story was adapted into a comic ghost yarn about golfing and love rivalry in the Ealing horror compendium *Dead Of Night*: the film which triggered Fred Hoyle's steady state theory and, inadvertently, his coining of the phrase 'big bang'. The influence of H. G. Wells, however subtle, knew no bounds. As George Orwell saluted: 'The minds of all of us, and therefore the physical world, would be perceptibly different if Wells had never existed.'

When *The War Of The Worlds* was first published in January 1898, *The Spectator* magazine nailed the source of its enduring fascination. 'As a rule, those who pass beyond the poles and deal with non-terrestrial matters take their readers to the planets or the moon. Mr Wells does not "err so greatly" in the art of securing the sympathy of his readers. He brings the awful creatures of another sphere to Woking Junction, and places them, with all their abhorred dexterity, in the most homely and familiar surroundings.'

It was this mischievous positioning of visitors from space on English soil, in the streets of London, which most alarmed and awed its readership; a calculated yank on the waxed moustache of Victorian society, teasing with an infinite, uncontainable fear of creatures from another world wreaking havoc in the belly of the British Empire. An alarm which, years after he wrote *The War Of The Worlds*, Wells believed still 'flickers about in people's minds, not quite dead'.

No, not quite dead. And soon to flicker in the mind of the most gloriously different Bromley boy since Wells himself.

FIVE
THE COLD REGION

The year 1922. A mere fifty years before Ziggy Stardust, and his approaching storm can be felt in the faint breeze of cosmic awe and sensory seduction fluttering the first pages of the twentieth century, ruffling gusts from a distant yet now unstoppable gale. A brave new world obliviously prepares to welcome the Starman as it has already the motor car, the aeroplane, the radio, the brassière and the knowledge to make an atom bomb. Music, once the confines of the concert hall, the church and the ale house, can now be caged like a songbird within the concentric grooves of a phonograph record. The ways and means for Ziggy to spread his gospel may yet be rudimentary but are safely in place. All but a few technological stepping stones remain between the crackle of a shellac 78 vibrating the horn of a wind-up gramophone to that of an under-the-covers transistor buzzing to Radio Luxembourg.

The recording process had yet to be properly electrified in 1922 when, on Friday 27 October, the London Symphony Orchestra crammed into the central studios of the Columbia Graphophone Company in Petty France, Westminster. They were there to tape the first in a series of seven discs which when grouped together in the days before the long playing album would comprise a popular new orchestral suite. Conducting the session in Petty France that day was the suite's composer, a physically sickly, intensely private 48-year-old girls' school teacher of Anglo-Baltic ancestry with such a severely cropped haircut even his own family likened his appearance on the podium to that of 'a newly released convict'. Yet this frail, shaven-headed spectre would fuse the strands of Beethoven and Wells as one, sweeping the century clear for Ziggy by unleashing the melodic force of that which Pythagoras and Kepler had only ever dreamed about – the audible harmony of the spheres. The suite was *The Planets*. The composer, Gustav Holst.

When Holst wrote his name-making masterpiece he was thinking in terms of astrology, not astronomy; an obsession he developed in his thirties hoping to make sense of a life which up to that point he considered an absolute failure. He was born Gustav Theodore von Holst in Cheltenham on 21 September 1874; the same day, a hundred miles away in Bromley, the young H. G. Wells had just turned eight. Gustav was a puny, asthmatic boy with poor eyesight who cut a dismal figure beside his hearty younger brother, Emil. Their mother died when Gustav was eight, leaving them in the care of their strict father intent on moulding his eldest son into a pianist despite neuritis, a muscular inflammation which plagued Holst till his death. When he came to write *The Planets* the pain was so bad he could no longer hold a pen, only capable of scribbling with a nib strapped to the middle finger of his right hand.

Untainted by the trauma of his dad's practice regime, music stirred the young Holst's soul like nothing else. He'd remember hearing a mass by Bach for the first time as an out-of-body sensation akin to levitation, clutching the sides of his chair for fear he might fall off. Moving to London to study at the Royal College of Music, Holst fell under the spell of Wagner; so poleaxed by a performance of *Tristan And Isolde* that he wandered the city streets all night in a transcendental stupor until watching dawn rise over the Thames.

Holst's late-nineteenth-century London odyssey sharply echoed the footfall of Wells but a few years earlier. Both were scrawny, impoverished vegetarian young men studying in South Kensington in the shadow of the Albert Hall; both were music lovers lured by the new English socialism movement. Like Wells, the young Holst also attended meetings at the Hammersmith house of William Morris, even conducting the affiliated Hammersmith Socialist Choir. After his boyhood dreams of becoming a concert pianist were thwarted by his worsening neuritis, conducting and composing became his life. Offered a place at the Royal College for an extra year, Holst chose to end his music scholarship in 1898, preferring to 'learn by doing' out in the world – a world which at that very moment was trembling to the descriptions of Martian heat rays in a new book by H. G. Wells.

The London concert circuit at the turn of the century was comparatively sober, save for one notable early Proms performance at the Queen's Hall. The conductor was a friend of Holst's, Henry Wood, who that night presented a new march by the most celebrated English composer of the day, Edward Elgar. At the end of the march the audience 'simply rose and yelled', recalled Wood. Unable to quell their applause and continue with the rest of the concert they played it a second time. 'With the same result,' exclaimed Wood. And so they played it a third time in a frantic bid to restore order. The piece would soon be supplied lyrics by the poet A. C. Benson as the 'Coronation Ode' of Edward VII, 'Land Of Hope And Glory'. But in October 1901 it was simply 'Pomp And Circumstance March No. 1 In D' – the tune destined to peal through a sea of sobs in the Hammersmith Odeon in the minutes immediately after the death of Ziggy Stardust.

The Hammersmith Odeon hadn't yet been built when Holst, now aged 30, took up a teaching post less than half a mile away from its eventual site. He would remain head of music at St Paul's Girls' School in the leafy avenue of Brook Green for the rest of his life, naming the key which allowed him access to the building to work any time of day or night as one of his two prized possessions. The other was a tuning fork given to him by an admirer, which had passed through many hands during the last hundred years since it left those of its original owner: Ludwig van Beethoven.

Teaching supported Holst, but as a composer he was struggling to make any impact in a world dominated by the pastoral reflections and sabre-rattling patriotism of the newly knighted Elgar. 'I'm "fed up" with music,' he mourned. 'Especially my own.' Sensing Holst's deepening depression, in 1913 his friend the composer Henry Balfour Gardiner rallied round to raise his spirits, offering to pay his way to join himself, fellow composer Arnold Bax and Bax's brother, the writer Clifford, on holiday in Spain. As they boarded the train to the coast at Charing Cross station, Holst and Clifford Bax discovered they shared a common interest in astrology: Holst still a novice, Bax an authority.

Their many conversations during the trip resuscitated Holst's wilting muse. Upon his return he bought a thin booklet by British astrologer Alan Leo called *What Is A Horoscope And How Is It Cast?* Its humble contents provided Holst with everything he needed: a readymade blueprint for an orchestral suite on the different human character traits associated with each of the planets. Mercury, Venus, Mars, Jupiter, Saturn, Uranus and Neptune.

He had found his spheres. Now, to give them harmonies.

By the late summer of 1914 Holst was still teaching in Hammersmith but now resident in Thaxted, a small country village in Essex. In this idyllic, earthbound setting he started to write *The Planets*, commencing with 'Mars, The Bringer Of War'. Historically, it seems obvious that its mood must have been sculpted, however subconsciously, by the outbreak of the First World War, even if Holst denied this. But the first drops of blood shed in Belgium and Prussia weren't the only influence. To any literate, culturally aware member of Edwardian society living and working in early 1900s London, as Holst had, the word 'Mars' and its association with 'War' would have meant only one thing: the slimy ovoid invaders and the indestructible tripod fighting machines of H. G. Wells.

As Holst wandered through the fields and meadows around Thaxted, it's not beyond reason to picture the germ of the tune's rhythmic ferocity beating between his ears conjuring hallucinations of Martian heat rays incinerating the hedgerows. Holst's 'Bringer Of War' could be a First World War symphony scored in blood and bullets upon a barbed-wire stave but, equally, a graphic Wellsian Martian invasion made music: the slow, rumbling approach as the cylinder falls ever closer to Earth through deep space; the crash of impact and the commencing battle; the relentless slaughter to a cold, cruel, military death beat; the respite of human despair; the holocaust resumed and the crescendo of total extraterrestrial victory.

Regardless of what Holst may have intended at the time, the sway of *The War Of The Worlds* was closer at hand in the village of Thaxted than he might have realised. Two miles down the road in Easton Lodge estate, the Countess of Warwick was renting out the rectory house on her grounds to a fellow socialist and successful author who'd just relocated from London. His friends called him 'Bertie'. The two 21 September birthday boys from Mars, Wells and Holst, were now practically neighbours.

In the last weeks before armistice, on 29 September 1918 *The Planets* was unveiled to a private afternoon gathering at London's Queen's Hall in its now familiar final order: the Wellsian overture of fear 'Mars, The Bringer Of War'; the sedate, spacey relief of 'Venus, The Bringer Of Peace'; the frolicsome 'Mercury, The Winged Messenger'; the royal salute of 'Jupiter, The Bringer Of Jollity' (which, the story goes, had the hall's charwomen waltzing with their mops in the corridors); the pensive epiphany of Holst's personal favourite, 'Saturn, The Bringer Of Old Age'; the discordant, dramatic 'Uranus, The Magician'; and the icy, inscrutable tranquillity of 'Neptune, The Mystic'.

Among the invited audience were his former Spanish holidaymakers the Bax brothers and Henry Wood, the man who'd conducted Elgar's infamous double encore under the same roof. Also present that Sunday was the critic Edward Dent, describing *The Planets* as 'extremely queer' yet 'very much alive'. Of the seven pieces it was the eerie 'Neptune' which impressed Dent the most. 'It was really mystical and exploratory,' he enthused, 'with a feeling of posthumous Beethoven, and a sense of getting on to a different plane altogether.'

Undoubtedly 'Neptune' was the most challenging for early-twentieth-century ears, involving a women's choir – hastily assembled for that performance from the girls of St Paul's – whose task it was to end the suite with a real-time live fade-out. Rather than simply lower the volume of their voices, Holst instructed that the choir should stand in an adjoining room, the door to be slowly closed until they could no longer be heard. His daughter Imogen vividly described its debut recital as like opening 'the doors on an unknown world'. Holst wrote *The Planets* as an astrological voyage through the human psyche. But its impact was infinitely more cosmic. In the days when the world had yet to punt so much as a satellite into orbit, using only a pen nib tied to his finger in a soundproof room in a Hammersmith girls' school, Holst, with the supernatural strains of 'Neptune', propelled humankind to the very edges of our solar system, weaving harmonies between the heavenly spheres. Exactly as Kepler had dreamed three hundred years earlier.

The Planets brought Holst the acclaim he'd been yearning for all his life, not only in England but internationally in Europe and America; the University of Michigan in Ann Arbor invited him to become their professor of music, a post he had to decline due to his enduring ill health. The sad irony was that having hungered for recognition, Holst failed to cope with his new status as a popular composer. Against his better judgement, he allowed 'Jupiter' to be fashioned into a jingoistic hymn with words by Cecil Spring-Rice, 'I Vow To Thee, My Country', a nationalist sentiment he deeply regretted. As his reputation grew, so did his wariness with the constant attention; his standard response to fan mail requesting autographs was a curt typewritten slip informing the recipient 'Mr Holst' never signed anything for strangers.

Holst's muse returned to space for a final fleeting visit in 1929, picking out a weird and appropriately alien piano dirge to accompany the words of Humbert Wolfe's poem about the star 'Betelgeuse' in the constellation of Orion, over six hundred light years from Earth. Yet when he finally heard his 'Betelgeuse' performed in public the cost of a life spent forever groping in the unknown darkness of non-human musical realms hit Holst with cruel force. The same concert ended with Schubert's 'String Quintet In C Major'. Hearing this one classical masterwork all but destroyed him. In the emotion and humanity of Schubert, he recognised everything his own music lacked. 'He felt imprisoned in a cold region,' recalled his daughter, 'where his brain was numb and his spirit was isolated.' Her father had spent so long composing among the stars he'd forgotten to fall back to Earth. The man who made twentieth-century music extraterrestrial had all but become one himself.

On 23 May 1934, the 59-year-old Holst was admitted to hospital for a stomach operation. Two days after surgery, he died of heart failure. His close friend and the inheritor of Beethoven's tuning fork, Ralph Vaughan Williams, paid poignant tribute in a foreword for Imogen Holst's biography of her father published four years later. 'Holst's art has been called cold and inhuman,' he wrote. 'The truth is it is supra-human... his music reaches into the unknown, but it never loses touch with humanity.'

In the supra-human melodies of Holst's *The Planets* blazed the sparkling prelude of the Starman's hazy cosmic jive. Strange, modern music from outer space, written at the birth of the recording age which found mass popularity through the new medium. In 'Mars, The Bringer Of War', it would eventually find its way into the repertoire of a young

London mod band called The Lower Third. And in the ethereal siren call of 'Neptune' it would one day echo around the expectant auditorium of an Odeon cinema mere streets from where it was composed, in the hour before the greatest pop star who ever lived stepped out on stage for the last time.

From the First World War to the 1970s. From Gustav Holst to Ziggy Stardust. The harmonic essence of alien mystique was born, and died, in Hammersmith.

SIX
LIGHTNING

The year 1932. Just forty years before the arrival of the Starman. He exists, for now, as a chorus of yet-to-be-connected whispers, no longer sequestered in the creative subconscious of a lone Ludwig, Herbert or Gustav, but subtly twisting the tongues and moulding the murmurs of thousands, an echo of dots waiting for the right DNA to smooth him out into a single coherent dash called Ziggy Stardust. All that's needed is for fate to gently tap the sides of the test tube, to delicately tweak the last vital pieces of genetic apparatus. But first, fate has to find them.

Life in the spiritually weakened England of 1932 was a life out of gear. 'Very seriously out of gear,' as the 65-year-old H. G. Wells told the nation across the airwaves of the BBC. 'There has been a creeping paralysis of business for some years,' mourned Wells. 'We are over-producing and under-consuming. None of us with investments feel safe with these investments and none of us who are gainfully employed, as the census forms put it, feel safe that that gainful employment will continue. Our political life is out of gear, even more than our economic life. We are taxed overwhelmingly, crushingly, to pay for the last war and to prepare for the next ...'

Four thousand years earlier, the Babylonians countered their fears of famine, war and poverty by building Ziggurats to their gods. The louder, faster, fidgety human race of 1932 wasn't so very different.

At 11.30 a.m. on Easter Monday, 28 March, the doors of a new temple opened to awestruck crowds in west London; a 190-foot-wide architectural marvel looking like a polished granite spaceship crafted by an infinitely more sophisticated alien species, now parked at the far end of Fulham Palace Road. Inside, the walls of the temple were as lavish as anything recently uncovered in the Egyptian Valley of the Kings by archaeologist Howard Carter. Gleaming columns and pilasters, tones of horizon green, grey, mauve, silver and various harmonising metallic tints enriched with gold lacquer. Even the atmosphere was heaven sent: five million cubic feet of pure air filtered through a complex system of pumps generating over 180 fresh tons per hour. The public called this temple 'the modern of moderns'. The press called it 'West London's Wonder Cinema'. The owners called it the Gaumont Palace, Hammersmith Broadway, later to change its name to the Odeon. Four decades before Ziggy Stardust landed, his gallows were already in place.

The Babylonians designed their Ziggurats to worship the stars. The British built their Gaumont Palaces for the very same purpose. Stars twinkling in silvery light, illuminating the darkness of a three-thousand-seater auditorium. Visions of exotic, sensual perfection beaming bigger than the tramcars which shuttled the cheer-starved audience of a sorry slump nation to its doors. Where the Babylonian priest of 2500 BC shook before the might of Ishtar, Marduk and Shamash, the British cinemagoer of 1932 cowered before Karloff, Dietrich and Garbo.

None were more spellbinding than Garbo: alleged Scandinavian flesh and blood living in the Californian Olympus called Hollywood but a mortal-mocking deity of desire when amplified through the lens of a 35mm film projector. When the *New York Herald Tribune* critic Percy Hammond made the mistake of criticising her performance in that year's

Grand Hotel, the ensuing fatwa of vitriolic mail from devoted Garboites forced him to publish an apology. 'When in a strange land,' Hammond noted to himself, 'worship the gods of the place, whatever they are.'

The first gods to grace the Hammersmith Gaumont Palace were of an admittedly lesser power than Garbo. Upon the screen, the latest 'Aldwych farce' *A Night Like This*, starring Tom Walls, and the American gangster drama *Bad Company* with Helen Twelvetrees. Upon the stage, a celebratory 'Easter Egg' variety bill featuring the noted Dutch violinist De Groot. Addressing the assembled public and members of the press that Easter Monday lunchtime, the Mayor of Hammersmith praised the Gaumont's thoroughbred British construction and, in particular, the ingenuity of its modern art-deco design. The latter was down to the brilliance of 44-year-old English architect Robert Cromie, already famed for similarly grand cinemas in Croydon and Epsom where he pioneered the widespread use of tubular steel furniture. The Hammersmith Gaumont confirmed his status as the country's leading creator of picture palaces – a reputation which belied his apprenticeship with a firm specialising in the construction of Edwardian mental asylums.

Two years later, on Monday 3 December 1934, the ribbon was cut on another of Cromie's cinemas in Tunbridge Wells. With its clever use of space, squeezing the foyer into a narrow street corner so as not to disturb neighbouring shops, and capped by a fifty-foot decorative glass tower, the new Ritz was hailed 'Kent's most luxurious theatre'. Upstairs was the added attraction of the Florida, 'Kent's most luxuriously appointed restaurant and ballroom'.

The Ritz complex tempted the townsfolk with such embarrassment of 'luxury' but the reality of its patrons' provincial life was all too poignantly summed up by the film chosen for its gala opening. *Sing As We Go* starred northern back-alley sweetheart Gracie Fields as a newly unemployed millworker merrily trilling her way through the country's worsening economic paralysis Wells predicted. '*Sing as we go although the skies are grey,*' grinned Fields. '*A song and a smile making life worthwhile.*'

Life in England in 1934 under Prime Minister Ramsay MacDonald – 'The Boneless Wonder' – wasn't nearly so 'gay' as Fields pretended. As Wells had previously argued, 'Plainly there is urgent need for some supreme control in the world to arrest this stalling of our economic machine.' By 1936, that urgent need had frayed disenchantment into desperation and hopelessness into hatred. In want of a common enemy, and in the absence of any Martian assault, men and women whose fathers had fought the war to end all wars found other aliens to attack.

In July that year, the Ritz in Tunbridge Wells proudly presented *Desire*, billed 'the sensational romance that took London by storm'. It starred Garbo-rivalling goddess Marlene Dietrich as a thief who cons a Parisian jeweller played by Cheltenham-born character actor Ernest Cossart – the professional pseudonym of Emil Holst, younger brother of Gustav. But while inside audiences watched Dietrich serenade leading man Gary Cooper – '*the stars looking down from above, seem to sing, you're in love*' – outside the Ritz the pamphleteers of the British Union of Fascists were marching to a very different tune.

There was no avoiding the apostles of Oswald Mosley in the town, a canvassing hotbed spearheaded by the local Tonbridge 'Action Press Squad' and its neighbouring Sussex branch, the East Grinstead 'Motor Propaganda Squad'. In late June the BUF preached isolationism and anti-Semitism to a rapt crowd only two hundred yards away from the Ritz on Newton Road. Many young minds in need of filling with something more tangible than idle dreams of Dietrich and Cooper or the wage-sapping escape of a Florida restaurant Saturday night dinner dance chose to listen.

Among them was a young woman of 22, the live-in nanny at a nearby family-run hotel. She was born Margaret Mary Burns but everybody knew her as Peggy. Whether bored, naïve or merely intrigued by the cut of their trousers, Peggy Burns' dalliance with the fascists didn't last longer than a couple of meetings and one march with her cousin from Tunbridge Wells to Tonbridge, passing along the London Road, a stone's throw from her parents' house. Word of her political allegiance quickly got back to her father, Jimmy, a veteran of the Great War who'd fought in the Royal Fusiliers. 'If you ever do that again,' he chastised Peggy, 'don't come back to this house.'

We can only wonder how much, or how little, Peggy drank in from this brief, best-forgotten episode which ended with her father's scolding. It's more than likely her friendly neighbourhood bootboys would have wooed her with their party's official newspaper, an eight-page weekly named after the movement's synonymous adopted uniform, *The Blackshirt*. Perhaps the eyes of young Peggy Burns glanced between the calls to 'sack the Jewish dictators', the cry to decide 'for alien or for Briton?', over the adverts for riding boots and John Bull razorblades and the columns of regular hate-monger Alexander Bowie, compiled that year in a special BUF volume called *Bowie's Annual*. If nothing else, she couldn't have escaped the graphic power of the paper's logo, only recently redesigned in May that year to incorporate the party's swastika-style symbol already used on banners, arm-bands and anti-Semitic graffiti streaked throughout London's East End. A fat, black zigzagging lightning bolt within a circle. The future insignia of Ziggy Stardust, indelibly branded in the psyche of 22-year-old Peggy Burns. Mother of David Bowie.

Mosley's blackshirts weren't the last to hurl Starman-shaped thunderbolts in late-thirties England. Another streaked through the darkness of Saturday morning cinemas, rippling upon the chest of an intrepid American football star turned saviour of the universe. In 1938, the second serial inspired by Alex Raymond's *Flash Gordon* comic strip hit screens across the country starring former Olympic swimming gold medallist Larry 'Buster' Crabbe. Where previously Gordon had fought the evil schemes of Ming the Merciless on the planet Mongo, *Flash Gordon's Trip To Mars* brought the action dangerously closer to home. The Martians Gordon encountered took human form, ruled by a vampish queen, an ally of his old foe Ming. Shortly after arriving on Mars, Gordon swaps his clothes for those of the queen's soldiers: a studded collar over a muscle-clinging long-sleeved top emblazoned with a large electric zigzag. Crabbe's Flash Gordon not only saved the world from Ming a second time but reclaimed the lightning bolt from the cheerless clutches of fascism for the high fashion of Mars.

In 1938 there was no hard scientific evidence to eliminate the serial's proposed fantasy of a habitable Mars of art-deco palaces, deafening rocket ships and cave-dwelling clay people. Forty years before Ziggy, no individual had yet to see its surface closer than the hazy distant refractions through a telescope lens, some astronomers distinguishing, or rather imagining, banks of vegetation and a purplish atmosphere called 'the violet layer'. Nor was anybody necessarily any wiser than Gordon's dour academic sidekick, Doctor Zarkov. 'I have repeatedly been asked the question, is there any likelihood of Earth being visited, or should I say invaded, by people from another planet?' remarks Zarkov. 'As to its likelihood, I cannot say. But as to its possibility, the answer must be yes.'

On 30 October 1938 that possibility became a reality. At 8 p.m., millions of American radio listeners tuned in to NBC's regular Sunday night variety programme *The Charlie McCarthy Show*, McCarthy being the cheeky monocled dummy of ventriloquist Edgar Bergen. Those who quickly got bored, if not by Bergen and McCarthy then possibly repelled by Nelson Eddy belting out 'Song Of The Vagabonds' two minutes in, turned their dials over to the CBS network where they heard Ramon Raquello and his Orchestra playing live from the Meridian Room of the Park Plaza Hotel in downtown New York. The concert was suddenly interrupted by a breaking newsflash from a strange meteorite crash on a farm in Grover's Mill, New Jersey. Reporter Carl Phillips narrated the events to listeners live as they happened. 'Ladies and gentlemen, this is the most terrifying thing I have ever witnessed,' gasped Phillips, describing in horror the emergence of 'a monster' from the crater which began to shoot a jet of flame destroying everything in its path. Twenty minutes later the station announcer described the scene from the roof of the CBS building, watching a mass exodus from Manhattan as the bells rang warning people to evacuate the city. 'As the Martians approach.'

It's estimated around six million heard Orson Welles and the Mercury Theatre's contemporary dramatisation of H. G. Wells' *The War Of The Worlds* that night, of which over one million who'd tuned in late took its fake news format as the real thing. The ensuing panic has since become broadcasting history if not, as detailed research suggests, slightly exaggerated myth, nevertheless based on proven instances of listeners jamming the switchboards of local police stations and newspapers in the New Jersey area to report murder, gas attacks and flame-throwing men from Mars. Armed with only words, sound effects and a genius for persuasion, Welles, via Wells, had demonstrated that the human race was ready and willing to accept as fact Zarkov's 'probability' of Martian invasion in the early twentieth century.

Those casual latecomers who tuned in to CBS that night were given no clues they were listening to scripted drama as they heard Raquello's orchestra strike up 'a tune that never loses favour'. The song in question was, by October 1938, an established standard already on its way to becoming one of the most recorded in the history of twentieth-century music. It began as an instrumental that fell into the head of a recently jilted young law student and jazz pianist named Hoagy Carmichael one night in 1927 as he sat alone on the 'spooning wall' of Bloomington University campus, Indiana. 'The stars were bright, close to me, and the North Star hung low over the trees,' he recalled. 'I looked up at the sky and whistled.'

As Hoagy Carmichael & His Pals, he first recorded his divinely inspired melody, then carrying the Spanish subtitle 'Estrellitas', for Indiana's local

Gennett label. Two years later lyrics were added by Mitchell Parish, taking inspiration from Carmichael's original title and a few suggestive opening lines. The result was a song about a song; an ode to the intangible allure of love and music; a romantic, almost cosmic, reverie in 'the purple dusk of twilight time'. A song fit for a Starman. Or at least in the case of the 1931 version by Bing Crosby, fit for those destined to duet with a Starman.

And so it was that on 30 October 1938, in Tunbridge Wells, the unmarried Peggy Burns, just turned 25, prepared to mark the following week's first birthday of her illegitimate son, Terry, while three thousand miles across the Atlantic millions of Americans oblivious to any imminent Martian attack sat beside their radios having just tuned in to Ramon Raquello and his orchestra playing one of their favourite pieces of music: Hoagy Carmichael's ever-popular song about a song. 'A tune that never loses favour.'

A song called 'Stardust'.

SEVEN
THE GOOD SOLDIER

The stars would have seemed especially bright above the blacked-out streets of Hammersmith in the early months of 1940. While the Blitz wouldn't begin until that autumn, London was already bracing itself for the Nazi's aerial lightning strike. Hindsight would rose tint a picture of wartime England digging for victory, keeping calm and carrying on. The reality was closer to the Armageddon panic of Welles' *The War Of The Worlds*. The first casualty of war was the nation's sanity. Six months after Neville Chamberlain's bleak announcement of September 1939 there were more suicides in Hammersmith alone than the local weekly paper could fit on its front pages. Mothers, husbands, nurses and company directors, throwing themselves off balconies, gorging on pills, slitting wrists, choking on belt nooses and mumbling farewell prayers to the god of the gas oven. Others fell victim to the blindness of the blackout: breaking their necks down stairwells, crushed under wardrobes as they toppled trying to hook up their blacking curtains or run down on darkened streets by invisible cars without headlights. Before a single doodlebug had fallen on London, its citizens were doing a grand job of killing themselves without any German assistance.

The cinema projectors rattled on regardless. The films on offer in the British spring of 1940 all but mocked their rationed, death-dodging audience. *Over The Moon. Return To Yesterday. The Stars Look Down. Escape To Happiness.* In *Ninotchka*, cinemagoers couldn't even depend on their supreme goddess Garbo for world-weary empathy. 'Garbo Laughs!' blurted the posters. Nobody in England was in any position to join her.

Over Easter weekend, 1940, Hammersmith's Gaumont Palace celebrated its eighth birthday with the big-screen version of comedian Arthur Askey's popular radio show, *Band Waggon*. But it was another film being shown down the far end of King Street in the ABC Commodore which better eased the effort of war for those fragile folk dangling at the end of their tether. The story of a depressed teenager who escapes the grey existence of economic recession for a Technicolor paradise of glittery shoes and dancing aliens. A premonitory tremor of Hollywood glam called *The Wizard Of Oz* with its yearning lullaby to flee 'somewhere over the rainbow.' Thirty-two years before the Starman arrived on Earth, his signature melody was already taking contagious effect.

Life was no rosier for Peggy Burns and her family down in Tunbridge Wells, doomed to fall in the west Kentish approach to London nicknamed 'doodlebug alley'. Entrusting the care of baby Terry to her parents, Peggy joined the home front women's workforce as a capstan machinist at the same factory in Hayes, Middlesex which later pressed records for EMI's Parlophone label. In the interim she fell pregnant to a co-worker, giving birth to a daughter, Myra, in August 1943. The father had agreed to marry Peggy but vanished. The stigma of a second child out of wedlock was too much for the Burns clan to bear. Aged ten months, Myra was given up for adoption and never seen again. In the wartime life lottery, Peggy Burns was nonetheless one of the lucky ones. Only random chance saved her, and the genes of the Starman, from being among the thirty-seven workers killed when a doodlebug hit the Hayes factory during the final frantic months of Nazi bombing.

Back in the blitzkrieged husk of London, the stress of war continued to drive desperate people to commit desperate acts as terrible in their human devastation as anything dropped by the Luftwaffe. One night in April 1944, a woman finished her late shift at the Ministry of War Transport in Berkeley Square where she'd been involved in preparations for the coming D-Day landings. Heading home during the blackout, she was cornered by four men. Their clothes were civilian but their southern American accents betrayed they were most likely GI deserters. They robbed her and kicked her unconscious, leaving her for dead, bleeding on the pavement. She'd also been pregnant and inevitably miscarried. It was the unenviable task of her friend Sonia Brownell – later to become second wife of George Orwell – to write and tell the victim's husband currently stationed with the Army Educational Corps in Gibraltar. Many years later this bewilderingly violent crime inspired him to write a novel duly dramatised on screen and rebuked by the Crown for the 'impressionable canker' stirred among the youth of the early 1970s. The wartime assault upon the wife of Anthony Burgess, author of *A Clockwork Orange*: a hideous yet vital molecule in the delicate double helix of Ziggy Stardust.

'What did you do in the war, Ziggy?'

We might well ask.

The heroic chorus of Beethoven's Ninth fluttered the Reich's swastika banners in Berlin's State Opera House for Hitler's pleasure. The sacred Japanese stages of kabuki strangeness perished in the flames of American carpet bombing. The strains of Holst's 'Jupiter' kept upper lips stiffened on the BBC while, just up the road from Broadcasting House, the ageing H. G. Wells kept fire watch over Regent's Park. The American Forces Network cheered GIs with the sweet comfort of Artie Shaw and his Orchestra's cherished bugle-tooting storm through Hoagy Carmichael's 'Stardust'. Judy Garland fell down from Oz to Camp Roberts, California, to sing the Starman-shaped melody of 'Over The Rainbow' to servicemen shortly to enter hell in the Pacific. And the mother of David Bowie sweated over a capstan in Middlesex doing her best not to get killed.

Over in North Africa, Peggy Burns' younger brother, named Jimmy after their father, had fought with the Lothians Yeomanry alongside Field Marshal Montgomery's Eighth Army before being shipped to Italy where he was awarded a Distinguished Conduct Medal for his part in the battle of Monte Cassino. Among his fellow 'Desert Rats' who'd similarly struggled to acclimatise to the punishing Saharan heat was a slender sharp-shooting Yorkshireman in his early thirties, calling himself 'John'. He'd been born Haywood Stenton Jones in Doncaster, 1912, second child of a bootmaker called Robert and his wife, Zillah, who died when the boy was four.

When Britain went to war with Germany in 1939, John Jones was a 26-year-old clerk working for Dr Barnardo's children's charity, living in a flat beside Regent's Canal in Camden with his wife, a nightclub singer called Hilda, and a baby daughter born out of his affair with a nurse he'd met on business in Birmingham. The 1930s had been a decade of repeated disappointments for Jones as he frittered away his parents' £3000 inheritance on his pipedream of becoming a showbiz entrepreneur. Blinded by love, he lost two thirds of the money funding a disastrous theatre revue for his new wife. The Joneses gambled what remained on a piano bar in London's Fitzrovia, then a regular drinking haunt of George Orwell. If Orwell himself ever did darken the door of the Boop-A-Doop club, where Hilda entertained in the exotic guise of 'Cherie, the Viennese Nightingale', it evidently wasn't often enough to keep the business afloat. Forced to make ends meet as a hotel porter, John Jones tempered his humiliating sense of failure with alcohol, eventually developing a stomach ulcer. Finding renewed purpose with the job at Barnardo's in 1935 rescued him from physical ruin. In much the same way, Hitler's invasion of Poland in 1939 rescued him from the charade of a by now unsalvageable marriage. When Jones was demobbed after victory in Europe he returned home to be told by his wife she'd found a new lover. They didn't argue, instead taking the pragmatic step of together investing their war savings and buying a house in Brixton, agreeing to proceed with an amicable divorce with Hilda taking custody of their eight-year-old daughter Annette; his child by another woman.

Meantime, John Jones went back to work as a promotions officer for Dr Barnardo's. In the spring of 1946, business took him south of the city, to Tunbridge Wells. A single man again, an innate magnetism to entertainment which cost him his pre-war savings must have still stirred within. Jones could have dined alone anywhere in the town. He plumped for the illusory glamour of the Florida restaurant upstairs in the Ritz cinema.

Minds as spectacular as Kepler, Newton and Einstein have attempted to clarify and comprehend the clockwork of the universe. But do any of us truly know what mischievous secrets power its obscure mechanism?; what cosmic chimes inspire the precise moment when a star decides to explode or another to form? For fate now tapped the sides of the Starman's test tube one last time. Humanity had waited long enough. The preparation was complete. The chemical solution was ready. And so John Jones took his table in the Florida and looked up from his menu at the waitress, a young woman whose beauty refused to betray she was already a 32-year-old mother of two.

John Jones meet Peggy Burns. Father of David Bowie meet mother of David Bowie. The hands of space and time, strike Ziggy o'clock.

In their critically intimate courtship weeks of late March and early April, the Ritz projectors flickered their fanfares of consummation. *The Seventh Veil*, a British romantic drama starring Ann Todd as a concert pianist who ends up a suicidal mental patient until cured by a radical hypnotherapy process using the music of Beethoven. And *Duffy's Tavern*, a star-studded if disappointing American radio spin-off featuring Bing Crosby spoofing the song he'd made famous in the previous year's Oscar-winning *Going*

My Way, 'Swinging On A Star'. Such were the currents of love, lust, Ludwig van, insanity, suicide and moonbeams drifting in the gulfstream of Burns and Jones nine months before the precious fruit of their union was born.

The end of that year, John moved Peggy and nine-year-old Terry Burns into 40 Stansfield Road, the vacant Brixton terrace house he'd recently bought in partnership with his first wife. It would be another year before their divorce became decree absolute. Meaning, for the third time, Peggy would give birth to a child out of wedlock. But, for the first, the dutiful father was finally standing by her.

The first days of 1947 were perishing. A cruel winter had instigated a national fuel crisis with the government forced to seize control of the collieries. The coal shortage was bad enough to halt production at the EMI factory in Hayes, Peggy's former wartime workplace. London staggered to a freezing halt as lorry drivers decided on an unofficial strike, causing a backlog of undelivered mail and animal carcasses, much to the despair of its still ration-couponed housewives.

On the afternoon of Tuesday 7 January, a fresh snow fell over the city. In Hammersmith, chattering jaws cowered for warmth inside the Gaumont Palace cinema to watch *The Jolson Story* – 'a lifetime of supreme entertainment in a cavalcade of Technicolor music and song!' In Westminster, a taxi skidded on the ice and killed a pram-pushing mother, while in Stockwell an 87-year-old man nearly died when he slipped after disembarking a double decker bus.

The streets were still sludgy on the morning of 8 January when, just after 9 o'clock, a brute half-masked in a blue handkerchief held up a bank on Gloucester Road, escaping with £163 and the stains from an inkwell launched at his head by a plucky cashier as he fled. At around the same time, across the river in Brixton, the son of Peggy and John was delivered in Stansfield Road. They named him David Robert Jones.

After his birth, the attendant midwife, a woman of evidently superstitious character, said something quite unexpected. 'This child's been on Earth before,' she told Peggy. 'It's his eyes, they're so knowing.'

The midwife was right. He had. The ideas yet to sparkle in the knowing eyes of Brixton-born David Jones were of ancient universal origin. But he, and he alone, would thread them into wild new ecstatic joys of pure being.

EIGHT
THE SOUND

The year 1947. Twenty-five years before Ziggy Stardust, whose human canvas fate had finally selected in the boy born David Jones. A canvas which now needed to be primed and stretched to the shape of the Starman by the gods of chance and circumstance. In 1947 those gods were already on his side.

That nativity Wednesday in January, in Brixton, the knowing eyes of the infant Bowie first squinted at the world with new-born dreams of domination, while over four thousand miles away a similar working-class fantasist lost in music, haircuts, flashy trousers and visions of lightning bolts, was waking up to his twelfth birthday in Tupelo, Mississippi. Another of history's different boys. Whose conception was so seismic his father blacked out after the moment of climax. Whose birth was so biblical it was said that night there was a strange bluish glow in the sky around the moon. Who was delivered thirty-five minutes after a stillborn twin brother his parents named Jesse Garon. Who later wondered, 'If my twin brother had lived, do you reckon the world could've handled two?' Who always knew, regardless, Planet Earth was only ever big enough for one Elvis Presley.

At the age of twelve, Elvis was already strumming his first guitar, a present from his previous birthday, if initially something of a disappointment. He'd asked for a bicycle, a luxury beyond the means of his poor, God-fearing parents – a besotted, heavy-drinking mother and a desperate, undependable father who missed three crucial years of his son's upbringing picking cotton on a chain gang as penance for doctoring a cheque he'd received in exchange for a pig. In his dad's absence Elvis pined for a male role model, finding one in the comic strip adventures of a boy named Billy Batson who, with a single splutter of the magic word 'Shazam!', transformed himself into the adult superhero Captain Marvel. His impressionable young eyes were especially enamoured with Marvel's costume: gold boots, a white cape and a red jumpsuit marked by a sharp, gold lightning flash.

Flashes of gold lightning were soon joined by the sound of rattling thunder thumping up the road to his Tupelo family home from Shake Rag, a nearby black housing project whose residents triumphed over daily dismay swinging a constant brickbat of rhythm and blues. For a boy on the cusp of adolescence his sneaks into Shake Rag offered a refuge from humdrum reality in a private Oz of alien music. The shrieking profanities from smoky juke joints and the liquor-stewed twangs of front-porch wailers singing the woes to befall them since they'd woken up that morning. Elvis heard and saw what those deafened and blinded by skin colour refused to. That the stark sound of Shake Rag was the same primeval roar and storm unleashed by Beethoven over a century earlier, fired in the post-war heat of the Mississippi Delta, a sound which set the metronome for the rest of his life. It took the genius of Beethoven to invent rock 'n' roll, but the voice of Elvis Presley to sign its belated birth certificate.

True to his vocation as the first rock 'n' roll superstar, the teenage Elvis understood his duty to stand out from the crowd – that pop music was all about the songs but, equally, the trousers. In his case, baggy black ones with pink piping down the side. When his family moved to Memphis it placed him in temptation's way of the zoot suits, pink peg slacks, ruff shirts, white buck shoes, sideburns, pompadours and ducktails as worn by the black dandies of Beale Street. Elvis, pop's original style magpie, reconstructed his wardrobe accordingly. In the corridors of Humes High School he was the solitary pink-clad pompadour punk bobbing amidst a disapproving sea of short back and sides. Even his gait was a source of fascination. 'It was almost as if he was getting ready to draw a gun,' recalled one of his few school friends. 'It was weird.' So Elvis bamboozled straight society, a weirdness of hips, lips, cotton and brilliantine oscillating an anomalous haze between white and black, male and female.

'I don't sound like nobody.'

So the 18-year-old Elvis told Memphis Recording Service office manager Marion Keisker when he walked into their reception at 706 Union Avenue on the humid Saturday afternoon of 18 July 1953. The studio doubled as headquarters of Sun Records, the new venture of established R&B producer Sam Phillips who offered the public a $4 vanity service to make a one-off 78 r.p.m. acetate. Their slogan: 'We record anything – anywhere – anytime.'

Well-worn rock 'n' roll legend would plead Elvis went there to cut a record as a gift for his mother's birthday – but that was another ten months away. In all likelihood he was just restless to hear himself on record. After Keisker set him up in front of the microphone, Elvis started strumming the same beat-up acoustic guitar he'd been dragging around since the age of eleven, opened his mouth and sang. '*Whether skies are grey or blue, any place on Earth will do ...*' He was right. He didn't sound like nobody. Not on this planet.

The two songs Elvis recorded that day, 'My Happiness' and 'That's When Your Heartaches Begin', were ballads. Keisker kept a copy of the songs and made a note of him in the studio log. 'Good ballad singer. Hold.' The following Monday Elvis returned to work cutting metal in a machinist's shop and waited. And waited.

While destiny kept Elvis at bay, Sam Phillips continued to show an instinctive genius for pickaxing black R&B gold on early Sun singles by Rufus Thomas ('Bear Cat', 'Tiger Man'), Little Junior Parker ('Feelin' Good', 'Mystery Train') and the harmonic Tennessee State Penitentiary inmates calling themselves The Prisonaires ('Just Walkin' In The Rain'). Only occasionally did his Midas touch desert him. In early 1954 he gambled on white country singer Doug Poindexter and a Hank Williams-style spur-trembler called 'Now She Cares No More'. The record flopped but a fleck of potential sparkled in the song's co-writer Scotty Moore, guitarist with Poindexter's backing band The Starlite Wranglers. Phillips sensed Moore's keenness to create new music. Moore sensed Phillips' ambitions for Sun to obliterate the racial barricades of the early-fifties American record industry. As Phillips supposedly confided to Keisker: 'If I could find a white man who had the negro sound and the negro feel, I could make a billion dollars.'

It was such a discussion on Saturday 3 July 1954 – nineteen years to the death of Ziggy Stardust – that prompted Keisker to remind Phillips of the unusual dark haired 'good ballad singer' kid who'd now auditioned three times without any success. Moore was intrigued and asked Keisker if she still had his details. She did, though she'd misspelled the name 'Elvis Pressley'. Moore laughed. 'That sounds like something outta science fiction.'

Phillips was still undecided. He knew 'there was something' about the Presley boy's voice but remained at odds where to channel it. Maybe, as Keisker suggested, Moore could help him find the answer. In the early hours of Tuesday 6 July, he did.

Moore had called Elvis, inviting him to join himself and Starlite Wrangler upright bass player Bill Black for a trial session at Phillips' studio booked for seven o'clock on the evening of Monday 5 July. All three fumbled in the creative darkness for a song they all knew, settling on Ernest Tubbs' country ballad 'I Love You Because', kicking it around for hours but making little impression on Phillips in the control room. Around midnight, the trio took a break, wondering whether they should call it a day and try again tomorrow. Until Elvis stood up with his guitar and began to sing ...

Four thousand miles away, dawn had already broken over Clarence Road in Bromley, where seven-year-old David Jones and his family had since moved from Brixton. Perhaps at that very moment the boy stirred in his bed, opening his eyes just as Elvis Presley opened his mouth. The two sons of 8 January awaking half a world away from each another, one physically, the other spiritually.

In Bromley, David Jones yawned.

In Memphis, Elvis Presley yodelled.

'Well, that's all right, mama ...'

Phillips' brain sizzled between his ears in flamed amazement. The fidgety white ballad kid was singing a black juke joint favourite, 'That's All Right', by Arthur 'Big Boy' Crudup. Recorded in 1946, more recently it had been among the first singles issued in a brand new recording format: the 45 r.p.m. vinylite seven-inch single, the destined holy vessel of pop perfection marking the death of the shellac 78 which had carried the sounds of Holst and Hoagy Carmichael. The seven-inch was launched in early 1949 by the label RCA Victor, whose trademark flicked a lightning bolt on the tail of the 'A'. To distinguish Crudup's disc as part of their generic 'blues and rhythm' series, it was pressed in a special coloured vinyl, officially 'cerise' but in the cold light of day more 'red hot red'.

As Elvis started hollering 'That's All Right' Moore and Black followed his lead and jammed along. Phillips told them to stop so he could switch the microphones on and tape it properly. A few takes later, they listened back. Nobody knew exactly what they were hearing, only that it was 'different', 'exciting', 'raw and ragged'. It was a white kid singing black blues attended by the giddy jangles of a country guitar picker and the rhythmic slaps of a gulping bass. So audacious a racial cocktail for 1954 that Moore nervously joked, 'They'll run us out of town.' The following night divine inspiration struck again, this time accelerating a frantic black R&B spin on a white country tune, Bill Monroe's 'Blue Moon Of Kentucky'. Phillips was elated. 'Hell, that's *different*,' he gasped. 'That's a *pop song*!'

Sun Records 209. 'That's All Right' b/w 'Blue Moon Of Kentucky'. By 'Elvis Presley, Scotty and Bill.' The big bang in the singularity of that which the twentieth-century would come to know as rock 'n' roll.

In Memphis, Elvis's fame was instant. Three nights after the spontaneous recording of 'That's All Right', local radio DJ Dewey 'Daddy-O' Phillips was playing a pre-release acetate on repeat, inciting so many requests he called Elvis to the station for his first live on air interview. The incredulous listeners of station WHBQ realised the voice they'd heard was that of a white kid.

The trio returned to Sun the following month, Elvis revealing a little more of his unearthly vocal prowess on the Rodgers and Hart standard 'Blue Moon': warped through his supernatural larynx to become a human distress signal ripping through the depths of the cosmos, a sub-zero shiver of solitude begging for an alien embrace to be told 'you're not alone'. In concert Scotty Moore and Bill Black now became his 'Blue Moon Boys'. To the Southern audiences who first witnessed them in the late summer of 1954 they may as well have come from space. It wasn't just the music, still blithely skipping over an unclassifiable minefield of 'race' and 'folk', 'blues' and 'pop', but the spectacle of Elvis himself, a knee-juddering, hip-wiggling, quiff-flouncing, lip-curling, nerves-a-jangling, 'mama'-yodelling tremble of flesh and trousers.

The shocking vision of Elvis Presley, the body, generated a new evolutionary swoon. A complete desertion of the female senses. A benign adolescent barbarism. A hitherto unseen sexual transfixion. An unquenchable desire to celebrate the absolute 'now'-ness of being alive. After Elvis, the Starman's only expressway to humanity was blindingly obvious. Not theatre, not the symphony, not literature, not poetry, not painting, not the cinema screen. Only pop music. Loud, screaming, seat-ripping, loin-bubbling, rib-breaking, heart-dissolving pop music in all its inscrutable ecstasy.

In May 1955 the ecstasy of Elvis turned to anarchy when the crowd of the Gator Bowl in Jacksonville, Florida started a riot. It was his own fault. 'Girls,' Elvis announced, 'I'll see you all backstage.' The majority of the 14,000 shrieking micro-boppers took him literally. By the time he'd managed to barricade himself in the dressing room they'd torn strips from his jacket and shirt and relieved him of his belt, socks and boots. Guarded by three policemen, the girls continued to pour through an open window like a plague of zombies. When Elvis finally escaped he found his car comprehensively vandalised by the scars of desire: names and numbers scratched into the metalwork and blinding the windscreen in thick smears of lipstick. Such things happened in Florida. A state in America. A cinema restaurant in Tunbridge Wells. Where hips drive kids to riot. Where starry genes collide.

And where pop music blossoms from despair.

The headline in *The Miami Herald* read 'DO YOU KNOW THIS MAN?' The accompanying photo was that of a corpse. He'd jumped from the window of his hotel room having deliberately destroyed all means of identification. The only clue he left was a handwritten note. 'I walk a lonely street.'

The story caught the attention of Tommy Durden, a singer–songwriter in Gainesville, who saw in its 'lonely street' the nucleus of, as he'd describe it, 'a good blues'. Durden took the idea to his friend Mae Axton, a fellow country songwriter in Jacksonville who'd witnessed the Gator Bowl riot first hand. She'd been there in the dressing room with Colonel Tom

Parker, the manager who would soon steer Elvis's career to unchartered agonies of exploitation. It took Durden and Axton no more than half an hour to concoct 'Heartbreak Hotel'.

Sam Phillips had always imagined a billion dollar price tag on any white man who 'had the negro sound and the negro feel'. When he finally found one, he sold him for $35,000 plus an extra $5000 in back royalties. After five records for Sun, Elvis was bought by RCA Victor. The label that created the 45 r.p.m. single and the promised land of Ziggy Stardust.

His debut for RCA was to do for America and the western hemisphere what 'That's All Right' had already done for Memphis and the South. The big bang may have already happened on Sun, but in the eyes and ears of the world rock 'n' roll wasn't properly born until January 1956 with the erotic, 'baby'-bereft pine of a quivering 21-year-old so lonely he could die. RCA Victor 47-6420. 'Heartbreak Hotel', by Elvis Presley.

Rock 'n' roll born from suicide.

Across the Atlantic, the new ration-free England of Anthony Eden, Jimmy Porter and the ghost of Ruth Ellis groped in the post-war darkness for dizzying rhythmic thrills of its own. For the time being it had to contend with the cupped-trumpet honk of trad-jazz, the washboard ricochet of skiffle and the chubby jive of a 30-year-old former American country singer in bowtie, plaid tux and kiss-curl called Bill Haley. Technically 'Rock Around The Clock' was, according to its label, a 'foxtrot', but when Haley and his Comets took it to number one in November 1955 it pumped a deluge of cement in the foundations of Anglo rock 'n' roll. The following April, readers of the *Daily Mirror* were forewarned of another 'Rock Age Idol' fast heading to their shores by histrionic Hollywood correspondent Lionel Crane. 'I have just escaped from a hurricane called Elvis Presley!' The perfect storm of 'Heartbreak Hotel' blasted into the UK charts a few weeks later. The alien had landed, not from Mars but from Memphis. Britain readily surrendered.

As *Mirror* readers braced themselves for Hurricane Pelvis and the anthem of Lonely Street, on London's Old Compton Street two entrepreneurial Australian wrestlers took over the lease of a split-level coffee bar. They kept the name of its previous owners, two brothers surnamed Irani: The 2 I's. Cheaper than most of its espresso-steaming Soho rivals, the new 2 I's began to attract idle teenagers looking for a basement hideaway to spend a few hours sipping on a single Coca-Cola, tapping the Formica to the latest skiffle and rock 'n' roll on the café jukebox, sometimes strumming a guitar and singing along, distorting their Thames-water vowels as best they could to an exotic Southern hillbilly twang.

Among them was a 19-year-old Bermondsey boy fresh from the merchant navy where he'd been hypnotised by one of Elvis's first US television appearances while on shore leave in New York. Tommy Hicks looked less like a rock 'n' roller than he did a Dickensian street urchin; a sweep's brush of hair atop a farthing-charming grin forever threatening to chuckle 'gor blimey!' But in the easily excited atmosphere of the 2 I's basement, Hicks' barrow boy approximation of The Memphis Flash struck a chord of awed admiration among his tea-chest-bass-plucking peers.

By late September, Hicks had been snatched from the 2 I's by Decca Records, renamed Tommy Steele and frogmarched into their West Hampstead studios to record his debut single, 'Rock With The Caveman'. Possibly intended as a pithy Darwinian thesis on the primeval origins of rock 'n' roll: '*The British museum's got my head/Most unfortunate 'cause I ain't dead.*' Or possibly not. Either way it booted Steele high up the top 20. Britain's first born and bred rock 'n' roll star. 'The English Elvis Presley.'

His overnight success demanded a hasty follow-up hit. Steele rushed off 'Doomsday Rock', a sliver of jitterbugging daftness about the end of the world; Ziggy's 'Five Years' in crude miniature. The single flopped, but Steele was already unstoppable, closing 1956 as the headliner on a countrywide variety package above 'television's crazy comedians' Mike and Bernie Winters and a 'Welsh wizard of the keyboards' calling himself 'Thunderclap' Jones. In early December, the latter's thunder confronted his lightning namesake when the tour spent a week at London's Finsbury Park Empire. Among the audience on its closing weekend was nine-year-old David Jones from Bromley, there with his dad and his 14-year-old cousin, Kristina. It was the boy's first rock 'n' roll concert. A foreshadow of a future legend. A shake, rattle and roll of things to come. A mirror image of what might be: Tommy Hicks, a London boy from south of the river much like himself but renamed, reinvented, reborn as a teenage god.

A handful of originals aside, the bulk of Steele's twenty-five-minute act put a Bermondsey beat on current hits by America's rock 'n' roll pioneers; he'd score his only number one early in the new year knocking 'Singing The Blues' by Detroit's Guy Mitchell off the top of the UK charts with his own rival version. 'Perhaps one day Tommy will sing songs as English as his speaking accent, or his grin,' pondered journalist Colin MacInnes, soon-to-be author of *Absolute Beginners*. 'If this should happen we will hear once again, for the first time since the decline of the Music Halls, songs that tell of our own world.'

Songs of our own world, and possibly others, electrified the mind of David Jones as he left Finsbury Park that night. His dad, the easily starstruck Boop-A-Doop dreamer of times past, had managed to squeeze him backstage, where David collected Steele's signature in his autograph book. On the return journey to Bromley he chatted with his cousin about their favourite Steele songs. David loved the one about a hound dog. Kristina told him it was by Elvis Presley. She had the original record.

Back in the Jones' family home, David watched spellbound as Kristina played him her copy of 'Hound Dog', jiggling her body and flapping her limbs lost in its rhythm. Never before had he seen her so physically possessed. Nor could he blame her. The firing-squad snare rolls. The razor-blade guitar solo. And that voice, a roar of savagery in a storm of sex. 'It really impressed me,' he'd remember. 'The power of the music.'

Like the alchemical 'Shazam!' transforming Billy Batson into Captain Marvel. Or Elvis Presley into The Memphis Flash. Or Tommy Hicks into Tommy Steele. 'The power of the music.' So on a Bromley winter's night in 1956, nine-year-old David Jones heard the first cry of destiny telling him to become Ziggy Stardust.

NINE
THE FEAR

As Elvis Presley writhed his way to immortality on US television screens in the early months of 1956, back in Memphis Sam Phillips, now $40,000 richer, faced the future in urgent need of a replacement to expand his Sun Records empire. Hope prospered in two recent signings, hillbilly bopper Carl Perkins and jail-bothering country roughneck Johnny Cash, not to mention the increased traffic of starry-eyed hopefuls beating a path to Sun's door believing themselves to be 'the next Elvis'.

Among them was a 20-year-old piano-savaging Bible-school dropout named Jerry Lee Lewis. His father, a poor farmer from Ferriday, Louisiana, had raised petrol funds for their three-hundred-mile trip to Memphis by selling close to four hundred eggs from the family chicken coop. Turning up unannounced at Sun, his hopes were scrambled to be told the legendary Phillips himself was out of town. Not to waste the journey, Lewis still cut an audition tape for producer Jack Clement in any case, singing 'everything' he could remember. Some blues, some gospel, and an ever-popular song about purple dusk and twilight time called 'Stardust'.

Clement liked Lewis but told him to go away and come back with an original rock 'n' roll song. A month later, he did, joining Phillips' roster as both a recording star in his own right – 'Jerry Lee Lewis and his Pumping Piano' – and Sun's in-house session pianist, lending his distinctive Ferriday fire to Perkins, Cash and a new novelty disc from the pen of reclusive Indiana songwriter Ray Scott. A few years earlier Scott had been at a drive-in movie when he noticed a strange object 'all lit up and shaped like a cigar' speeding high over the horizon – eventual fuel for a song about '*little green men*' landing on Earth in a UFO to teach humans how to bop: '*They were three-foot high, hit a few bars/ Started rock and roll all the way from Mars.*' Sun passed Scott's demo to Arkansas-born singing truck driver Billy Lee Riley who eagerly kicked it into familiar rockabilly shape, embellishing the concept by naming his backing band the Little Green Men and tailoring matching green baize suits to wear on stage.

So it came to pass in February 1957, fifteen years before Ziggy, that the fuses of pop music and visitors from outer space were finally soldered together as one on Sun Records 260. Billy Riley and his Little Green Men. 'Flyin' Saucers Rock & Roll'.

When David Jones was born on 8 January 1947 the term 'flying saucer' didn't exist. Nor would it for another six months. Not until 32-year-old American pilot Kenneth Arnold reported the sighting of several 'peculiar looking' objects flying over Mount Rainier, south of Seattle, Washington. On the afternoon of 24 June, Arnold was alone in a two-seater plane when he spotted a wedge-shaped formation of nine unidentified aircraft all seemingly without tails streaking through the sky at unnaturally high speed. When later giving statements to the FBI and news reporters, Arnold described them as 'saucer-like'. Simplified by the press for ease of headlines, the 'flying saucer' was born.

Only two weeks after Arnold's sighting, on 8 July in New Mexico, the front page of the *Roswell Daily Record* declared 'RAAF CAPTURES FLYING SAUCER ON RANCH IN ROSWELL REGION'. An official statement issued by the Roswell Army Air Field intelligence office announced that they had 'come into possession of a flying saucer', which had crashed on a local ranch. According to the *Record*, 'No details of the saucer's construction or its appearance had been revealed.' The following day, the same paper reported it had all been a false alarm – the 'saucer' was really part of a weather balloon. Yet the seeds of the century's most famous UFO conspiracy theory had now been sown: that the US military had recovered a genuine interplanetary craft and its occupants; that six months to the day David Bowie popped into the world in Brixton, a Starman had already fallen to Earth on a ranch in Roswell, New Mexico.

Flying saucer scares were symptomatic of an age shivering with the onset of Cold War and the shock and awe of atomic power. An age more than ready to rekindle the panic ignited by Welles via Wells not ten years earlier. Those first flinches of invasion paranoia in the press quickly led to shrieks of low-budget hysteria on the soundstages of early-fifties Hollywood. Among the first and best flying saucer films was 1951's *The Day The Earth Stood Still*, a political plea for anti-nuclear global pacifism masquerading as sci-fi drama. Klaatu, a humanoid alien, and his eight-foot robot Gort, arrive in Washington DC in a giant silver saucer. On disembarking Klaatu announces, 'We have come to visit you in peace,' only to be promptly shot by the trigger-happy National Guard. He survives, escaping government custody and returning to his planet after delivering a stern warning to humanity – that it should cease its present course towards atomic war or risk obliteration by his peacekeeping space police.

As a benign extraterrestrial missionary come to save Earth from itself, Klaatu was something of a Ziggy-in-the-rough, one who in actor Michael Rennie boasted almost as fabulously feline a set of cheekbones. He was also one of few exceptions to the rule of fifties Hollywood sci-fi with its endless assault from slimy interplanetary aggressors intent on world domination – the perfect climate for producer George Pal's 1953 film version of *The War Of The Worlds*, its Martians attacking a Commie-fearing gung-ho America, foregoing Wells' original tripod fighting machines for stingray-shaped flying saucers.

In Britain, Wells' old friend, Prime Minister Winston Churchill, was becoming increasingly agitated by recurring UFO stories in the press. He'd been aware of the phenomenon since 1944 when, during the final months of the war, an RAF pilot logged the first official military report of a flying metallic disc. As with all future military sightings, Churchill ordered an official silence on the subject for fear of destabilising the still-victorious national morale. But by the summer of 1952, as the low-budget Hollywood hokum of *Flight To Mars* hit British cinemas and fresh press reports of UFOs over the White House bounced across the transatlantic newswire, Winston's nagging unease was serious enough to contact his Air Ministry. 'What does all this stuff about flying saucers amount to?' he demanded. 'What can it mean? What is the truth?'

The ministry placated him with the assurance that a full intelligence study had already been undertaken and 'all the incidents reported could be explained'. But not all of them could. In the high summer of 1956, months after Churchill had retired from office, an incident occurred within British air space which would forever alter the Ministry of Defence's stance on flying saucers.

The date was Monday 13 August. In Bromley, nine-year-old David Jones was enjoying the school holidays. In America, the unstoppable Elvis Presley was whoopin' and a-hollerin' towards his third number one with 'Hound Dog'. In London, Tommy Hicks was still busking for the Soho slickers in the basement of the 2 I's, while over in Hammersmith the Gaumont Palace projector shone the tale of *Jedda* the aboriginal girl, 'as wild as the land she loved'. And just after 5 p.m. in the radar traffic control room of RAF Lakenheath in Suffolk, Technical Sergeant Forrest Perkins began the late shift as watch supervisor.

As night closed in, Perkins took a call from another RAF base in Norfolk warning of a mysterious object heading their way at such an extraordinary speed those who saw it could only describe 'a blur of light'. The object soon showed up on Lakenheath's radar. Perkins monitored its odd behaviour for the next half hour: a blip remaining static for five-minute periods before gliding in straight lines at a constant six hundred miles per hour then stopping still for a few minutes' rest only to glide on again. The same movements were tracked by neighbouring RAF bases in Bentwaters and the air surveillance unit at Neatishead. Assessing the risk posed by the UFO, the decision was taken to scramble a de Havilland Venom night fighter to intercept it.

Perkins guided the Venom towards the still stationary object. Half a mile from contact, the pilot radioed. 'I've got my guns locked on him.' Seconds later the Lakenheath radar showed the UFO had mysteriously slipped behind the Venom and was now shadowing its flight path, in Perkins' words, 'Like it was glued right behind him.' The pilot spent the next ten minutes trying in vain to shake the UFO with a series of desperate ducks, dives and loop the loops. As Perkins noted, they could tell from the pilot's radio tone, 'He was getting worried, excited and also pretty scared.'

Low on fuel, the pilot announced he had to return to base. Perkins watched him on the Lakenheath radar, tailed by the UFO for a few miles until it stopped, resuming a stationary position. 'I saw something,' said the pilot, 'but I'll be damned if I know what it was.'

A second fighter was scrambled to intercept the UFO. Before it had a chance to approach its target, the engine inexplicably started to malfunction. The second pilot was forced to return to base also. Minutes later the UFO moved out of radar range and was lost.

The next day, anxious top brass from the Ministry of Defence swooped upon the RAF bases concerned, interviewing all pilots, crew and radar technicians involved and reminding them of their obligation to the strict thirty-year rule of silence under the Official Secrets Act. Log books were taken away for expert analysis, never to be seen again. Relevant papers were 'accidentally destroyed'. Shaky footage from the first Venom's gun camera, allegedly containing images of the UFO, was also removed to MoD headquarters in Whitehall. It too has since vanished without trace.

Ten years after the 'Lakenheath–Bentwaters Incident' – its official name in the annals of ufology – in 1966, American physicist and flying saucer sceptic Dr Edward Condon at the University of Colorado accepted his government's offer to compile a detailed scientific report into the UFO phenomenon, examining a number of cases from around the world. For security reasons the names of locations were changed, with Lakenheath becoming 'Greenwich'. Condon's committee analysed all data, including Perkins' testimony. Their conclusion made for the most stunning extract of his otherwise fiercely dismissive report published in 1969 as *Scientific Study Of Unidentified Flying Objects*. 'Although conventional or natural explanations certainly cannot be ruled out,' wrote Condon, 'the probability of such seems low in this case and the probability that at least one genuine UFO was involved appears to be fairly high.'

Those who lived to speak of the events of 13 August 1956 beyond any stipulated MoD embargo were left in no doubt that on Lakenheath, Condon was right. At least one genuine UFO. 'No aircraft then or since has shown the flight envelope demonstrated by that object,' protested Flight Lieutenant Freddie Wimbledon, chief controller on the night at RAF Neatishead. 'Are we so arrogant,' he concluded, 'as to think we are the only intelligent life in the universe?'

The morning of 14 August 1956. Mere hours after an unexplained blip vanished from a radar screen in Lakenheath, David Jones awoke in Bromley; a nine-year-old boy who in only a few months' time would have his juvenile senses irreversibly blinded by the fiendish light of rock 'n' roll. Who for the time being knew nothing of Tommy Steele, nor Elvis Presley. Nor, like the rest of Britain denied all knowledge of the incident in the press, the unidentified blur of light which had freaked and foxed the major resources of the Royal Air Force one hundred miles away over East Anglia as he slept.

The Starman still wasn't due for another sixteen years. The boy David had yet to assemble him. Yet Her Majesty's government was now poised and ready. For they knew what he didn't. That, as of 13 August 1956, Ziggy Stardust might land any time tomorrow.

TEN
THE PROFESSOR

David Jones wasn't like other boys. Other boys his age played cowboys and Indians and followed the adventures of 'Dan Dare, Pilot of the Future' in the *Eagle*. Other boys his age didn't suddenly announce 'I think I'm dying,' and lie still for hours trying to convince their parents rigor mortis had taken effect. Other boys didn't pull melodramatic 'moodies'. They weren't mysterious. They weren't, as even he'd later admit 'slightly camp'. They weren't anything like an alien pop messiah in hibernation.

Even his earliest taste in music was askew of the norm. Before discovering rock 'n' roll his mother encouraged him through the national ritual of Sunday lunchtimes listening to the BBC Light Programme's *Family Favourites*, kitchen aromas wafted through the furnishings by the strains of 'With A Song In My Heart' and the comforting cut-glass tones of 'forces' favourite' Jean Metcalfe. Except that David's ears were piqued not by comfort but by upset. Musical awkwardness. Hidden within this seemingly safe, morally chaste ark of pleasantries were the Trojan horses of hazy cosmic jive. The Weird Notes. The kind that jack-knifed the melody of Danny Kaye's 'Inchworm' and 'Tubby The Tuba' or his mother's favourite, Mendelssohn's 'O, For The Wings Of A Dove' aria as trilled by the famous boy soprano Master Ernest Lough. Notes that didn't travel straight but zigged and zagged, as if veering off their intended path. These were the strange sounds of David Jones' childhood. And then came stranger visions.

On Tuesday 2 June 1953, with the 18-year-old Elvis Presley yet to darken the door of Memphis Recording Services and bump the world off its axis, in Britain some twenty million people spent most of their day staring at a small oblong window in a hulking wooden coffin, peering into a new dimension of monochrome majesty. Largely thanks to the public anticipation of this, the spectacle of the Coronation of Queen Elizabeth II, in the weeks beforehand an estimated million extra households invited these bulky, fuzzy, murmuring aliens into their living rooms as sales of the hitherto middle-class luxury of the television set rocketed.

One such cathode monolith landed in the front room of the Joneses, then living in Bickley to the south of Bromley. Like the other million families who'd succumbed to Coronation fever, in the weeks that followed the Joneses adjusted to life with their costly new invader in the corner of the living room. Weekday afternoons at 4 p.m. sharp brought *Watch With Mother* featuring the antics of Andy Pandy and, David's favourite, The Flowerpot Men. Evenings ushered in serious political chat with *The Voice Of The People* and the informative natural history of *Animal Patterns* presented by a young David Attenborough. Saturdays were devoted to sports coverage until the tea-time *Children's Hour* starring Sooty and Sweep. And at 8.15 p.m. Saturday nights starting 18 July, the first part of a new thriller serial called *The Quatermass Experiment*.

Six-year-old David would have been packed off to his bed before the programme started. Only perhaps, as he'd later claim, on that first Saturday he silently crept on tiptoe down the stairs and watched, unseen by his parents, from behind the settee. And his ears, already attuning to the scales of weird, would have smouldered at the discordant awe of its theme tune. And his pliable mind would have swollen with wonder to watch the story unfold of the first manned rocket flight into outer space, of some unexplained malfunction sending the vessel crash-landing to a terraced street just like his own in south London with only one of its three crew emerging alive.

And if he did, then at 8.50 p.m. in Bromley as the boy David crept back to bed 'rigid with fear', disturbed by all he'd seen and heard – a rocket scientist named Quatermass, strange things falling to the London suburbs from space, news reporters talking about 'flying saucer scares', men with sandwich boards proclaiming the end of the world and the sense-numbing assault of its theme tune – then simultaneously in Memphis where it was just approaching 3 p.m., Elvis Presley would have first set foot in the studios of 706 Union Avenue, loitering in the queue until it was his turn to tell office manager Marion Keisker, 'I don't sound like nobody.'

So, on Saturday 18 July 1953, the stars aligned between Tennessee and Greater London as the two eighth of January boys turned their respective corners. The stars aligned, and also the planets. For the tune seared into young David's head by the opening of *The Quatermass Experiment* was from a pre-existing piece of classical music. A recent recording of Gustav Holst's famous astrological suite. Its ferocious Wellsian overture: 'Mars, The Bringer Of War.'

The first *Quatermass* series was itself a literal experiment in a dramatic medium still finding its feet in a post-war climate of 'radio with pictures' beamed live from the studios of Alexandra Palace. An experiment much like that described in its narrated prologue, 'an operation designed to discover some unknown truth', born as much out of administrative oversight as the brilliantly daring mind of its creator, Nigel Kneale.

With all BBC hands to the pump preparing the schedule surrounding the Coronation, it had somehow escaped the attention of controllers until the very last minute that they'd left a six-week gap in the Saturday-night schedule over the summer period from mid-July through to the end of August. As a matter of extreme urgency, the head of drama asked the staff scriptwriters to come up with something – 'anything!' – to fill the looming dead air. Luckily their department had already recruited Kneale, a 31-year-old writer of Lancashire–Manx heritage who'd previously studied at RADA and published an award-winning collection of short stories.

Kneale's response was a science-fiction idea called *Bring Something Back …!* Its ambitious premise of manned spaceflight seemed a little far-fetched for 1953 – a year when humans had only just conquered the summit of Mount Everest but had yet to lob so much as a frisbee beyond the Earth's atmosphere. The BBC were nevertheless as enthusiastic as they were desperate. Kneale was given the go-ahead for the six-part series, soon retitled when he came to christen its central rocket scientist, a respectable professor whose authority should command the audience's full trust. He chose Bernard as a first name in homage to the head of Jodrell Bank Observatory, astronomer Bernard Lovell. The surname he found at random, flicking through the London telephone directory and plumping for that of a firm of East End grocers. Quatermass.

The first original science-fiction drama on UK television, *The Quatermass Experiment* was uniquely – defiantly – British. Resisting the ray-guns and flying saucer kitsch of contemporary Hollywood, Kneale brought something of the 'Martians-in-Surrey' mischief of H. G. Wells to the small screen, stirred up with a generous helping of Mary Shelley's *Frankenstein*. Professor Bernard Quatermass is head of the British Experimental Rocket Group, who launch three astronauts into space from a base in Australia. Once in orbit, ground control lose contact with the rocket fearing it, and its crew, are lost for ever. To their relief the rocket reappears on their radar screens, now way off target and falling back to Earth. It crashes in a terraced street west of Wimbledon Common, where Quatermass, the police and the prying press gather to retrieve the crew. Quatermass is horrified to discover that only one of the three men has survived, the other two pilots having mysteriously vanished. The more horrifying truth is all three pilots have been subsumed into a single being by an unknown extraterrestrial presence which gradually mutates into a murderous and gruesome space monster.

Much like H. G. Wells, who conjured a Martian invasion from thin air in an age when no scientist could yet disprove the possibility of such an attack, so half a century later Kneale stared into similar chasms of cosmic mystery and filled the gaping hole with terror. It would be another eight years before Yuri Gagarin became the first human being in space. In the summer of 1953, the fear of what might happen if we ever placed our bodies beyond our planet's atmosphere was still a legitimate scientific concern.

Quatermass returned to TV screens in October 1955; David now eight and his family finally settled at 4 Plaistow Grove, a terraced two-up two-down within shaking distance of trains passing through Sundridge Park station on the short branch line to Bromley North. Two years older, two years more mysterious, David's memories of Kneale's *Quatermass II*, still thundering with the dread of Holst's 'Mars', must have imbedded even deeper into his mind. Between the two series Kneale had confirmed himself a peerless televisual dramatist with his adaptation of George Orwell's *Nineteen Eighty-Four* for the BBC, retaining something of its dystopian gloom for his second *Quatermass*. This time the professor becomes roped into exposing a government cover-up surrounding a futuristic factory complex which has taken over the southern coastal town of Winnerden Flats. The plant is supposed to be developing a new kind of synthetic food, the official whitewash for its giant domed silos harbouring an alien species in the process of colonising Earth, fed and maintained by zombified human workers under its power. Once again, Kneale wickedly plonked unimaginable cosmic menace bang in the heart of a Thermos-flask-and-sandwiches provincial England. In one of its most memorable scenes a working-class family who make the fatal mistake of picnicking too near the alien factory find themselves at the mercy of the zombie guards. 'Look 'ere, mate,' says the scrawny father, unaware of imminent death at the hands of interplanetary evil. 'You stop shovin' us around or I'll write to the papers!'

By its fourth episode, broadcast 8 p.m. Saturday night, the BBC felt it necessary to forewarn viewers that in the corporation's opinion 'it is not suitable for children or for those of you who may have a nervous disposition'. The real horror of *Quatermass II* wasn't that of the aliens – seen briefly through a silo hatch as an amorphous gurgling compost heap of space toxins – but of an omnipotent unseen enemy, one whose spectre is that skulking conspiratorially in the corridors of Whitehall. Kneale's plot placed civil servants under the aliens' influence, dressing up the threat from beyond our world as the figure of authority, the man from the ministry, the kind of trenchcoat and briefcase commuter to be seen any day of the week scurrying between London and its suburbs. In the eyes of an eight-year-old Bromley boy, the *Quatermass II* model of the thing from outer space looked exactly like his own father.

It would be three years before the two worlds of David Jones and Bernard Quatermass, fact and fantasy, boy and man, collided again. For David, they were the years of rock 'n' roll baptism, a chain reaction of epiphany after sonic epiphany.

1956: the jumpstart of Tommy Steele at the Finsbury Park Empire and cousin Kristina freaking out to Elvis Presley's 'Hound Dog'.

1957: David turned ten and heard 'God'. Little Richard's 'Long Tall Sally' was released in January, but it was the B-side, 'Tutti Frutti', which blew a hole in his cerebrum with, as he'd describe, 'energy, colour and outrageous defiance'. His discovery of Little Richard was compounded when an American serviceman donated his record collection to Dr Barnardo's head office, where John Jones picked out a few rock 'n' roll discs for his son. Among them was a 45 r.p.m. copy of Richard's 'The Girl Can't Help It', not out in Britain for another month, galvanising his faith in a rock 'n' roll idol he'd yet to clap eyes on. 'I had heard

God,' he'd recall, 'now I wanted to see him.' He'd get the chance in mid-February when Richard's film debut *Don't Knock The Rock* blasted into the Gaumont at the end of Bromley High Street, just around the corner from H. G. Wells' birthplace. David's new God was a gorgeous pompadoured black Elvis with a smile like a supernova, making camp foreplay with his piano in an oversized silvery suit, throwing the occasional leg over the keys and flanked by four saxophone-tooting disciples. It was a vision as heavenly as the accompanying sound. A new awareness, a new dream formed in ten-year-old David's head. 'To be in a band playing saxophone behind Little Richard.'

1958: Aged eleven, David's doors of perception were battered afresh by the gut-bucket guitar boogie of Chuck Berry. 'Sweet Little Sixteen' reached the UK top 20 in late spring, igniting the passions of David and his best friends George Underwood and Geoff MacCormack. Sadly for Berry his follow up, 'Johnny B. Goode' – a song so otherworldly it would one day join Beethoven in outer space as the only rock 'n' roll tune on Voyager's Golden Record – failed to chart in Britain. Upon its B-side was the first physical portent of the sound of Ziggy Stardust, a song Berry composed during a pre-concert jam, finding a riff which refused to leave his memory. 'I waxed in a tune with words about a dance hall that stayed open a little overtime,' he'd explain. 'Rockin' 'til the early morning had been used so 'til the moon went down was the same time of day.' So the first song from the Starman's future repertoire silently struck England in May 1958. The B-side of London Records 45-HLM8629. The 'crazy, crazy sound' of Chuck Berry's 'Around & Around'.

That same summer of '58, UK pop suffered its first alien invasion courtesy of American actor Sheb Wooley's one-horned, one-eyed 'Purple People Eater', still bothering the charts in August when David joined the Bromley cub scouts' annual summer camp on the Isle of Wight. He insisted on dragging along his ukulele and the plywood tea-chest string bass John Jones had indulgingly built for him. Sword and shield for his first public performance that summer camp when he joined his best friend George on a handful of skiffle favourites, including Lonnie Donegan's previous number one 'Gamblin' Man' and its double A-side, 'Putting On The Style'. Aged eleven, Ziggy's boyhood vessel had found his singing voice. *'Putting on the agony, putting on the style, that's what all the young folks are doing all the while ...'*

For television's most famous rocket scientist, the three years between *Quatermass II* and his return, Christmas week 1958, in *Quatermass And The Pit* had narrowed the gap between science and fiction. 'Time has caught up with Quatermass,' agreed Kneale, noting that since his creation's first outing, 'We have all been shot into a factual Space Age.' In October the previous year, Russia launched the world's first satellite, the four-pronged aluminium sphere Sputnik I. In the words of the BBC's Reg Turnill, Sputnik 'acted as the starter's pistol in the Soviet–American race to put men on the Moon'. It also acted as a premature death knell to the immediate career of David's hero, Little Richard. Already unsettled by hallucinations of angels and burning plane wings during a flight between concerts in Australia, Richard interpreted the launch of Sputnik as 'a big ball of fire' in the sky – a commandment from the Almighty to give up rock 'n' roll and become a preacher.

The third Quatermass was Kneale's smartest, bleakest and most philosophically profound variation on the extraterrestrial invasion yet, aided by a dramatically improved production budget and a new theme tune: the alarming fanfare of Trevor Duncan's 'Mutations' replacing Holst, a switch which wouldn't have bothered David – having since bought a budget LP of *The Planets* he could hear 'Mars' any time he liked.

Kneale's 'Pit' is an excavation on a London underground station in Knightsbridge where work ceases when builders discover a strange, primitive skull. Analysis reveals it to be five million years old, before known human history. Quatermass is called for assistance when the archaeological investigation exposes a giant cylinder deep in the earth, much like an unexploded bomb. It turns out to be an ancient spacecraft from Mars, marked with Kabbalistic symbols and containing the dead bodies of insectoid, lobster-like beings with three legs – Kneale's subtle anthropological nod to the tripod Martians of H. G. Wells. The professor gradually pieces together the abominable implications of the capsule's contents. Millions of years ago, the innately aggressive Martians executed a mass purge of their own race, exterminating any defects and mutations, effectively destroying their own world before seeking to colonise another. The dark secret of human evolution – *we* are the Martians. The final episode aired on Monday 26 January 1959. In the closing scene, Quatermass is shown addressing the British nation in an explanatory TV lecture. 'Every war crisis, witch hunt, race riot and purge is a reminder and a warning,' seethed Quatermass. '*WE ARE THE MARTIANS*! If we cannot control the inheritance within us, this will be their *second* dead planet.'

Little David. Twelve years-old. Headful of Little Richard, saxophones and skiffle. Sat in his living room in Bromley amidst the same suburban streets where, at his age, H. G. Wells committed fantasy genocide, a copy of Holst's *Planets* in his bedroom and a face staring out of his TV screen telling him that he, David Robert Jones, is a Martian.

As the programme finished just past 8.35 p.m., fourteen miles away in the BBC's Riverside Studios, Quatermass actor André Morell and the rest of the cast congratulated themselves on a successful broadcast. While some of the action had been pre-recorded out of necessity, the majority was acted live as transmitted, the climactic Martian speech included. Heading homewards, those actors and technicians who didn't have their own transport would have made the short walk to the nearest underground station. A few minutes' stroll up Queen Caroline Street to Hammersmith Broadway. Just past the Gaumont Palace cinema.

ELEVEN

MATEUS!

She'd long been Peggy Jones but her first son still carried her maiden name, Burns. After three years' national service with the RAF, Terry Burns returned home a few weeks before the Quatermass Christmas of 1958. In Plaistow Grove he found that the kid brother he'd left behind mesmerised by *Watch With Mother* was now an alert rock 'n' roll apostle with a hunger for knowledge, a clear gift for drawing and painting, and an obsession with all things American. David Jones was a juvenile sculpture already showing its future adult form but still susceptible to moulding by the 21-year-old wisdom of one who'd been and seen the world. Or at the very least Malta and North Africa.

And so, during that fragile first passage into adolescence, Terry Burns delicately tweaked the pliable clay of youth. With the sounds of modern jazz. John Coltrane, Eric Dolphy and Charlie Parker. And with the bible of the beats.

In July 1947, while baby David gurgled in Brixton, and America took its first twitchy glances at the skies for Kenneth Arnold's flying saucers, a 25-year-old Columbia University dropout and discharged marine named Jack Kerouac hitched from New York to Denver to visit his friend, the freewheeling poet, drug addict and bisexual petty criminal

Neal Cassady. Kerouac made similar pilgrimages back and forth across the country over the next few years, bumming rides to Los Angeles and San Francisco and south of the border to Mexico, either with Cassady or visiting similar likeminded – outminded – bohemian desperados including poet Allen Ginsberg and novelist William Burroughs. Together these trips formed the autobiographical narrative of *On The Road*, Kerouac's groundbreaking second novel, published in America in 1957 and in the UK the following year.

As the adult David recalled, 'I liked school until I was twelve. I have an older brother and he was always a reader, more than I was. He made me read *On The Road* by Jack Kerouac. From then on I didn't go to school much.' In the pages of Kerouac, the Bromley boy became frantically, demonically and angelically drunk on its cast of exotic characters: the pseudonymous Sal Paradise (Kerouac), Dean Moriarty (Cassady) and Carlo Marx (Ginsberg). New escapist reveries bevelling the brain of a twelve-year-old into that of the Starman. Even Ziggy himself would one day tell the American press that reading *On The Road* 'was the most important thing that ever happened to me'. He wasn't alone.

By the late 1950s many a young English heart was tempted by the United States of Make Believe. Who'd be a David Jones when you could be a Sal Paradise? Who'd be a Reg Smith when you could be a Marty Wilde? Or a Ron Wycherley when you could be a Billy Fury?

And who'd be a nobody from Isleworth when you could be a somebody from Hollywood?

He said he came from Hollywood and his name was Vince Taylor. The now 'world famous' 2 I's coffee bar of Tommy Steele legend hadn't seen anything like him. His hair was just like Elvis Presley's, he spoke with a lip-curling 'crazy, man!' twang and his clothes were genuine 'Made In America'. The real deal. When he danced it was a wobble of wayward limbs, like a marionette whose strings were being yanked by four different people in opposite directions at once. When he sang he was out of tune and out of time. But it didn't matter. Vince Taylor was the physical embodiment of fifties cool. A blessed gift, to them, from the gods of rock 'n' roll.

It didn't take long before the buzz around this American alien in the heart of Soho snared him a record contract. Calling his backing band the Playboys, he released his first single in November 1958, pairing two covers of tracks originally recorded for Sam Phillips' Sun label: Roy Orbison's 'I Like Love' and Ray Scott's 'Right Behind You Baby'. It made no impact. The songs were fine, but his singing wasn't. Still, no one could deny Vince's contagious effect on audiences. When the Playboys appeared on a Saturday morning bill at the Gaumont cinema in Shepherd's Bush the owners had to call the police to calm the seat-ripping scenes of screamage Taylormania.

He hoped to inject the dynamism of his stage act into his next record, a song he'd written himself called 'Brand New Cadillac' – a twang-barbed basilisk of a tune with Vince straining at the wheel of his Ford desperately trying to keep pace with his baby as she vanishes over the horizon in her shiny new convertible. The B-side was the ballad 'Pledging My Love', popularised by tragic bluesman Johnny Ace who'd accidentally killed himself in a catastrophic game of Russian roulette; a rock 'n' roll suicide in all but name. Released in April 1959, the cloth-ears of *New Musical Express* critic and future *Ready Steady Go!* presenter Keith Fordyce dismissed it for lacking 'any distinguishing feature'. Cursed by similar apathy elsewhere, 'Brand New Cadillac' missed the charts and skidded into pop's cheated abyss.

Still without a hit to his name, Vince could always fascinate the press with stories of the life he'd left behind in America. He said he'd been in the US Army, just like Elvis Presley, who was currently serving out his draft in Friedberg, Germany. He said he'd been a member of a Los Angeles hot-rod gang called The Roadmasters. That he came close to being mortally wounded in a knife fight, just like James Dean in *Rebel Without A Cause*. That he'd been discovered battered and bruised by a kindly stranger who allowed him to convalesce in their home for three days while he reassessed his life, coming to the conclusion he should travel to England and become a rock 'n' roll star. Always ready with a great story was Vince Taylor.

Except there was no Vince Taylor. While it was true he'd grown up in Hollywood, he wasn't American. He was British, born in July 1939 in Isleworth, west London, before his family emigrated to California when he was seven years-old. And his name wasn't Vince Taylor. He'd taken the 'Vince' from Elvis's character in *Jailhouse Rock* and the 'Taylor' from actor Robert Taylor, star of *Quo Vadis* and *Ivanhoe*. His real name was Brian Holden. Vince was merely a character 18-year-old Brian created out of thin air in an intrepid, if doomed, bid to conquer British rock 'n' roll. A singing, shaking figment conjured by a fragile, feeble mind …

Vince Taylor didn't officially exist but neither did David Jones until 5 April 1960. The boy who would be Ziggy had lived the first thirteen years of his life without a birth certificate. Born out of wedlock, he'd been left absent from all parish records until he needed a passport for a family trip to France.

Stepping into adolescence, young David's was a world where rock 'n' roll and death were already interchangeable. The previous year Buddy Holly had been killed in a plane crash alongside Ritchie Valens and The Big Bopper. In the spring of 1960 their spectres were joined by that of Eddie Cochran, cut off in his 21-year-old prime in a car collision while touring England. Cochran's disembodied croon, a message from the other side frozen in black vinylite, would haunt David's ears in the listening booth of Medhurst's department store on Bromley High Street where he'd spend most afternoons after school, investing all his pocket money and boyish charm in special discounts from the 17-year-old sales girl. Two months after Cochran died he reached the top of the UK singles chart with the clairvoyant 'Queen Bitch'-alike shake of 'Three Steps To

Heaven'. Cochran had paid the ultimate price but was finally number one. Three steps from Earth, Ziggy took note.

While a nation of rockers swooned over Cochran, nobody paid much attention to the deteriorating fortunes of Vince Taylor and his ever-changing Playboys, slipping further off the pop radar with their third and fourth singles, unable to compete against the stronger Brit beats of Johnny Kidd and the Pirates or Cliff Richard and The Shadows. By the end of 1960 England had seen and heard enough of Vince Taylor, sweeping his sham existence off the White Cliffs of Dover. Across the channel, the rebel-starved French were more than happy to dredge him ashore.

In Paris, Brian Holden began his hip-swivelling medicine show all over again, now stealing the same guise of demonic Black Leather Prince adopted by Gene Vincent, the American 'Be-Bop-A-Lula' idol who narrowly avoided death in the same crash as Cochran. Unlike the British, the French knew no immunity to the Vince Taylor virus. Flapping on the floor of Parisian nightclubs in a leather blouson and oversized medallion, black-gloved hands shaking a bicycle chain, legs bandying back and forth in rubbery spasms as if his bone marrow were made of gin, while pouting and screaming his way through popular American hits, Taylor was everything the French believed rock 'n' roll ought to be. A handsome, oily-quiffed cartoon amalgam of hoodlum and heartthrob straight from the finger-clicking script of a Hollywood B-movie.

Signed by record boss Eddie Barclay, Vince Taylor became the fake American labelmate of some of France's biggest singing stars. Among them was Belgian-born chansonnier Jacques Brel, who'd move to Barclay's eponymous label having already made his name on Philips with a string of albums toxic with mad love, loneliness, disease, the devil and death, including his own: 1959's 'La Mort'; 'My Death'. Brel's third album for Barclay, a 1964 live recording from the Paris Olympia, would also include his ode to the drunken sailors, whores and fish heads waltzing around the port of 'Amsterdam'.

In his first few months on Barclay, Vince jiggled off some half dozen singles, all knockabout covers of Elvis, Chuck Berry, Little Richard, Jerry Lee Lewis, Johnny Kidd and Eddie Cochran. It seemed in France the ruse was finally working. Barclay were smart to exploit his image in a series of short films for the popular Scopitone cine-jukeboxes, Vince acting out his role as the licentious leather hooligan, leaping up on pool tables wielding his bike chain with a come-hither sneer. In interviews he'd shyly try to play down the violence. 'My stage act is an act,' he'd stutter. 'As far as in the street or a way of life, I'm like everyone else. I'm a normal person.' Only Vince's fans weren't interested in normality.

In November 1961 he was due to headline the third Paris Festival of Rock at the Palais Des Sports. Before Vince had so much as walked on stage the three-thousand-strong audience ran riot. Fourteen gendarmes were injured and one girl seriously hurt as his French fans spontaneously destroyed over two thousand seats in a slam-bang exorcism of raw, teenage anarchy. After the hall was cleared of fans, Vince crept from his dressing room and skulked through the wreckage, still dressed in his black leathers, press photographers capturing his glazed expression as he fondled the shards of devastation. Brian Holden had wanted to convince a nation he was a rock 'n' roll bad boy. Bike chains, broken glass and, 'If you're looking for trouble, you've come to the right place.' This was his reward. Splinters of wood and twisted metal. The hollow spoils of victory for the legendary lie that was Vince Taylor.

Back in Bromley, Terry continued to drip-feed David's appetite for the wilder sides of American jazz and beat literature on weekend trips to the record booths and coffee bars of London's West End. The allure of performance beckoned ever lustier after he was taken to see the new musical co-written by and starring Anthony Newley at the Queen's Theatre, *Stop The World, I Want To Get Off*. The only male actor in an otherwise female cast, Newley mixed singing, comedy and elements of mime in his central role as Littlechap, the Cockney clown who achieves success at the expense of love and happiness, bowing out with his equivalent rock 'n' roll suicide ballad 'What Kind Of Fool Am I?'

On Christmas Day, 1961, David's perpetual pleas for a saxophone were finally answered when he received his first, a white acrylic Grafton model with gold keys. Alone in his bedroom, he squawked on his new best friend in tuneless dreams of Little Richard and heading west with Sal and Dean. But from the outside, he still looked like a normal teenage boy. Time and space had chosen David Jones as the one who would be Ziggy Stardust. Now, with just ten years before he was due, the moment had arrived to properly brand him. The extraterrestrial circumcision. A rite of passage from human to alien from which there could be no return.

Her name was Carol and David fancied her. So did his best friend, George. It was George who asked Carol if she'd like to go out with him to the youth club that Friday. Carol accepted. George was thrilled. David was jealous.

The night of their date, David rang George out of the blue to tell him Carol had asked him to cancel the date on her behalf. David was lying. George believed him. Carol waited at the youth club in vain.

The following Monday morning, David regaled his friends on the bus to Bromley Technical College with the news he was now going out with Carol. George realised he'd been had. When they arrived at school, George grabbed David in the playground and threw a single punch at his face, striking the left side of his head like a lightning bolt.

The deed was done.

George had only meant a retributive thump but realised immediately he'd hit David harder than he should have. So hard the headmaster drove David to the emergency department of Farnborough Hospital while he clutched his face in agony.

Two days later he was taken to specialists at London's Moorfields Eye Hospital. He'd suffered lasting damage to the sphincter muscles in his left eye, leaving its pupil permanently dilated. He could still see but would spend the rest of his life with different sized pupils, the medical condition known as anisocoria. His right eye was blue but his enlarged left pupil made its surrounding iris look green. David Jones, just 15-years-old, suddenly had different coloured eyes. The boy who *would be* was now the boy who could *only be* Ziggy.

Once branded, the paving stones of David's and Ziggy's destinies rapidly fell into place towards their due crossroads. Recuperating from the accident, his friendship with George remarkably unscathed, he devoted himself to his saxophone. Looking through old copies of *Melody Maker* he found the number for popular jazz bandleader Ronnie Ross, six miles away in Orpington. David cajoled Ross into giving him lessons, spending Saturday mornings being taught the basics of blowing and breathing control. Terry was impressed, as much by his half-brother's sax progress as his continued passions for bebop pioneer Charlie Parker and more modern jazz albums. In particular, *Oh Yeah* by Charles Mingus, released in 1962 but, to David's ears, sounding 'very 2001', especially the pulpit raving 'Ecclusiastics' and the car-jam chaos of 'Wham Bam Thank You Ma'am', a phrase Mingus attributed to drummer Max Roach. 'I'm trying to play the truth of what I am,' said Mingus on the album's back cover. 'The reason it's difficult is because I'm changing all the time.' Ziggy's teenage chrysalis softly crinkled in solidarity.

A fierier baptism awaited David that October when he saw 'God' in person: Little Richard, now back on the live frontlines of rock 'n' roll after his brief Sputnik-inspired holy meltdown. Halfway through his set at the Woolwich Granada, Richard stood on top of his grand piano, suddenly grabbing at his chest, face wrinkled in agony. The band slowed to an uneasy halt. Richard collapsed on the floor. The compere pelted on stage, took the mic and asked if there was a doctor in the house. David was convinced he was watching the death of God in front of his very eyes. Moments later, Richard was back, coolly cocking a leg over his piano, a smile the size of Saturn. The whole dying stunt was merely a regular feature of Richard's act.

So time took a cigarette and delicately put it to David's spluttering young mouth.

ritish rock 'n' roll in 1962 was still anchored to the ground by the terrestrial yodels of Frank Ifield, the bruvverly bop of Joe Brown and the clean Telecaster prangs of The Shadows. The only stardust to fall between was in that year's joint Anglo-American pop showcase film *It's Trad, Dad!* where a white leather Gene Vincent (looking like Vince Taylor in negative) serenaded his strange, discordant 'Spaceship To Mars', and the interstellar crackles and ice-rink screech of The Tornados' 'Telstar', the first, and very probably last, number one hit written in honour of a communications satellite.

'Telstar's creator was Gloucestershire eccentric Joe Meek, famous for working in his home studio above a leather goods shop on London's Holloway Road. Along with séances, Buddy Holly and his unhealthy lust for the Tornados' blond-haired teenage bassist Heinz Burt, space ranked high among Meek's obsessions. Two years earlier he'd produced a concept album about extraterrestrial life called *I Hear A New World*. Meek and his writing partner Geoff Goddard were also habitual UFO spotters: the source of inspiration for their wonderfully wonky and commercially doomed country-bumpkin 'Starman' prototype, 'Sky Men'.

Yet as 'Telstar' slid down the charts in November, the writing for the likes of Meek, The Tornados and even The Shadows was already boring through the concrete of pop history as a song called 'Love Me Do' craftily shunted its way towards the top 20. David was the first boy in his class to buy a copy of The Beatles' debut, its wobbling grandpa's harmonica one of many seeds now planting itself deep in his starry subconscious for future use. Another was sown the second time he saw Little Richard, in the puckering sight and precious sound of the young London blues band supporting called The Rolling Stones. Others, in Dobell's jazz shop on Charing Cross Road, the seeds of John Lee Hooker and the first album by new American folk sensation Bob Dylan. Seeds which effortlessly took root and flowered with the realisation David's saxophone skills weren't up to those of a jazz musician. He'd never be a John Coltrane or a Roland Kirk. But he could, as he'd later confess, 'fake it pretty well on rock 'n' roll'.

And so David faked it, his life's blinding bright pretence beginning as saxophone player and co-vocalist in dear, eye-denting George's covers band, The Konrads. Soon he was experimenting with his first aliases. 'Dave Day', 'Alexis Jay', 'Luther Jay'. He tried, in vain, to convince the band to swap their tidy bowtie and dinner-jacket image for a cowboy theme, similar to that already tried by another of Joe Meek's instrumental acts, The Outlaws. He even suggested they call themselves The Ghost Riders so he could take the name of Alamo folk hero 'Jim Bowie'. The Konrads were happy as they were.

Splintering away from the band with George, he nailed his colours to American R&B as The Hooker Brothers. Until The Hooker Brothers became The Bow Street Runners who in turn became Dave's Reds & Blues, his now the face in front of the mic and the name above the title. Until he changed his Mingus-quick mind again and thought about calling himself after Henry Fielding's rakish hero *Tom Jones*, at that time the other Tom Jones was still 'Tommy Scott', trying to repel the amorous advances of his first producer, Joe Meek. Until, in temporary defeat, David Jones decided to become simply Davie Jones and call his band The King Bees.

It was as 'Davie Jones With The King Bees' that he'd finally hear his teenage voice chiselled for all eternity in the crannies of a black plastic seven-inch disc. David's tenacity in firing off requests for professional investment paid off when he caught the interest of 34-year-old pop hustler Leslie Conn. By June 1964 The King Bees were on a contract with Conn and on record with Decca's Vocalion subsidiary. The Starman-in-waiting's vinyl debut was 'Liza Jane', a song cheekily credited to Conn but freely adapted from a traditional American folk standard. David sang lead, played saxophone and proved, above all else, that he wasn't lying when he'd said he could fake rock 'n' roll, wailing desire for his woman with mock Memphis grit over a cutthroat twang and his own seductive sax tooting. 'Liza Jane' was a song about lust and screaming, about girls and madness (*'she drives me insane!'*) but above all else about a 17-year-old kid from Bromley being given his chance to convince the world he was as potentially godlike as Little Richard. Even if in press photos, dressed in a dustman's leather waistcoat and hunting boots, he looked unnervingly like Tommy Steele in panto as Robin Hood.

Barely a month after the single's release, between its failure to sell and David's restless Mingusitis, he was driven away from The King Bees into the arms of another of Conn's groups, The Manish Boys. He also packed in the day job he'd been struggling to hold down since leaving school with one art O-level, a junior paste-up artist with Nevundy–Hurst, a commercial graphic company in Mayfair. With some financial support from his dad, David turned to Conn for any chance to earn an extra few bob. As it happened, Conn did have a chore, one that made the lightest of demands on David's artistic streak. Repainting the walls of his Denmark Street management office.

When David turned up for work he discovered his boss wasn't so daft as to overestimate his enthusiasm to finish the job alone. Conn had roped in another of his skint and eager young charges, a short 18-year-old kid from Hackney who fancied himself as King Mod.

'Hello,' said David. 'Who are you?'

'I'm a singer,' said the other boy.

'Oh, yeah? So am I.'

The air spat and crackled over the paint pots between them.

'Are you a mod?' asked David

'Yeah, I'm King Mod.'

Fizzle!

'Your shoes are crap,' said the boy.

'Yeah?'

'Yeah.'

SNAP!

'Well, you're short,' said David.

The tense air steamed and popped until it finally cooled, revealing the brittle frame of a strange, fragile new friendship. By the time Conn returned to his office, David and King Mod had downed brushes and scarpered, leaving a tardy half-finished undercoat.

The Manish Boys offered David only marginally more satisfaction than interior decorating. Unable to steer their sound away from the strict confines of R&B, he instead concentrated on their image, leading by example as a long-haired Carnaby Street dandy and leader of the entirely fictitious International League for the Preservation of Animal Filament. 'It's really for the protection of pop musicians and those who wear their hair long,' he told the *Evening Standard*. 'It's time we united and stood up for our curls.' Aged 17, he was fast becoming a master faker.

The BBC gobbled the same bait, inviting the Fauntleroy-locked David, his best friend George and the shaggy members of The Manish Boys to discuss the issue on the *Tonight* programme with Cliff Michelmore. The League had since changed its name to the Society for the Prevention of Cruelty to Long-Haired Men. 'I think we're all fairly tolerant,' David told Michelmore, 'but for the last two years we've had comments like, "Darlin'" and, "Can I carry your handbag?" thrown at us. I think it's just had to stop now.'

It was David's first interview on national television and he was talking about something which didn't actually exist. He never even mentioned The Manish Boys, who'd record just one single with him before disbanding. A cover of Bobby Bland's soul ballad 'I Pity The Fool', it fell on a nation of deaf ears in March 1965. At least its B-side marked the first 'Davie Jones' original to make it on record, a stomping beatnik-jive called 'Take My Tip', which saw the phrase 'playing with the spider' bubble between his jinky teeth. He'd have sung it twice but the second time fluffed the line as 'bider', time constraints leaving the take as it was. It wouldn't matter. 'Spider.' A sleek word with a precise punch. Given time, David Jones would learn to sing it better.

In May 1965, Bob Dylan rolled into London's Savoy Hotel, currently touring England being followed by American documentary maker D. A. Pennebaker and simultaneously pursued by a strange blonde woman from Germany who sang like a bassoon with scurvy. He was also rolling high in the UK top ten that month 'lookin' for a friend' while in the want ads and tin pan alleyways north of the Savoy, David Jones was looking for a band. And somewhere amidst the dankest tumbledown dives of nearby Soho, the man born Brian Holden was looking for what was left of his sanity as he scraped the bottom of the barrel he'd christened Vince Taylor.

Vince had left his destitute backing group behind in Paris on a Monday morning, telling them he needed to hop across the channel to demand outstanding payment from their London booking agent. He was gone four days. Time enough to recover the £200 owed. Time enough to crash a party for Dylan and drop his first tab of acid.

By the time he returned to Paris on Friday evening Vince had managed to spend most of the money on a bag of LSD, half of which he'd already gobbled. When he stumbled back into the band's hotel they barely recognised, let alone understood, him. Unwashed and unshaven, he carried a roll of purple material under one arm and a bottle of Mateus rosé wine in the other. Met with their confused daggering stares, he tried to explain himself.

'You think I'm Vince Taylor, don't you?'

Nervous silence.

'Well, I'm not. My name is Mateus.'

Not a squeak.

'I'm the son of God.'

After a deathly pause, his long-suffering drummer, Bobbie Woodman, tentatively broached the subject of the missing money. Vince, or maybe Brian, or maybe even Mateus, took out the few notes left in his pockets along with a cigarette lighter.

'That's all you guys are interested in. Money! The root of all evil.'

He burned the lot.

The next morning, Vince Taylor resurfaced from his room, freshly shaven, his familiar black quiff newly slicked, much to the relief and reassurance of his band. Until they arrived at La Locomotive club where they were due to play that Saturday night. Vince noticed a poster outside advertising their gig. He calmly walked over, took a felt pen from his pocket, crossed out the name of Vince Taylor and scribbled 'MATEUS'.

Woodman and the rest of the band still clung to the skinniest of hopes they could carry off the show without incident. As was now their standard intro, they walked on stage first and kicked into the opening riff of Eddie Cochran's 'C'Mon Everybody', increasing the tension until their leader's entrance. When Taylor finally emerged from the wings he was carrying a jug of water. He never made it to the microphone. Instead he wandered among the audience, baptising them with wet sprinkles from his jug.

'God bless you. I am Mateus. The son of God.'

Vince Taylor continued preaching out into the streets of Pigalle, spreading the gospel of Mateus through the city centre, across the river Seine to the bohemian byways of the Left Bank. It was another twenty-four hours before his band saw him again. When he returned to their hotel he told them they were all catching a plane to California.

'God is the pilot, and he's going to fly us to Hollywood.'

The next day the human husk that once was Brian Holden left Paris in the care of his sister on his way to a psychiatric clinic in England. Back to where Ziggy Stardust needed him to perform one last feat of messianic influence.

By the summer of 1965, the 2 I's in Soho was no longer the favourite hang-out of London's young and desperate musicians. The smartest mod heads and hemlines had shifted camp to an Italian café on Denmark Street, the small nucleus of pop publishers, agents and management offices known as 'Tin Pan Alley'. La Gioconda was the 'in' place where a band could form at any moment at any table over the steam of a few espressos. Where a beat group from Margate called The Lower Third could come looking for a singer and find one called David Jones, formerly of The Manish Boys. And where, one day in that same '65 summer of 'Help!' and 'Mr Tambourine Man' the former Manish Boy, David Jones, could have a chance encounter with the former Brian Holden, Vince Taylor.

The way David told and retold it, Taylor was still quaking in the aftershock of Mateus, dressed in a white robe and sandals like a biblical prophet. He said he was the son of God. David wasn't frightened, only fascinated. The same fascination which would soon see him cherish a paperback by Frank Edwards called *Strange People,* a compendium of true tales of folk 'who have baffled the world', including Victorian deformities, lunatics and his nineteenth-century namesake, a David Jones of Indiana who functioned perfectly despite never going to sleep. Vince Taylor was as strange as anything in Edwards' book, his every word a bell jangling completely out of tune. It seemed very appealing to David. 'I'd love to end up like that,' he thought. 'Totally nuts.'

They chatted in La Gioconda about God, the rebuilding of the lost sunken city of Atlantis and flying saucers before walking together up Charing Cross Road. It was now rush hour, Taylor's appearance squeezing stern glances from the stream of commuters marching towards Tottenham Court Road underground. Just outside the station, Vince asked David to sit down with him on the pavement, pulling out a battered map of the world and spreading it out on the ground oblivious to the stamp of tired feet all about him. He then took out a magnifying glass and began to scrutinise it in detail, pointing out various locations.

'There's money buried here,' Vince told David, prodding his fingers across the paper.

'And the UFOs are going to land here ...'

A finger dabbed somewhere in the Arctic circle.

'... here and here.'

The curious 17-year-old drank in the ravings of a drug-damaged rock 'n' roll star who believed himself to be the Messiah. Who believed that aliens were going to land any day soon. 'I'm going to remember this,' thought David. 'This is just too good.' So ended the gospel of Vince Taylor. And so twinged the first conscious labour contractions of Ziggy Stardust.

With David's new band, The Lower Third, came a new manager, Ralph Horton, who convinced him to shed his persecuted long locks for a shorter crop from the court of King Mod. Sonic pop art master Shel Talmy, producer of hits by The Kinks and The Who, agreed to record his third single, backed by The Lower Third but, to their annoyance, credited only to 'Davy Jones'. 'You've Got A Habit Of Leaving' and its B-side 'Baby Loves That Way' were both Jones originals, already staples of the group's live set, which stretched to feedback-heavy struts through 'Chim Chim Cheree' from *Mary Poppins* and a tune David had loved since the first time he heard it pressed up against the back of the settee at the age of six. The *Quatermass* overture 'Mars, The Bringer of War' by Gustav Holst.

Horton maintained high hopes for 'Davy Jones & The Lower Third' but knew accelerating them into pop's fast lane would take the added investment of a management co-partner. He first threw the invitation to Kenneth Pitt, a theatrical agent who'd handled the publicity for Bob

Dylan's recent UK visit. Pitt politely declined due to work commitments but was generous enough to offer Horton one piece of free advice. Perhaps they weren't yet aware, but there was already a young singer from Manchester called Davy Jones, currently attracting rave reviews on Broadway for his performance as the Artful Dodger in the musical *Oliver!* It might, suggested Pitt, be in The Lower Third's best interest if their singer reconsidered his name.

Two days later, Pitt received a letter from Horton overflowing with gratitude. 'May I say that I enjoyed our meeting the other day and it was indeed a pleasure to be introduced to you.' The typed note continued. 'I have taken the liberty of writing to you and advising you that I have now changed Davie's name … '

Somewhere deep, deep in the velvet ink of outer space, a storm of dust, a blizzard of gas and a new star punctured the blackness.

'… to David Bowie.'

TWELVE
VINYL

David Bowie. So the 19-year-old David Jones began the year 1966 one shedded skin closer to Ziggy Stardust. The Starman's evolutionary jigsaw was still an incomplete, disjointed confusion of gaping holes and missing pieces but now, slowly, the edges were taking shape. A picture roughly the shape of Vince Taylor begging order from a bric-a-brac mosaic of Elvis Presley, Little Richard, *On The Road*, Quatermass, Martians, Mingus, saxophones, sexual discovery, suburban frustration and the symphonic discord of Holst's *Planets* and, another classical favourite, Stravinsky's *Rite Of Spring*.

He released his first single as David Bowie that January, the moodily moddish 'Can't Help Thinking About Me'. A beautifully honest mission statement, it sang of teenage remorse and childhood longing, severing family ties and seeking new realities, burying the body of David Jones beneath that of David Bowie. In its recognition of his '*long way to go*' and the blind hope he will '*make it on my own*', 'Can't Help Thinking About Me' was also a scream for help into the cavernous womb of time, one whose Ziggy-shaped echo wouldn't be heard for another six years.

Thinking about himself, David was still unsure who that 'Me' was. When interviewed by *Melody Maker* to promote the single he referred to his new fascination with Tibetan Buddhism, the religion of Kerouac, which scrutinised and obliterated all conventional Western philosophy of the self. That there was no such thing as a 'David Bowie', or even a 'David Jones'. Already growing weary of rock 'n' roll, he also spoke of his plans to write musicals and his ultimate ambition to act. 'I'd like to do character parts,' he confessed. 'I think it takes a lot to become somebody else. It takes some doing.'

The charts of spring 1966 would remain as untroubled by the name of David Bowie as they had been by Davie Jones; the top ten a stronghold of The Rolling Stones, The Walker Brothers, The Kinks and The Yardbirds with their H. G. Wells-inspired art pop 'Shapes Of Things'. David hoped to retaliate with a new backing band, The Buzz, joining him in April for a regular residency at London's Marquee club.

'The Bowie Showboat' was a Sunday afternoon slot directly inspired by the same venue's Sunday evening 'Spontaneous Underground' showcase for The Pink Floyd, an experimental R&B band who used fancy liquid projections and other strange mechanised light machines. The Floyd's frontman, Syd Barrett, cut a spookily detached figure, his make-up, nail-varnish and exotic shirts jarring with an unexpectedly soft home counties accent. Over the next year, David followed their progress from the Marquee to the psychedelic haven of the UFO club, gorging his imagination on the Floyd's 'Interstellar Overdrive' and 'Astronomy Domine', entranced by Syd cooing '*Neptune, Titan, stars can frighten*' between a cacophony of Holstian power chords.

In contrast 'The Bowie Showboat' offered audiences a different kind of pop experiment: part rock 'n' roll gig, part cabaret, jumbling originals with chart covers and a handful of West End showstoppers including Anthony Newley's 'What Kind Of Fool Am I?' The second week, David's manager Ralph Horton brought along Kenneth Pitt, the agent who'd already nudged the name change from Jones to Bowie. As Horton had hoped, Pitt was thunderstruck, as much by David's sense of theatre as his singing voice, enough to reconsider the offer of becoming a business partner. He accepted, not only managing Bowie but, in time, becoming a close confidante and trusted mentor.

Pitt's Marylebone flat immediately offered David another new haven of inspiration, an oasis of Victorian collectibles and antiquarian books. Among the first volumes he plucked from Pitt's shelf was Antoine de Saint-Exupéry's children's classic *The Little Prince*, the story of an airman who crashes in the Sahara desert where he meets a wise and charming boy from a distant asteroid. The tale ends with the sad little prince only able to return to his starry home by allowing his body to perish in an act akin to extraterrestrial suicide.

David nevertheless still remained blind to his blindingly obvious destiny, for the time being distracted by other characters stalking his mind demanding immortality in song. The overgrown, comic-reading mummy's boy 'Uncle Arthur'. The bitter old soldier who loses his love to the leader of the 'Rubber Band'. The innocent children of 'There Is A Happy Land' borrowed from the Keith Waterhouse novel of the same name. The rain-sodden child killer of 'Please Mr Gravedigger'. And, tantalisingly, his first self-proclaimed 'Messiah', the population-crunching prophet of a future world-state turning 'a blind eye to infanticide' in 'We Are Hungry Men'.

Such musical playacting offered creative sanctuary away from the R&B pop world he'd already tried and so far failed in. A semi-autobiographical exception was 'The London Boys', not only David's best song of the period but one of the best he'd ever write: a slow-building ballad belittling the empty promise of the city's club scene through the eyes of a lonely young mod who falls prey to Soho's vicious circle of drugs and false friends. The Rise And Fall Of David Jones, as narrated by his older, wiser reincarnation. Already popular in concert, David thought 'The London Boys' had single potential. Sadly his new label, the Decca subsidiary Deram, didn't want to risk controversy over its lyrics mentioning amphetamine 'pills' but, as consolation, agreed to release it as the B-side of the safer, trumpet-tooting 'Rubber Band'.

In early November, Pitt left London on a business trip to New York, among his aims: to drum up American interest in David, both as a recording star in his own right and a potential songwriter for hire. David enviously wished him luck, wondering when the day would come when he'd finally get the chance to visit the promised land of Sal Paradise, Elvis Presley and Little Richard. To a seldom-travelled boy from Bromley, America, and New York in particular, remained an elusive fantasy. He admitted as much in another new song, 'Did You Ever Have A Dream', pondering on the ease with which somebody could imagine walking around Manhattan as they slept in Bromley's neighbouring suburb. Dearest, glamorous Penge.

Nobody in New York dreamed of Penge. Nobody in New York knew or cared where Penge was. Certainly not Andy Warhol, who knew where Pittsburgh was because he was born there, but was still happier in Manhattan dreaming of Marilyn Monroe, Jackie O, Campbell's soup cans, Brillo boxes, Coca-Cola bottles, Bloomingdale's, Elaine's restaurant, electric chairs, wanted men, beautiful boys, high heel shoes, paint and glue. Andy Warhol, pop-art god, created from thin air around the Slovak-American vapour that once was Andrew Warchola. Whose greatest work of art was himself: silver-haired, sunglass-eyed, cruising through life in catatonic gear, never fully in the room he appeared to be in, forever clinging to the surface of reality. The artist who didn't have a studio but a 'Factory' on the fourth floor of a midtown warehouse which used to trade in upholstery. The socialite who collected friends like ornaments and called them 'superstars'. Youthquaking heiress Edie Sedgwick. Shaggy-maned *Vogue* model 'Baby Jane' Holzer. And the spooky blonde sex phantom known simply as Nico.

Nico came from Germany and spoke, as some described, like a computer trying to impersonate Greta Garbo, a foggy moan of flat, elongated vowels creaking at the speed of an hour hand. She sang that way too: the bassoon with scurvy. Nico arrived in New York from London

HOW TO MAKE
A STARMAN

Left to right: The ancient space face of Japanese kabuki theatre; An interplanetary immigration crisis awaits the citizens of Surrey in H. G. Wells' *The War Of The Worlds*; Teenage David's 'God', Little Richard, cocks a divine leg in *The Girl Can't Help It*.

Left to right: Professor Bernard Quatermass (actor André Morell) prepares for the worst; Halfway to 'Mateus', the doomed black leather lunatic, Vince Taylor; Waiting to hitch a ride on a Gemini Spaceship, The Legendary Stardust Cowboy.

Left to right: Andy Warhol unpeels slowly; The invincible Iggy Pop; Alex (Malcolm McDowell) and his droogs cut the cloth for Ziggy's wardrobe in Stanley Kubrick's *A Clockwork Orange*.

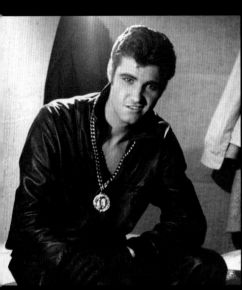

COSMIC COSTUME DRAMAS PART 1
The Freddie Burretti Collection. Top left: Original art-deco droog top and matching bipperty-bopperty hat, May 1972. **Top right:** The Technicolor Starman and his golden Spider lift off with Ayshea, June 1972. **Bottom left:** Ziggy proudly packs out Freddie's number outfit on stage in Cleveland, September 1972. **Bottom right:** Ice blue Burretti suit as worn for Mick Rock's 'Life On Mars?' promo, June 1973.

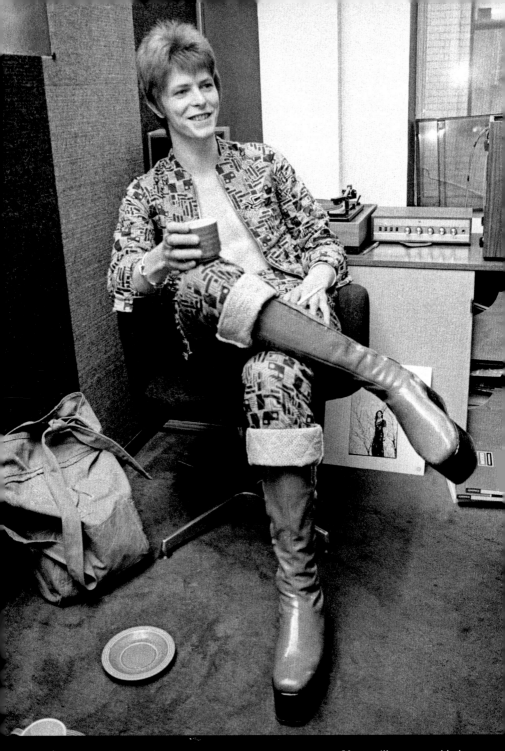

Previous page: The dye is cast.
Newly 'red hot red' Ziggy prepares for
Invasion Earth: 1972 AD at home in
Haddon Hall. Portrait by Mick Rock

Above: 'I'm gay and I always
have been.' Ziggy comes out
over a cuppa in his Regent Street
management's office, January 1972

Top: The Unholy Trinity. MainMan impresario Tony DeFries (rear) laughs on as Ziggy, Iggy and Lou provide a crash-course in raving at London's Dorchester hotel, 16 July 1972.

Bottom: Jimmy Dean from Mars meets Marilyn from Venus. New York sex-bomb Cyrinda Foxe and Ziggy play *Nighthawks* in Los Angeles, October 1972.

***That* photo.** Ziggy slides between the mellow
thighs of the greatest guitar player on planet Earth,
Mick Ronson, Oxford Town Hall, 17 June 1972

where she spent the same acid summer of 1965 which destroyed Vince Taylor sinking her fangs into Bob Dylan. By the age of 27 she'd already appeared in European films including Federico Fellini's *La Dolce Vita*, rolled with the Stones' Brian Jones and cut an unsuccessful folky single for their manager Andrew Loog Oldham's new label, Immediate. As Nico told Warhol, her next priority was to record the song groaning Bob had given her in London called 'I'll Keep It With Mine'.

Warhol saw the art in pop but had never thought about dirtying his hands in the record industry. He loved girl groups, especially The Crystals' 'He Hit Me (And It Felt Like A Kiss)' and his all-time favourite, 'Sally Go Round The Roses' by The Jaynetts. He'd also used pop music in his 16mm underground films, most recently March 1965's *Vinyl*. A very loose interpretation of *A Clockwork Orange*, Anthony Burgess' novel of teenage violence first published three years earlier, *Vinyl*'s soundtrack included the Stones, The Kinks and Martha & The Vandellas. As the first to mix rock 'n' roll with droogy delinquency, Warhol and his director Paul Morrissey were already seven years ahead.

Out of everyone in and around the Factory, Paul Morrissey was Nico's biggest fan. She was his 'most beautiful creature that ever lived' and, he thought, a born superstar if she could front her own rock 'n' roll band. Warhol agreed that, if only physically, she was gobsmacking: glacial Dietrich cheekbones; irresistibly sensuous pillowy Bardot lips; an ideal subject for one of Andy's 'stillies', his short 16mm moving portraits or 'screen tests' of regular Factory hangers-on and his many celebrity visitors, from Salvador Dali to Allen Ginsberg. His discovery of Nico also coincided with an offer from Broadway producer Michael Myerberg, who wanted Factory endorsement of a new discotheque in a disused aircraft hangar over in Queens. Morrissey intervened to advise Myerberg that, location-wise, it was too far off Manhattan and, Warhol-wise, would only be worthwhile for them if Andy could use the club to present his own rock 'n' roll group. Myerberg agreed – unaware that Warhol didn't yet have one.

Since Morrissey was already excited about hiring a band for Nico, it now became his mission to find one worthy of the Andy Warhol trademark. He didn't have to search long.

A week or so after Myerberg's proposal, Morrissey's friend and fellow underground filmmaker Barbara Rubin asked if he'd help her shoot footage of her friends' band currently in residence at a Greenwich Village beatnik club. Marooned on a dead go-go strip of West 3rd Street, the best days of the Café Bizarre were long behind it by December 1965; a cartoon goth tourist trap of Morticia Addams-a-like bar staff and fishnet lamps where every day was Halloween. Its last booking of any great interest was a couple of years earlier when it was home to 50-year-old Herman Blount, a 'cosmic jazz' pianist and philosopher who in his own inimitable hum-defying way bravely tested the waters for Ziggy by calling himself 'Sun Ra', telling everyone he came from Saturn and wearing far-out spacey Egyptian pharaoh costumes. If only Blount had been thirty years younger and learned to play three-minute rock 'n' roll instead of ten minute abstract mood-jams, the Starman's glory might even have been his.

Any other time, Morrissey wouldn't have bothered trudging down the Café Bizarre with Rubin and their mutual friend Gerard Malanga, a Warhol assistant and actor who'd played the equivalent 'Alex' role in *Vinyl*. But since he needed to find a group in any case he had nothing to lose by poking his head through the door.

The band Rubin had raved about were a four-piece, led by a curly and surly 21-year-old singing about whips, razors and what it felt like shooting heroin, sometimes dispensing with words altogether and making funny 'shhhh'-ing noises. Beside him stood a sullen rhythm guitarist and a distracting Richard III lookalike in a turtleneck sweater and rhinestone necklace bowing havoc with an electric viola. Their drummer, who wasn't allowed to drum because it was a folk venue so had to make do with bashing a tambourine, looked like the Beatle that time forgot, possibly male, possibly female, Morrissey couldn't quite tell. He only knew that Rubin had saved him the trouble of weeks of fruitless talent scouting by handing him Andy's dream band on a plate. Even the name resonated with tailor-made Warholian perfection.

The Velvet Underground.

The curly, surly singer–songwriter was Lou Reed, born in Brooklyn before moving out to Freeport in Long Island just before his teens. Lou made his first record as part of a doo-wop group while still at high school, an act which appalled his straitlaced middle-class parents. As he'd painfully understate, 'I represented something very alien to them.' Anxious over his preoccupation with rock 'n' roll, his undesirable friends and general behaviour they conservatively deciphered as 'homosexual', they sent him to a psychiatrist. The doc's recommended 'cure' for the 17-year-old was an eight-week course of electroshock therapy at a local psychiatric hospital. It 'cured' him of nothing.

As an English student at Syracuse University, Lou fell under the rhythmically liberating spell of modern jazz and the guru-like influence of his creative writing lecturer, the poet, paranoiac and fellow electroshock victim Delmore Schwartz. 'The unhappiest man I ever met in my life,' said Lou, 'and the smartest.' Fate had also thrown him on to the same campus as Long Islander Jim Tucker, older brother of androgynous drummer Maureen 'Moe' Tucker and friend of guitarist Sterling Morrison, both destined to eventually join him in The Velvet Underground.

Finishing his degree, Lou moved back home, finding work writing low-budget copies of the latest rock 'n' roll trends for Long Island's Pickwick Records. Shackled to soulless production-line pop, he embraced the absurdity, developing his bellicose subway-bum drone fronting daft tunes attributed to non-existent acts comprised of his own house band. Lou's trash masterpiece was a screeching dance-craze pastiche, 'The Ostrich', a musical rip-off of The Crystals' 'Then He Kissed Me' released under the name The Primitives. The record's producer, Terry Philips, thought it had a genuine chance of chart success. But first, they'd need to recruit desperate young musicians to make a 'real' Primitives line-up to promote it. Philips met his first volunteer at a party in downtown Manhattan. A 22-year-old Welshman with a Beatley haircut named John Cale.

A classically trained violist and pianist, Cale had moved from London to New York in 1963 to study avant-garde composition with his heroes John Cage – experimental theorist best known for his piece '4'33"' consisting of four minutes and 33 seconds of absolute silence – and minimalist pioneer La Monte Young. On paper, Lou's apprenticeship in disposable rock 'n' roll and Cale's radicalism weren't an obvious match. But when they met at the first Primitives rehearsal, something clicked. Cale was especially impressed when Lou told him 'The Ostrich' was a cinch to play as all the guitar strings were tuned to the same note. Not uncommon in rock 'n' roll – Lou's hero, Bo Diddley, had made a career out of 'open tuning' – Cale recognised its shared stripped-bare methodology with his own avant-garde teachers.

They'd quickly forget about The Primitives, moving into the same flat on New York's Lower East Side, writing, rehearsing, experimenting (Cale now amplifying his viola using an electric pick-up) and laying the foundations of their own band named after a book one of their friends found littering a nearby street. *The Velvet Underground* was journalist Michael Leigh's titillating survey of sexual deviancy in contemporary America, from suburban wife-swapping to bestiality and sado-masochism. They didn't much care for the book itself, even if Lou already had a song in a similarly kinky vein called 'Venus In Furs' inspired by a different book by Leopold von Sacher-Masoch. But the title, especially the word 'Underground', summed up the sonic no-man's land between Lou's beatnik rock 'n' roll and Cale's ear for the chaotic and unconventional.

In the summer of 1965, Cale made one of his sporadic trips back to London armed with the band's first rudimentary demo tape. His inexperienced efforts to stir interest went as far as thrusting a copy upon fluttering pop songbird Marianne Faithfull in the hope she in turn would pass it on to her mentor, Stones manager Andrew Loog Oldham. As Cale recalled, Faithfull closed the door in his face; ironic considering her great-great-uncle was none other than Leopold von Sacher-Masoch; 'Venus In Furs' featured on the same tape.

At least being in London meant Cale could gauge the city's ever-changing pop trends, stocking up on the latest mod noises from The Who's 'Anyway, Anyhow, Anywhere' to 'What'cha Gonna Do About It?', the debut from The Small Faces whose singer, Steve Marriott, was a La Gioconda regular and friend of David Jones. Both records whistled with feedback: an encouraging omen the Velvets were already clanging up the right path. Returning to New York, Cale made a point of repeatedly playing them to his bandmate. 'Shit, Lou!' Cale teased him. 'We gotta get a deal. They're catching up to us.'

The Velvet Underground settled on their final line-up with Morrison and Tucker only weeks before they landed the residency at the Café Bizarre. Their friend and superfan Barbara Rubin acted as human flyer about town. Ed Sanders, singer with local obscenity-courting anarchist hippies The Fugs, was among the first she dragged to see them. A mutual acquaintance of Warhol who, like Nico, would be filmed at the Factory for one of his stillies, Sanders was impressed by their droning repetitiveness and Lou's obvious star quality. Next Rubin brought Gerard Malanga who, halfway through their set, stood up and started dancing with a whip right in front of the stage. Afterwards Lou told Malanga he should come and do that again. The next time, Malanga and Rubin came with Paul Morrissey. Their velvet road to Warhol was almost complete, bar the consenting nod of approval from Emperor Andy himself.

A few days before Christmas 1965, the downbeat Café Bizarre was blessed with a rare visitation from His Warholness and a Factory entourage including Morrissey, Malanga, Rubin and Edie Sedgwick. Also present was Nico, who'd remember it as 'the most beautiful moment of my life'. Morrissey made the crafty suggestion that as she needed a band, maybe they'd allow her to sing with them. Warhol watched Malanga repeat his whip dance, entranced by the noise and their grotesque beauty. He agreed, The Velvet Underground should be his Factory's rock 'n' roll band. That is, pending one non-negotiable caveat. Concerned over Lou's 'lack of charisma', Morrissey pressed Warhol to insist Nico join the group. If they accepted, he'd manage them, buy them new equipment, pay their rent and provide free rehearsal space at the Factory. If they declined, the deal was off, leaving Lou and Cale to continue eking out a threadbare existence dealing drugs or hawking themselves out as models for trashy crime magazines offering a flat fee to pose as rapists, murderers and child-molesters. It wasn't even a choice.

Myerberg's original offer for the disco in Queens had since fallen through. Instead Warhol began integrating the group, now conjoined with Nico, into his own New York multi-media happening, 'Andy Warhol, Up-Tight'. By April it developed into 'The Exploding Plastic Inevitable' at The Don in the East Village, the Velvets and Nico playing live upon a stage flickering with strobe lights and film projections (including his droogy *Vinyl*) as Malanga and Factory star Mary Woronov cast sado-masochistic shadows frugging in leather boots and flicking whips. By May, lured by the Warhol branding, MGM Records had signed them as a five-piece. 'But they didn't really want The Velvet Underground,' noted Cale. 'They thought they had a better chance of selling records with Nico as a blonde bombshell than they did with four irascible individuals trying to make noisy cacophonous music.'

Cale's suspicions were more than justified. Having recorded the bulk of their debut by the summer of '66, MGM chose two of its three tracks featuring lead vocals by Nico as a promo single, 'All Tomorrow's Parties' and 'I'll Be Your Mirror'. Stalling on a release date for the album, as feared the label insisted it needed 'more Nico'. Lou's obstreperous response was to write the Nico-worthy 'Sunday Morning' only to sing lead himself. Group tensions were further compounded by their European siren's romantic follies, plotting a messy love triangle with, first, Lou, then Cale. 'I've had it with the dramatic bullshit!' fumed Lou. 'Yeah, she looks great in high contrast black and white photographs, but I've had it!'

With 'Sunday Morning' as a late addition to the running order, in late October the album was finally complete bar the sleeve. Except that Warhol's design, a pop-art banana which could be physically unpeeled to reveal a pink fruit beneath the yellow skin, was so complex it required the building of special machinery, adding to the already exasperating delay. His band splitting at the seams and temporarily paralysed, Warhol tried to stay focussed on the future, considering whether, as his friend and actor Denis Deegan suggested, they could bring the 'Exploding Plastic Inevitable' experience overseas to Europe. As fortune had it, in early November a mutual friend introduced Deegan to an English pop manager who'd just arrived in New York on business. His name was Kenneth Pitt.

On Deegan's invitation, Pitt came to the warehouse on East 47th Street, took the famously slow antique elevator to the fourth floor and stepped into the silvery foil-lined neverland of the Factory. There he met Warhol and told him he'd be more than willing to help with any promotion in London. Before he left, Pitt also met Lou and was given an advance copy of his group's unreleased album, a coverless test pressing bearing only a sticker with Warhol's signature. Pitt thanked him, and packed the record away safe in his luggage where it spent another month bumped and shunted by baggage handlers from New York to Australia and Singapore before arriving safely back in London. In all likelihood the first copy of *The Velvet Underground & Nico* in Britain. Property of Kenneth Pitt. Present for David Bowie.

Pitt returned in mid-December to a Britain shivering to the Yuletide comfort of Tom Jones' 'Green, Green Grass Of Home' just as David's

'Rubber Band' single was released to positive reviews if indifferent sales. As requested, Pitt brought him back some original American Batman comics, a reading preference David shared with his own fictitious 'Uncle Arthur', and some records of 'weird stuff' he thought he'd appreciate. One was the second album by The Fugs, carrying a liner note by his beatnik favourite, Allen Ginsberg. It was 'great drinking and getting stoned music' thought David, especially the bad taste blues of 'Dirty Old Man', a self-explanatory character sketch he'd soon learn to play live.

The other was the sleeveless album with the Warhol sticker. The first track, 'Sunday Morning', didn't really register. Then came the delinquent head-rush 'I'm Waiting For The Man', Lou's account of riding uptown to score drugs in Harlem.

'Lexington, one-two-five.'

As it sledgehammered towards the first chorus, David was seized by a euphoric queasiness. Everything he already felt and didn't yet know about rock 'n' roll at the age of 19 trepanned his skull simultaneously. Streams of silver pouring through the sky into his eardrums. A thousand 'fuck you's thunderbolting his thoughts. An undiscovered galaxy of infinite possibilities, all past parameters blown to sick smithereens.

'Hey, white boy ...'

The body of David Bowie was still geographically closer to Penge. But in the sweet taste of *The Velvet Underground & Nico* his soul had come home to New York City.

THIRTEEN
THE LONELINESS

As the circuitry inside David Bowie's skull melted with the surge of 'I'm Waiting For The Man', some twenty-seven miles north of the parents' house he still called home, another New Yorker was in the process of melting all human understanding of our known universe on a closed film set in Hertfordshire. The same multinational corporation which signed the Velvets, MGM, were pumping ten and a half million dollars into a project taking up the majority of space at their studios in Borehamwood. Its director was Stanley Kubrick, then 38 years-old and already regarded by many in his profession as a cinematic genius. Some might add he was also impossible, insensitive and, quite possibly, insane.

Raised in the Bronx, Kubrick began his career as a professional photographer while still in his teens, documenting the everyday lives of post-war New Yorkers for *Look* magazine. When not snapping Frank Sinatra, showgirls and shoeshine boys, he'd exploit his precocious intellect by hustling chess games downtown in Washington Square, just a block away from the site later to become Café Bizarre. By the time the beatniks invaded Greenwich Village he was already making a name for himself in cinema, effortlessly mastering low-budget crime thrillers, period war drama and, with 1960's *Spartacus,* the star-studded sword-and-sandal blockbuster. Ill at ease in Hollywood, when it came to shoot his adaptation of Vladimir Nabokov's inflammatory *Lolita* for MGM, Kubrick moved production to England, deciding to settle there with his family just outside London, close to the studio's main soundstages in Borehamwood. He followed it with *Dr Strangelove*, his satirical masterpiece about Cold War nuclear annihilation subtitled *How I Learned To Stop Worrying And Love The Bomb*. When the mainstream American media back home tore into him for its 'unpatriotic' poke at US military procedure it only highlighted the intellectual sanctuary and artistic freedom he'd found in exile.

After *Strangelove*, Kubrick had no concrete ideas for his next film, only a foggy notion to make 'the proverbial really good science-fiction movie' based on his belief that until then nobody else had. To do so, he'd need a collaborator. Which is why, in April 1964, Kubrick invited English sci-fi author Arthur C. Clarke, then living in Sri Lanka, to visit him in New York where he still kept an apartment on the Upper East Side.

Their first meeting took place over lunch in Trader Vic's, the basement restaurant of the Plaza Hotel beside Central Park where Andy Warhol sometimes dined. 'Don't laugh,' Kubrick told Clarke, 'but I'm fascinated with the possibility of extraterrestrials.' Clarke didn't laugh. He was intrigued by Kubrick's passion and impressed with his knowledge. Aged ten, Kubrick had been among the millions tuning in live to Orson Welles' *The War Of The Worlds* broadcast and could still recite its opening speech off pat.

As a starting point for an original film about extraterrestrial contact, Clarke offered Kubrick half a dozen of his previously published short stories. The director eventually singled out 'The Sentinel'. Written in 1948, it told of a future exploration of the Moon, when astronauts uncover a strange pyramid structure, a 'fire alarm' left by an alien race millions of years earlier to alert them when life on Earth had evolved enough to venture into space. Over the next few months Clarke remained in New York, staying at the bohemian sanctum of the Chelsea Hotel –

home at one time or another to Bob Dylan, Nico and Jack Kerouac – working on a rough script for a film he and Kubrick eventually announced as *Journey Beyond The Stars*.

Constantly rewritten and amended throughout production, the core of their story took the alien 'fire alarm' premise, swapping a pyramid for a smooth black rectangular monolith. It also called for the most meticulously detailed designs – everything from suspended animation units to zero-gravity lavatories – and ingenious pioneering camera techniques to achieve as scientifically accurate a vision of humanity's future in space as was possible. When filming began in late December 1965, their speculation vastly outweighed solid data from the two dozen or so manned flights of the American and Soviet space programmes to date; both sides in the Cold War having only progressed as far as one spacewalk apiece. The scale of the sets and effects involved quickly set the budget soaring and the schedule stalling. Early reports that *Journey Beyond The Stars* would be in theatres by Christmas 1966 proved laughably ambitious. As David Bowie lay rigid in Bromley stupefied by the pulse of 'I'm Waiting For The Man', Kubrick was still filming, finessing and deliberating on its final shape.

Their biggest unresolved problem remained the question of how to depict its climactic scenes of human and alien contact without resorting to sci-fi clichés of slimy bug-eyed monsters. Clarke sought guidance by arranging an informal meeting with Brooklyn-born cosmologist Carl Sagan, the man who'd later put Beethoven and Chuck Berry in space on Voyager's Golden Record. Sagan's advice to Kubrick was very straightforward. Any explicit attempt to portray extraterrestrial life 'was bound to have an element of falseness about it'. Far better, said Sagan, to 'suggest' rather than 'display' such an alien presence. There was also the matter of the title which, purely in terms of physics, made no sense. 'A film about such a place "beyond the stars" would have to be two hours of blank screen,' laughed Sagan. 'A possible plot only for Andy Warhol.'

For the time being Kubrick persevered with his art department, trying to concoct convincing aliens from 'rubber gargoyle monsters' to gaseous shapes made of dancing polka dots. But he did, to Sagan's relief, change the title to reflect the script's Homeric themes of wandering, exploration and adventure. *2001: A Space Odyssey.*

Twenty-year-old David Bowie squared up to the new year with high hopes of *1967: A Hit Odyssey.* But while London was swinging, David's first post-teenage beat was more a demented lollop, closer to a German bierkeller than Carnaby Street. As if he'd been told his future was writing songs about a strange creature from a different world by a drunken gypsy who'd hiccupped and belched over all the fine details. As if everything he'd felt listening to The Velvet Underground had been erased from his mind and replaced by a big fat bowl of jelly and ice cream laced with whatever Vince Taylor took to make him believe he was the son of God. How else to explain the pristine oom-pah daftness of 'The Laughing Gnome'?

In its favour, it was catchy. And funny, if you liked puns. But it showed all the wounds of a worrying severance between the cosmic crotchets ringing inside David's head and the queer semi-quavers he was putting on record. And so he sang his song of 'The Laughing Gnome' while his mind's jukebox drowned out its '*ha-ha-ha*'s with The Velvets and The Fugs, and its '*hee-hee-hee*'s with Syd's Pink Floyd, the left-handed wizardry of The Jimi Hendrix Experience and Cream, a trio formed by ex-Yardbird Eric Clapton who started the year crashing close to the shores of the top ten ringing the Ziggy-ready liberty bell 'I Feel Free'.

Cream's first big hit was still ebbing out of the charts in late February when they played David's local Bromley Court Hotel. David invited Terry along, hoping he could turn his 29-year-old brother on to something other than his old bebop jazz favourites. But as Cream began their set, he noticed Terry starting to swivel and moan, as if the sound was physically assaulting him. He grew worse as the gig continued, eventually so bad that David had to lead him outside for some fresh air. Terry clung to David until they were in the car park, where he fell to the ground, ranting and screaming. He described the pavement cracking open beneath his feet and a ring of fire slowly encircling him, like flames were licking up all the way from hell. David knew this wasn't booze or a bad trip. He'd seen the same schizophrenic glaze in the eyes of Vince Taylor. Now it shone in those of his poor half-brother, frightened and shaking on the cold ground of Coniston Road for all the world to see. There, in public, David's great undiscussable family secret. The streak of insanity marbling through the Burns gene on his mother Peggy's side, a bloodline dammed by lobotomy, shock therapy and early death, now destroying Terry. How much, he wondered, would it destroy him?

Terry Burns wasn't alone in choking on the smog of madness to fall over London that month. The pop world was stunned by the rock 'n' roll suicide of 'Telstar' producer Joe Meek. An insufferable combination of chart failure, paranoia, blackmail threats over his then-illegal homosexuality, drug abuse, pending bankruptcy and perhaps one séance too many drove him to murder his landlady moments before blowing his brains out; the date, 3 February, was also the eighth anniversary of the death of his idol, Buddy Holly. The last record of Meek's to be released was a single by London mods The Riot Squad whose singer, Keith Gladman, was so affected by the tragedy he decided to quit. His determined bandmates began looking for a replacement. A few weeks later they found one. His name was David Bowie.

As an artist under contract currently recording their debut solo album, David had no need to seek another group. But The Riot Squad offered him an escape from his own storybook 'Gnome-man's land', a chance to test the new ideas and influences playing havoc with his self-image. David completely restyled the band, ripping the threads from Syd Barrett's wardrobe with bright flowery shirts and face paint. He made them rehearse covers of his newfound New York thrills, 'I'm Waiting For The Man' and The Fugs' 'Dirty Old Man'. He also supplied some unique and uniquely risky originals, the marijuana fantasy 'Silver Tree Top School For Boys' and the downright kinky 'Little Toy Soldier' stealing its chorus from the Velvets' 'Venus In Furs'. A premature, wastepaper basket rehearsal for The Spiders From Mars, his Riot Squad experiment ran its course after one demo and a handful of low-key gigs.

David returned to the day job of being simply David Bowie just in time to promote the release of his first album – titled simply *David Bowie*. As a bolthole from Bromley he was now lodging at Kenneth Pitt's Marylebone flat, and it was Pitt whose flattering fanfare graced the back sleeve. 'David's keen sense of perception and unusual powers of observation enable him to view the world around him with the eye of an articulate eagle,' wrote Pitt. 'He moved so fast that everything he did was two years too soon. Why, he was even photographed in 1964 wearing a military jacket.'

Pitt's latter comment assumed a cruel poignancy when the album was released on 1 June 1967. The same day as the decade's decisive pop zeitgeist *Sgt Pepper's Lonely Hearts Club Band*. In its instantly iconic pop art cover by Peter Blake, The Beatles assembled a dream cast of their personal heroes, among them portraits of H. G. Wells, Bob Dylan, William Burroughs and Kubrick's *Dr Strangelove* co-writer Terry Southern. At the centre of the celebrity scrum in day-glo military jackets stood The Beatles themselves. Or rather, *not* The Beatles. The strain of their delirious 'bigger than Jesus' totalitarian conquest of every human nervous system in the western hemisphere had forced them to cease playing in concert the previous summer. It was Paul McCartney who suggested it 'would be nice' to lose their identities by assuming the military alter egos of Sgt Pepper's band. 'To submerge ourselves in the persona of a fake group,' McCartney added, 'we could make up all the culture around it.' Pop had always been full of alter egos in as far as Reg and Brian sweeping their birth certificates under the rug of a glamorous Marty or Vince. But the ruse of *Sgt Pepper* blasted open a totally new dimension of illusion and suspended disbelief. A ruse that wasn't lost on the young David Bowie.

Bitterly, *Sgt Pepper* also highlighted the shortcomings of the *David Bowie* album as a defining pop artefact of 1967. While both records looked back through sepia spectacles to a fuzzy, arcane Lord Kitchener's Empire, The Beatles had done so plugged into the mains of modern psychedelic rock 'n' roll. The songs of David Bowie sounded strictly vaudeville by comparison. His debut album had been an end rather than a beginning. Such an end that he wouldn't release another record for the next two years. Two long years in which to reassess who or what 'David Bowie' really was.

Unable to make any headway in pop, he first rebounded into delusions of thespian grandeur. A director friend of Pitt's offered to cast him in a comedy film based on the classical legend of Orpheus in the underworld. The role was that of a pop singer who is eventually ripped to pieces by his own fans. The film was never made.

Potentially more disastrous was his escalating interest in Buddhism. David attended regular meetings at the Tibet Society, studying their literature and philosophy and meditating with lama monks. His next move towards enlightenment would have involved retreating to a monastery in Scotland, a vow of abstinence and a shaved head. The Scottish bit didn't bother him so much as the lack of sex and hair. He wisely stayed in London, his locks and libido unsnipped.

Still resisting the straighter path of pop, his next tangent was thankfully more fruitful. David decided he wanted to study mime after being introduced to Lindsay Kemp, a 29-year-old Scottish actor and dancer currently performing a one-man show off Covent Garden. Kemp was to become David's mentor, friend and one of his many lovers. But more importantly he pruned away the dead wood of David Jones to reveal a little more of the Starman lying in ambush within. It was Kemp who first opened David's eyes to the exotic costumes, make-up and mannerisms of Japanese kabuki. It was Kemp who properly taught his body to 'exteriorise' the soul through movement. And it was Kemp who embedded his love for the work of a Belgian songwriter and former labelmate of Vince Taylor, Jacques Brel.

David's first dose of Brel came in the autumn of '67 with the solo debut of ex-Walker Brother Scott Walker, himself an aloof pop enigma whose mass appeal was neatly summed up by his publicist as 'isolation inviting adulation'. The *Scott* album featured three of Brel's English translations by Brill Building veteran Mort Shuman, including both 'Amsterdam' and 'My Death'. Walker covered more Brel on his second and third albums of '68 and '69, by which stage David had since been 'absolutely floored' by the off-Broadway hit *Jacques Brel Is Alive And Well And Living In Paris*, a theatrical showcase of the Belgian's songbook which he and Kemp saw many times during its five-week London run.

Between kabuki and Jacques Brel, Kemp's influence boded well for the coming of Ziggy Stardust. So too David's discovery of a poem by Liverpool's Roger McGough, 'At Lunchtime', about bus passengers freaking out thinking it was the end of the world – a lyrical spore for 'Five Years'. Only the fact he was currently reciting the poem as part of a one-man cabaret act where he also sang 'The Laughing Gnome' to a glove puppet seemed the action of someone who'd willingly allowed their once promising pop career to slip into the doldrums. His record label obviously agreed. They'd since scheduled his next single, a song presumably born of his thankfully aborted Scottish exodus, 'London Bye Ta-Ta', only to cancel its release at the last minute. The same month, they dropped him.

David Bowie was 21-years-old. Now a singer–songwriter without a label, without a band. In bloody-minded defiance he drew up a radical new masterplan making full use of Kemp's training. He would re-launch himself as a mime artist in a one-man show enacting the Chinese invasion of Tibet. He was also, as he'd later admit, smoking a lot of marijuana at the time.

Then again, sometimes it helped being out of one's gourd. David could forget about all his recent frustrations and failures and vanish in the clouds of future fantasy. He could do what a lot of trippy hipsters were doing that summer of '68. Get high. Go to the pictures. Maybe try losing his mind in that far-out new Stanley Kubrick film …

Nearly four years after Kubrick's first meeting with Clarke at Trader Vic's, *2001: A Space Odyssey* was finally complete. The original cut was close to three hours long and included a ten-minute prologue of edited interviews with physicists, astronomers and theologians discussing the possible existence of extraterrestrial life and its impact on our concepts of God and the universe. After the first press previews, Kubrick decided to lose the prologue, along with another nineteen minutes of film, before its official American release in the first week of April 1968. Even so, at two hours and twenty minutes with minimal dialogue the film was still 'too long' and 'boring' for test audiences. The critics were no kinder. The *New York Times* wrote it off as 'somewhere between hypnotic and immensely boring'. Many agreed it was 'dull' and 'banal', while in *Harper's Bazaar* the notorious cinematic reaper Pauline Kael hacked into it as 'a monumentally unimaginative movie'.

Kubrick was bulletproof. He confidently dismissed all negative comments as clear-cut evidence of a generation gap, attributing the 'poor reaction' to the wrong preview audience voicing a blinkered opinion of a film their senses weren't equipped to understand. 'There's a basic problem with people who are not paying attention with their eyes,' he argued. 'They're listening. And they don't get much from listening to this film. Those who won't believe their eyes won't be able to appreciate this film.'

There was more to Kubrick's conviction than bullish vanity. A generation of kids softened by the age of *Sgt Pepper* and flower power were, as he'd guessed, ready and willing to believe their eyes. Kubrick had given them the gift of a mind-bending widescreen psychedelic spectacle. The ultimate trip. With *2001: A Space Odyssey*, the hippies could now join the space race.

The film premiered in London the same month, beginning a year-long run at the Casino Cinerama Theatre in Soho, just along Old Compton Street from the 2 I's coffee bar. Which is where a soporifically stoned David Bowie wandered in and sank into his seat.

The lights dimmed and for the first three minutes he sat in inky darkness, the moaning unease of György Ligeti's *Atmosphères* pricking his ears like a scream of insects. And then there was light. Blinding starlight curving white arcs around the edges of planets, stabbing his eyes from the great beyond, sucking him up out of his chair into the unimaginable softness of the cosmos. Light and music. The sound of all life awakening. The big bang hallelujah chorus of Richard Strauss' *Thus Spake Zarathustra*. *Daa. Daaa. Daaaa. DA-DAAAAA!*

Bom, bom, bom, bom, bom, bom, bom, bom, bom!

For the next two hours his senses were whiplashed through time and space. Back millions of years to the dawn of man's docile primate ancestors who learn the art of war through the first apparition of Clarke's giant monolith. Then forward to a future of space stations spinning above a pale watery planet to the graceful waltz of Johann Strauss' *The Blue Danube* and another monolith unearthed by astronauts under the surface of the moon. Forward again to NASA's first mission to Jupiter, sabotaged by the artificial intelligence of the spaceship's on-board computer, HAL, until he's de-programmed by the sole survivor, Dr Dave Bowman. *'Stop, Dave. Will you stop, Dave?'* And finally climaxing with the psychedelic crescendo 'Beyond The Infinite'; Bowman's mind and body wrung through an alien kaleidoscope of light and colour until his journey's end, evolving into a luminous humanoid foetus, the 'Star-Child'. The now familiar kettle drums of *Thus Spake Zarathustra* beat deep into David's ribcage. Alien contact had been made and, Sagan was right, Kubrick only had to 'suggest' it. The final frames of the Star-Child drifting towards Earth peeled back another layer of David's brain. The superbeing born on Earth, reborn in space, seconds from returning to save mankind.

Bom, bom, bom, bom, bom, bom, bom, bom, bom!

The End.

For David Bowie, *2001: A Space Odyssey* wasn't just a film. It was a commandment. A burning bush in Super Panavision 70. He returned to see it several times, telling friends he felt completely 'zapped', yanked through his own cosmic wringer just like Dr Dave Bowman – Dave, Bow, he was only a syllable away himself. The future vision of *2001* was also that of David Bowie. One day he'd look back and agree. 'It predicted my lifestyle for the seventies.'

Nor was it only about the psychedelic kick, the jaw-swinging special effects, the fact that when it was released humans had yet to set foot on the Moon but Kubrick realised it so eloquently that when they finally did astronauts remarked the real experience 'was just like *2001*'. It was something far deeper, a bleak human truth, a sense of isolation which touched the absolute core of his latent Starman. An understanding *2001* wasn't really about space, or aliens, but loneliness. The pure, beautiful loneliness that exists at the centre of all great art, from Beethoven's Late Quartets to Elvis Presley's 'Heartbreak Hotel'. Loneliness. Isolation. Or like Scott Walker, 'isolation inviting adulation'.

If he could find a way to capture that same feeling, sat in the darkness of the cinema, staring at the sad little rock of human life so blue, so helpless, hanging in the unthinkable emptiness of deep space. No comedy gnome voices or wobbling Anthony Newley tics but a song from the soul with all the pathos of Jacques Brel. The ballad of the loneliest man in the universe. Floating in his tin can. Far above the world.

Yes. A musical space odyssey. He just might have the making of a great pop song …

FOURTEEN
THE RIVAL

The idea for the musical space odyssey kicked and thrashed inside David's head like an impatient foetus desperate to escape its womb. Until in the last weeks of 1968, the waters of inspiration finally broke. On Christmas Eve, David was among the millions watching a satellite broadcast from NASA's Apollo 8 command module containing the first men to fly around the Moon. They beamed back pictures of the Earth as seen from the far side of the Moon accompanied by their reading of the opening 'let there be light' passages from *The Book Of Genesis*. Speaking to mission control, astronaut Jim Lovell confessed 'the vast loneliness is awe-inspiring'. It made David imagine himself in the same situation, piloting the Apollo 8 from Earth to the Moon and back. Had it been him, he thought, something would have almost certainly gone wrong.

And so he took *2001*'s Dave Bowman and Apollo 8 captain Frank Borman and created his own astronaut, called Major Tom, on a solo mission to the Moon. He leaves Earth a national hero but becomes overwhelmed by the intense alienation. Ground control lose radio contact with Major Tom who is left stranded alone in space, staring helplessly at the blue planet he once called home. A simple tune about a tragic spaceman. A hymn to human isolation and our planetary solitude in the wider universe. In wordplay homage to Kubrick, David called it 'Space Oddity'.

One of the first to hear David's new song was his old comrade in Carnaby clobber, the handsome young upstart he'd met over a tin of paint in Denmark Street a few years earlier. The one who called himself 'King Mod'.

Life had been good to King Mod in the interim, more so than it had been for David. After a few false starts, flop singles and changes in haircut he'd finally clawed his way into the charts with a hippy folk stupor about a girl named 'Debora' (who looked like 'a zebra'). King Mod wasn't even a mod any more, more of a fairytale pixie fallen from the pages of Arthur Rackham made wild trembling hair and bleating flesh. The papers were already nicknaming him 'The Bóppin' Elf'. While David's muse was lost in space, King Mod's was somewhere in the bowels of J. R. R. Tolkien's Middle-earth, a fantasy realm of wizards, unicorns and silver satyrs. He wrote songs with odd titles like 'Frowning Atahuallpa' exclusively for voice, acoustic guitar and bongos. But with two albums and two minor hit singles by the age of 21, he was winning in a race where David was forever struggling to get off the blocks.

In early 1969, King Mod was living in the epicentre of west London hippiedom in a pokey basement flat off Ladbroke Grove. It was there, in what he jokingly called his 'chateau in the west', that David sang him 'Space Oddity' on acoustic guitar. King Mod sat nodding his head in rhythm to its slow, melancholic chords. Afterwards he told David he thought it sounded a bit like The Bee Gees' 'New York Mining Disaster 1941', a resemblance some of his other friends had also picked up on. But King Mod liked it. 'It's going to be a hit,' he predicted. David left overjoyed with encouragement. But as he closed the door behind him, King Mod's eager smile collapsed in a brimstone scowl.

Yes, it was going to be a hit, all right. But if David Bowie believed the tiny planet called pop was big enough for the pair of them, he certainly didn't. Not King Mod. Not The Boppin' Elf.

Not Marc Bolan.

They were born the same year, 1947, in the same sacred city of London. January 8's David Jones a Wednesday's child, full of woe. September 30's Mark Feld a Tuesday's child, full of grace. All that separated them was 265 days and the river Thames. While, to the south, David came of age in Brixton and Bromley, on the north bank Mark Feld was learning to preen and pose on the streets of Stoke Newington and Stamford Hill. He received a similar baptism of rock 'n' roll fire at the age of nine from Elvis Presley. In the winter of 1956, as David was watching cousin Kristina dance herself delirious to 'Hound Dog' the young Mark was already on his first guitar trying to learn 'Blue Suede Shoes' from a treasured 78 r.p.m. single. By 1958, as David was strumming skiffle tunes at scout summer camp, ten-year-old Mark was at the heart of the action in Soho scampering behind the counter of the 2 I's, helping serve coffees in the hope of a first-hand encounter with a real life pop star – a tinkling teaspoon away from Vince Taylor.

Mark Feld was short but pretty, a pint size rock 'n' roller who sculpted his dark quiff and curled his lips just like his hero, Cliff Richard. Until the pint size rock 'n' roller became a teenage dandy. At 14, he was a walking mannequin of sharp-suited Italian fashions plucked from the rails of Petticoat Lane or Sportique, the Soho mod paradise two doors along from the 2 I's on Old Compton Street. Until the teenage dandy became a Cockney Dylan. At 17 he made his first demo warbling a version of Bob's 'Blowin' In The Wind' in a fisherman's cap and rollneck jumper, swapping his birth name of Mark Feld for that of Toby Tyler. Until Toby Tyler went on holiday to Paris in early 1965, returning with preposterous tales of meeting a black-magic wizard and another change of name. Keeping 'Mark' but swapping the hard Hackney 'k' for a softer French 'c'. The surname he adapted from his current flatmate, actor James Bolam, star of the BBC comedy *The Likely Lads*. Until forever, Marc Bolan.

Like David, Marc knew the importance of not being himself, of burying his birth certificate in a cocoon of self-mythologising bluster.

When they met in Leslie Conn's Denmark Street offices during the brief period he managed both – Davie the mod, Marc the self-appointed 'King Mod' – they saw in one another a strange alternate self, at once alien yet unnervingly familiar. Different hair, different eyes, different height, different voices, different affectations ... but an uncanny kindred rock 'n' roll spirit. The Starman and the Metal Guru, neither entirely sure which was destined to become which. It was mutually fascinating, and a bit alarming, more so to Marc who felt the first bruise of competition when he learned David had already beat him to releasing a couple of singles.

Marc didn't have to wait long to catch up. His first, November 1965's 'The Wizard' was, he insisted, inspired by that life-changing trip to Paris, supplying the press with cock and bull anecdotes of befriending the magician he claimed levitated before his eyes, ate human flesh and crucified cats. The song itself was a simple yarn about meeting a wizard in the woods, sung with a hazy Dylanish twang over an urgent Motown thump, a mesmeric riff and some bewitching woodwind. Recorded in the same Decca studios where David cut his respective debut, 'Liza Jane', in a straight comparison 'The Wizard' was the better pop record – gently bizarre, intriguingly brief – if no more successful.

It took Marc another year and a half of failed follow-ups, vocal tweaks, visual tucks and a liberating interlude with riotous noise-mods John's Children before he settled in his role as the tinker sprite wrapping his gizzard around gems of fantasy gibberish in hippy duo Tyrannosaurus Rex. His spaced-out partner went by the name of Steve Peregrin Took (by birth, Steve Porter) and restricted himself to bothering bongos and vocal harmonies. Together they sounded like a Hare Krishna playing nursery rhymes on a ukulele being pursued by a frantically clopping pantomime horse. A sound which, even within the post-*Pepper* watershed of psychedelic nonsense perfuming the charts of late 1967, wasn't the easiest on human eardrums.

Luckily for Tyrannosaurus Rex, their biggest fan was also their most influential. The BBC's John Peel was so besotted with the duo that he invited them to play his regular DJ nights at a cellar club in Covent Garden. It especially suited Marc's love of Tokienesque gobbledygook that the club was called Middle Earth. It also attracted a young American producer just relocated from New York to London, now on a mission to sign his own pet project. A mission which ended one night in Middle Earth when 23-year-old Tony Visconti caught Tyrannosaurus Rex in all their indefinable eccentricity.

Visconti introduced himself after their set and asked if they needed a producer. Marc told him he'd have to join the queue, being the eighth to approach them that week, somewhere behind John Lennon. An outright lie, as Visconti only suspected when Marc rang his office the next morning haggling for an audition. Over the coming weeks, the producer's New York world-wisdom was sharp enough to scythe through Marc's havering bravado and befriend the lovable charmer beneath. When he learned Marc lived in a bedsit with a shared toilet and no bath, he invited him to come and use the tub in his own flat once a week. There they'd drink wine with their girlfriends, discuss books and poetry and listen to favourite records. And sometimes there was the added surprise of other visitors. Like another young and slightly odd singer Visconti had just been paired with. A queer coincidence, thought Marc. There, in the cosy bohemian den of his producer's flat, finding himself saying 'hello' again to the boy with the crap shoes and teeth like a broken zip he'd first clapped eyes on over some tins of paint in a Denmark Street office three years earlier.

'Marc, David. David, Marc … have you guys met?'

In their subconscious pop marathon of tortoise and hare, by the summer of '68 Marc was many miles out in front. David's career had decelerated since his debut album. He'd only just started working with Visconti, producer of the doomed 'London Bye Ta-Ta' which put an end to his Deram contract. While David floundered without a label, in desperate thoughts of monks and mime, Tyrannosaurus Rex's debut single 'Debora' rattled its way to number 34. By no means 'a smash', but definitely 'a hit'. The band's first album also made the top 20 despite the burden of its exhausting title: *My People Were Fair And Had Sky In Their Hair … But Now They're Content To Wear Stars In Their Brow*. Adding to David's envious indignation, its cover was designed by his best friend, George.

Marc could comfortably afford to be magnanimous in victory over his old acquaintance, inviting David to support Tyrannosaurus Rex that June at a prolific headline show at London's Royal Festival Hall. Providing, that is, he didn't sing but performed his mime act about the Chinese invasion of Tibet. Which he did, his turn ruined by the heckles of left-wing students and hippies irate over his damning portrayal of China's communist Red Guard. In the wings, Marc couldn't help but laugh.

Possibly by way of consolation prize, in the aftermath Marc gave David a present. It was a new toy instrument, a miniature battery-powered synthesizer with a flat metal keyboard played with a stylus which produced a noise like a bumblebee trapped in a toaster. It was a trifling gesture. An innocuous token of a strange, uneven camaraderie. A whim of generosity from winner to loser.

Marc Bolan would live to regret it.

As Frank Borman and his Apollo 8 crew splashed down safely back to Earth in the last week of 1968, David was still trying to create a new career for himself outside pop music. False hope teased with his first screen role in the war drama *The Virgin Soldiers*. He'd impressed at his audition, turning up with a cropped military haircut before he'd been cast. For his troubles, he was given a blink-and-miss walk on.

Kenneth Pitt, meanwhile, had his own masterplan to reboot David's career. A half-hour film showcase, *Love You Till Tuesday*, featuring songs from his debut album, a short mime sketch and a preview of David's latest band project, a folky trio called Feathers. Pitt suggested it could also probably do with a brand new song. David obliged and added 'Space

Oddity', acting out the plot in silver spacesuit, crash helmet and a chunky wig to disguise his now redundant soldier cut. An ignominious unveiling of a tune which, as Marc had just told him, sounded like a hit. Or it would have been had the film been shown at the time. Sadly for Pitt his investment in *Love You Till Tuesday* paid no dividends, remaining unseen by the public until the 1980s. The film's obscurity was a definite blessing for its shaky first draft of 'Space Oddity', even if it denied the world the prophetic Ziggy fable of its mime sketch. 'The Mask' was David's story of a man who finds a mask in an old junkshop. First he wears it to amuse his family and friends until, after a local concert, the mask makes him a famous star. 'Autographs, films, television, the lot … it had a very strange effect on me, though.' One night at the London Palladium, basking in the applause, he tries to remove the mask but finds it permanently affixed. He struggles to wrestle it off his face only to strangle himself, dying on stage in front of his fans. 'The papers made a big thing out of it. Funny, though – they didn't mention a thing about a mask.'

Marc Bolan's begrudging enthusiasm for 'Space Oddity' wasn't shared by Tony Visconti. When Pitt finally found David a new label, the fittingly planetary Mercury Records, Visconti declined the offer to produce the song. With Moon fever in the press as NASA's Apollo programme gathered momentum, he thought it much too obvious a gimmick. Instead, the job was handed to the engineer on David's first album, Gus Dudgeon, no stranger to cosmic pop having just co-produced The Bonzo Dog Doo-Dah Band's novelty hit 'I'm The Urban Spaceman' with Paul McCartney (together under the alias 'Apollo C. Vermouth').

Completed in the last week of June 1969, 'Space Oddity' was David's first session at Trident, tucked in a Soho back alley just round the corner from the Marquee club and already the studio of choice for Visconti and Tyrannosaurus Rex. Dudgeon helped illuminate the song's human drama with arranger Paul Buckmaster, his orchestral crescendo nicely echoing the Ligeti strings used in *2001*. The finished 'Space Oddity' was a masterpiece of zero-gravity pop; Jacques Brel sings Stanley Kubrick with eerie robotic accompaniment from what sounded like HAL himself. The latter was David's spontaneous finishing touch, writing a harmony part and solo for his new toy instrument, the Stylophone. A recent gift from a friend. Without ever wishing to, Marc had accidentally gilded David's career-saving breakthrough.

Visconti's suspicions about 'Space Oddity' were vindicated when it was rush-released five days before the launch of NASA's Apollo 11 mission to place a man on the moon. A week earlier the single received its poignant world premiere through the PA system of The Rolling Stones' free concert in Hyde Park on 5 July, an event overshadowed by the death two days before of their founding guitarist Brian Jones. On stage, Mick Jagger read an excerpt from Shelley's poem 'Adonais' inspired by the death of his friend, Keats. 'He is not dead, he doth not sleep.' Later that evening on the other side of the park David witnessed his boyhood hero Chuck Berry support The Who as part of the Royal Albert Hall's 'Pop Proms'. The Who played their new album in its entirety, their 'rock opera' *Tommy* about a deaf, dumb and blind pinball prodigy who starts a youth cult until his followers rise up against him. David's companion that night was his new A&R man and confidante, Calvin Mark Lee, an American-Asian with a doctorate in philosophy, famed in London party circles for wearing reflective diamond 'love jewels' in the centre of his forehead.

Eleven days later, Apollo 11 launched successfully from Cape Kennedy, Florida, carrying astronauts Neil Armstrong, Edwin 'Buzz' Aldrin and Michael Collins towards the moon. A trio of real life Major Toms, they spent the next three days floating in their tin can staring down at the blue planet slowly receding into the darkness of space. Just after 9.15 p.m. British Summer Time on Sunday 20 July, the same lunar module Arthur C. Clarke had seen during construction while still writing and researching *2001* touched down on the surface of the Moon. Six and a half hours later, Armstrong made his giant leap for mankind. Three hundred and fifty years after Johannes Kepler had his first lunar dream, human beings had finally reached the Moon. There were no camel-legged, frail-skinned aliens waiting to greet them. Nor any black monoliths to pierce the cosmos with their 'fire alarm'. Just craters, rocks, Moondust and, by the time they left, an American flag.

Over five hundred million people watched the Moon-landing live by satellite. None were more gobsmacked than David, hearing his 'Space Oddity' used during the BBC's broadcast, stunned that the programme makers couldn't have listened closely to its lyrics which left Major Tom marooned in orbit. The Beeb wouldn't make that mistake again. Sharing the same distaste as Visconti, the corporation placed a temporary embargo on broadcasting any songs with an exploitative 'space theme' in the weeks surrounding the Apollo 11 flight, stalling the success of 'Space Oddity' for another two months. Two months of momentary consolation for Marc Bolan whose latest single, a warning of the electrical storm to come called 'King Of The Rumbling Spires', cartwheeled to a halt at a dismal 44. Two months where Marc was more than happy to have his 'hit' prediction for David proved wrong. Until, in late September, 'Space Oddity' managed to drift just inside the top 40. By early October it was inside the 20. Two weeks later, it was in the top ten.

Sat in the Notting Hill basement flat where David had first played it to him less than a year earlier, Marc fixed his evilest eyes on his television where 'Space Oddity' now vibrated from the speaker. On screen, David Bowie making his debut appearance on the BBC's *Top Of The Pops*, surrounded by images of the Apollo 11 mission. And in his hands, the silly musical toy that had once belonged to Marc, its every fuzzy note stinging his ears and thrashing his ego with cruellest irony.

In early November, as 'Space Oddity' peaked at number five, David was sent on a short solo tour of Scotland. On the first night in Perth at the Salutation Hotel, 'the Sally' to its locals, as he began strumming the single's B-side, 'Wild Eyed Boy From Freecloud', the fair maids of Perth rushed to the front of the stage and began screaming at his feet. It was a sensation David had never experienced before. The shriek and sigh of unconditional adulation. 'I would never have believed in a million years that people would scream at me,' he said afterwards. 'I stand bemused by it all.' In the stratosphere high above the Sally, the approaching phantom of Ziggy Stardust smiled down fondly. His human vessel was almost ready to be occupied.

The end credits of the 1960s rolled to the tune of 'Two Little Boys' by Rolf Harris, the Australian entertainer who'd been first to endorse the Stylophone, a good year before 'Space Oddity'. Ending a decade epitomised by pop's cultural revolution, its last number one was an atypical sentimental relic of early-twentieth-century music hall: the simple yarn of childhood best friends whose love of playing on wooden horses leads to a poignant moment in adulthood fighting in the American Civil War. 'Two Little Boys' was a song of undying friendship, of a brotherly love never to be broken. A song which said next to nothing about the relationship between David Bowie and Marc Bolan as 1970 began.

In less than two years the see-saw had shifted. David was now the star, on *Top Of The Pops* and in the pages of *Jackie* magazine. Marc was still gargling madrigals about dragons' ears and druids' spears for fuggy student bedsits a-choke with joss-sticks. It wasn't enough that Tyrannosaurus Rex still had the cult kudos of John Peel and the underground bible *International Times*. For Marc, their façade of hippiedom was gossamer thin. He still wanted to be Cliff Richard. Worshipped. Adored. Screamed at by girls sprinting to the front of the stage in Perth or wherever else.

For David, the year of 'Space Oddity' had been a life-changing maelstrom of euphoria tempered with despair. He had the hit single he'd always craved. He'd also met the woman who'd soon become his wife, a 19-year-old American-Cypriot called Angie Barnett. Casting the die for their future marriage, they met through mutual bisexual lover, the love-jewelled Calvin Mark Lee. Casting the die for the future David, Angie was also studying marketing at Kingston Polytechnic, a skill she'd apply to her husband and herself as human products in the years to come.

But he'd also lost his father. John Jones died that August, only a few weeks before 'Space Oddity' entered the charts, never living to see his son achieve the dreams of showbiz success he'd shared all those years earlier in the doomed days of the Boop-A-Doop club. And, in a different sense, David was also losing his brother. After further schizophrenic outbursts, Terry Burns was admitted to Cane Hill, a late-Victorian psychiatric hospital on the south edge of Croydon. As David later claimed, 'he'd be happy to spend the rest of his life there.'

David followed 'Space Oddity' with his second album, confusingly sharing the eponymous title *David Bowie* with his debut. But by the start of 1970 the pressure was already on for new material to maintain its success. Eager to make his mark on the new decade, eight days in, on his twenty-third birthday, he returned to Trident with Visconti this time to record what he hoped would be his next hit, 'The Prettiest Star'. Not, as the title teased, another space ballad, but a love song written for his bride-to-be Angie. Its sentiment unconsciously echoed his own parents' courtship with its mention of old movies and darkened cinemas, its prettiest star being the Garbo, not the galactic kind. The romantic mood was complemented by a sweet toe-tapping tune, a little too sweet for Visconti who decided it needed something, or rather someone, to add some missing rock 'n' roll fire.

Visconti had just such a secret weapon up his sleeve, one which anyone listening to BBC Radio 1's *John Peel Concert* that New Year's Day would have already heard for themselves. Marc Bolan had become increasingly amplified over the last year, taking sneaky lessons from Cream's Eric Clapton, as his performance for Peel that Sunday made obvious. He ended his gig with a new song, 'Elemental Child', a typical Tyrannosaurus Rex chant about damsels and gemstones but violently electrified, his guitar disintegrating in a white hot climax of fuzz, feedback and the sort of fretboard voodoo a January 1970 audience would have expected only of Jimi Hendrix. Placed in a unique position as the producer of both David and Marc, it was Visconti's brainwave to bring the two together on 'The Prettiest Star'. The record was David's baby, but Marc could rock it. Or so Visconti hoped.

David was the least resistant. His was still the name above the title. And Marc had already been something of a lucky talisman for 'Space Oddity' thanks to the Stylophone.

'OK,' David told Visconti. He'd do it.

Marc, on the other hand, was cagier. He didn't like the idea of being anybody's second fiddle. But, then again, it could be a chance to steal the limelight from under David's nose. And, besides, it would only be a few hours' work at most.

'OK,' Marc told Visconti. He'd do it.

On the day of the session, David played the song to Marc, who very speedily improvised a guitar riff based on the main vocal melody. Marc's soon-to-be-wife and manager, June Child, sat in the control room with Visconti. She hated the song and said as much. Marc seemed to agree, unwilling to share his precious 'Elemental Child's play on a slurry solo, the musical equivalent of a disinterested yawn.

'That'll do.'

The tension fizzled with every minute that limped past, Marc and David reaching a non-cooperative stalemate where both somehow kept out of the other's way. Visconti breathed a sigh of relief when Marc finally left after less than two hours' non-graft. His guitar part was usable, but it stuck out on the record like a bent rusty nail in a varnished plank of wood, a spiky tribute to its creative unease. If Marc's intention was to jinx David's single, it worked. 'The Prettiest Star' sold less than a thousand copies.

One year on from 'Space Oddity', David Bowie remained a one-hit wonder. The situation didn't change with his next single, 'Memory Of A Free Festival', a rambling Ziggyish tease about communal love, spaceships and visitors from Venus. Nor the one after that, 'Holy Holy', a Satanic love song capsized by the lumpy arrangement of its producer and bass player, Herbie Flowers. It certainly didn't help David's cause that the week of its release in January 1971 Flowers was basking in his own number one success as the co-author of 'Grandad', a daft coffin-knocking pop novelty for *Dad's Army* actor Clive Dunn.

Yet for David, the failure of another single was the least of his worries. It wasn't Flowers' 'Grandad' being at number one that bothered him. It was the record at number two, one which had taken twelve weeks to climb its way within kicking distance of Dunn's walking stick. The song was 'Ride A White Swan'. The group was listed as T. Rex – Marc Bolan's facelift for Tyrannosaurus Rex, his drug-ravaged sidekick Steve Peregrin Took last seen 'in a wardrobe in New York looking for God' and since replaced by smouldering new bongo devil Mickey Finn.

Marc and David had both undergone a conscious electric transition in 1970. In David's case, epic power jams about madness, despair, Aleister Crowley and Friedrich Nietzsche soon to be heard on his next album, *The Man Who Sold The World*. But in Marc's case, amplification was the key to a magical new kingdom of sensation and simplicity. As a trial run, he cut a cathartic bubblegum stomp called 'Oh Baby', released under the pseudonym Dib Cochran & The Earwigs. A colossal flop sales wise but enough of a drag on the sweet cigarette of unashamed pop bliss to convince Marc that's where he wanted to spend the rest of the decade.

For Marc the future wasn't about finding the right song but the right sound. And on 1 July 1970, he heard it ringing in his headphones as he stood in Trident, plugged in waiting for Visconti to roll the tapes. The producer had been playing around with the ambience of Marc's guitar, adding a ricochet of reverb hiccupping all the way back to Sam Phillips'

Sun label. The tune was a simple rock 'n' roll pattern shook up with some typical Bolan hippy jive about long hair and druids. There were no drums, just Marc, his guitar and Finn banging a tambourine. But with that chrome echo on Marc's Les Paul the effect was hypnotising.

After the first take, Visconti wasn't sure if it was what Marc was after. 'Thank you, man,' Marc assured him. 'I *want* that sound!'

They continued layering overdubs, double-tracking Marc's vocal, adding bass, backing harmonies and some group handclaps recorded using the natural resonance of the studio toilet. Visconti's polishing Midas touch was grafting on a string section, fanning the melody ever higher into the heavens. Listening back, Marc knew nothing else had ever sounded like 'Ride A White Swan' before. It was a sound that was intoxicating, colourful, elusive and glamorous. Yes, *glamorous*. The sound of glam rock. The sound of the Starman.

Except it was coming from the wrong Starman. A sudden crisis in the cosmos. A missed stitch in the fabric of space and time. An administrative mix-up in destiny's sorting office had accidentally delivered the sound of Ziggy Stardust to another human vessel. It was an easy mistake to make for a package marked '1947 London boy, ex-mod, pseudo-hippy, fancy second name beginning with B'.

But where the hell did that leave David Bowie?

FIFTEEN
NAMING BABY

It left David Bowie feeling sick but relieved. Sick with fear to be on a plane hurtling towards take-off on Heathrow's runway. Relieved to be leaving 'Holy Holy', Clive Dunn and T. Rex behind him, their painful memories instantly wiped from his mind in the rush of foggy whiteness through the cabin window.

With his curly nemesis pirouetting at number two, the last week of January 1971 was a good time for David to get out of England. His label had decided to send him on an overseas trip to promote his new album, *The Man Who Sold The World*. A trip to the promised land of Sal Paradise, Elvis Presley and Little Richard. At the age of 24, David was finally going to America.

Angie, now his wife, was five months pregnant and unable to travel. In any case, Mercury were only prepared to pay for one ticket. So when the plane landed at Washington Dulles Airport, David stepped off alone, golden tresses down past his shoulders, eyelids faintly dabbed with shadow and shielded from the winter in a blue fake fur coat. A look in keeping with his latest metamorphosis from the cosmic hippy of 'Space Oddity' to the cross-dressing Graham Garbo of his new album sleeve. But nothing like the 'David Robert Jones' it said on his passport. After an hour of intense questioning, the immigration officers were unable to find a decent reason not to allow their limey transvestite freak into the country. With a look of disgust and a begrudging entry stamp, they sent him through border control where his panicking US press officer, Ron Oberman, was there to greet him. 'For some reason, they seemed to think I looked strange,' shrugged David.

The schedule of press and radio interviews began the next morning, moving up the East Coast until, on his fourth day in America, David finally set foot in the hallowed 'frosty fagtown New York' he'd been fantasising about since he was twelve years-old. Mercury booked him into the midtown Holiday Inn, a few blocks away from the corner of 54th and Sixth, home to a blind middle-aged busker with a wizard's beard and horned helmet. He was born Louis but called himself Moondog. Because of his costume locals nicknamed him 'The Viking of Sixth Avenue'. He'd been making records since the fifties, some of the earliest issued on the short-lived jazz label Mars, summoning exotic sounds on homemade instruments as he sang sad songs of isolation. 'All Is Loneliness'. 'Death, When You Come To Me'. Moondog was just the sort of crazy David liked, Vince Taylor meets Odin, a self-made creation with a name that literally howled with the wonder of outer space.

On first impressions, New York was as wild and frantic as David had always imagined lying in Bromley listening to the sound of The Velvet Underground. It only got better when he discovered yet more Velvet Underground. A local journalist named Ed Kelleher introduced him to *Loaded*, their latest album, currently unavailable in Britain. In the lazy sneer of 'Sweet Jane' and the gospel of 'Rock & Roll', songs of riding Stutz Bearcats and lives saved by the radio, he felt a fresh twist in his star-shaped ignition. A twist which intensified when he learned the Velvets were actually playing downtown that weekend at the Electric Circus, formerly The Don where Warhol first staged his 'Exploding Plastic Inevitable'. Four years after his manager had visited New York on his behalf and returned with a test pressing of their debut album from the clutches of Lou Reed, he was finally going to get to see his beloved Velvets sing and play in the flesh.

The band who walked on stage at the Electric Circus that night looked a bit different from the one David had seen in photos, apart from the unmistakably androgynous Moe Tucker. But to his ears they still sounded stunning, especially when they played his favourite, 'I'm Waiting For The Man'. Not long after the Velvets finished their set, David nervously banged his fist on the backstage door. It opened ajar. Softened by his English accent and intrigued by his appearance, they welcomed him through into the dressing room. David immediately gravitated towards Lou Reed. He told Lou he'd been a huge fan of his work for many years. Lou seemed a little embarrassed. David continued praising the songs. Lou grew more fidgety until eventually he cut David off mid-sentence.

'Er, look, buddy,' said Lou. 'I'm not Lou Reed.'

Because he wasn't Lou Reed. He was somebody else called Doug Yule. He'd been in the band since late 1968 after Lou ousted co-founder John Cale. David didn't even know that Cale had left, never mind that Lou himself had since quit forcing Yule to take centre stage in a desperate attempt to keep the name of The Velvet Underground alive. For the last fifteen minutes, David had been talking to the 'wrong' Lou Reed.

David was mortified. Then amused. Then, the more he played it over in his mind, quite fascinated. As far as he was concerned, he *had* seen and met Lou Reed. Yule had played the role so brilliantly.

What must that feel like, he wondered. Going on stage, pretending to be a completely different character? Doing it so well that everybody in the audience truly believed you were someone you weren't? Hadn't he mentioned something similar in the press five years earlier?

'I think it takes a lot to become somebody else.'

Yes. That was it. *To become somebody else.*

'It takes some doing …'

Before he became somebody else he was plain old Norman Carl Odam. He was born the same year as David and Marc, 1947, in the Texas town of Lubbock, and went to the same junior high school as Lubbock's most famous son, Buddy Holly. Norman was an extremely quiet boy who rarely spoke. At the age of six he began fantasising about what it must be like to visit the planet Mars. By seven, he'd convinced himself that one day he was going to be famous, by whatever means necessary. And so Norman started making up songs, singing them in the street and around the school playground. Only he couldn't sing to save his life. So, instead, he learned to whoop and holler like an Indian brave and built up his own peculiar bag of bird calls and animal growls, ungodly noises which became his lyrics.

Norman tried to learn guitar so he could look like Elvis Presley and impress the girls. He wasn't much of a guitar player either. The girls ignored him but Norman kept trying. He tried teaching himself to play the bugle, the harmonica and the drums. He couldn't even master the kazoo. It didn't stop Norman. He continued to strum and scream outside school, in parking lots and standing on car bonnets at the local drive-in. He was, if nothing else, determined.

Then, one night sitting in his backyard staring up at the Texan twilight, Norman had a brainwave. He loved cowboys and he loved outer space and started to wonder how he could maybe squeeze the two together. He came up with a name. The Stardust Cowboy. It sounded, he thought, 'like a living legend'. And so that night Norman Odam from Lubbock, Texas ceased to be and became somebody else. The Legendary Stardust Cowboy.

Norman customised his car, a Chevy Biscayne, painting the sides with the words 'NASA presents The Legendary Stardust Cowboy'. He grew his hair long and cultivated a chunky pair of sideburns. He'd turn up uninvited at traditional honky-tonks and try singing to crowds who only wanted to lynch him. He was a legend, all right, but for all the wrong reasons.

A tone-deaf, shrieking buffoon. A magnet for abuse, bottles and threats of violence. Until one day a woman strode right up to him and stamped her boot straight through his guitar. Heartbroken and humiliated, he decided to quit his job at a factory drill press and leave town.

Norman headed west, taking a bus to San Diego, then moving on to Hollywood. He still believed himself to be a Legendary Stardust Cowboy and bought himself a buckskin coat to prove it. But Tinsel Town quickly chewed him up and spat him back to Texas.

Norman next thought about heading east instead, to New York, where he hoped to convince the producers of *Tonight With Johnny Carson* to put him on national television. They'd recently done the same for Tiny Tim, a long-haired ukulele-plucking ghoul who crowed old music-hall tunes in a queer, spinsterish wibble. Norman knew that, given the chance, he could be 'the next Tiny Tim'. With $160 in his pocket he loaded his new guitar in his painted 'NASA' Chevy and headed towards New York. He never got there.

Norman never even made the Texas border. He'd pulled over for gas in Fort Worth, where his customised car attracted curious locals who invited him to a music club. After loosening their jaws with a typically tuneless Legendary Stardust Cowboy routine, instead of running him out of town Lubbock-style that same night they ran him into the studio of local producer Joe 'T-Bone' Burnett.

By dawn, Norman had cut his first single. It was called 'Paralyzed' and sounded like the dying confession of a man under Gestapo torture, a hyena in a wheelchair falling down a fire escape, and the rodeo delirium of Slim Pickens astride the falling H-bomb at the end of Kubrick's *Dr Strangelove*. All at the same time. Two minutes and 17 seconds of blasting blue murder.

To Burnett's surprise, the AM radio station upstairs from his studio played it straight away. Listeners were shocked but captivated. It was so abysmally weird they asked to hear it again.

To Burnett's even greater surprise, after Norman paid for five hundred copies to be pressed on his own 'Psycho-Suave' label, the song's cult infamy caught the attention of Mercury Records, who agreed to distribute it nationally. Somehow 'Paralyzed' screamed and spluttered its way inside the Billboard top 200 singles chart.

In November 1968, Mercury managed to squeeze Norman a cameo spot on NBC's new hit sketch show *Rowan & Martin's Laugh-In*. Maybe not the dream of Johnny Carson he'd hoped for, but if it was good enough for Tiny Tim, already a regular of the show, then it was good enough for The Legendary Stardust Cowboy. Wearing a white ten-gallon hat, his beloved buckskin jacket and bright yellow chaps, he was introduced by Dan Rowan as 'the discovery of the week'. As he sang 'Paralyzed' – barking, whooping and bouncing around like a frog on a hotplate – co-host Dick Martin stood beside him mimicking his funny dancing. The audience laughed. They asked him if he wanted to play another. Norman launched into the single's equally demented B-side, 'Who's Knocking On My Door'. The show's ensemble cast of comedians joined in, pretending to dance to its irregular rhythm and drowning out Norman's screams with their own crude imitation. The audience laughed louder. Finally, Norman gave up in frustration and slunk off set. The first television appearance by The Legendary Stardust Cowboy, and also the last.

Mercury persevered with Norman for another couple of singles. They managed to curtail his screaming but his singing voice remained a slurry off-key honk. The best of them was 'I Took A Trip On A Gemini Spaceship', a lovesick cowpoke's groan echoing among the stars. A bit like 'Space Oddity' sung by Hank Williams during morphine withdrawal. But neither it nor the dreary ballad 'Kiss And Run' matched the freak novelty of 'Paralyzed'. Inevitably, Mercury dropped him. They assumed Norman had returned to Texas in his beat-up 'NASA' wagon. Somebody heard a rumour that he'd been arrested for vagrancy. Nobody knew for certain. But every once in a while, his name would creep up in conversation.

'Oh, man! Remember The Legendary Stardust Cowboy?'

Ron Oberman remembered. Mercury's head of press still held back copies of Norman's three singles. Sometimes he'd pass them on to people he thought might dig them. People like David Bowie.

Ten days into his press trip, David reached Chicago where Oberman brought him into Mercury's headquarters, housed in a 1920s skyscraper overlooking the river with a domed restaurant atop its forty storeys, once a speakeasy in the days of Al Capone. On his way inside, David stopped to admire its ornate clock mounted on the north-east corner, crowned by an imposing sculpture of a winged Father Time carrying a scythe and hourglass while below each of its four clock faces yelled the simple, stark insignia: 'TIME'.

Up in Oberman's office, David mentioned that he liked listening to 'weird shit'. He was immediately handed the complete works of The Legendary Stardust Cowboy.

'This is the weirdest shit we've got,' said Oberman.

David had to agree. The first, 'Paralyzed', wasn't so much music as contained anarchy. But somewhere within its calamity David could still hear a soul. 'I Took A Trip On A Gemini Spaceship' was even more impressive. There was a touching loneliness in its obvious lunacy. He especially liked the bit where he drawled, '*I shot my space gun, boy did I feel blue.*' Oberman told him about the *Laugh-In* incident, how Norman had gone on television in all earnest only to be made a fool of. It touched David, who'd had enough jeers in his 24 years to know exactly how that must have felt.

Over the next few days, as he travelled through the Midwest towards the South, his mind kept returning to The Legendary Stardust Cowboy. The madness of the music. The story of this weird little guy from Texas who everyone laughed at.

And the name. 'Stardust Cowboy'. Whatever anyone said about his records, nobody could deny it was an amazing name. It got David thinking all over again. The familiar echo.

'I think it takes a lot to become somebody else. It takes some doing ...'

Before he became somebody else he was plain old Jim. James Newell Osterberg, Jr, another of 1947's boom babies, raised in a trailer park outside Ann Arbor, Michigan. A quiet and thoughtful kid prone to debilitating attacks of asthma, he first acknowledged a hidden 'wild streak' around the age of five; by the time he reached high school he was swaying in the corridors pretending to be a giant flower and calling himself 'Hyacinth'. Rock 'n' roll baptism came courtesy of drummer Sandy Nelson's savage instrumental hits, inspiring Jim to buy his first kit and form his first band at the age of 15, The Megaton Two. He remained on drums in his next group, The Iguanas. Other kids thought the name was hilarious and started to call him 'Iggy' for short. Jim didn't like it at first. He tried to think of his own pseudonym but his best shot was 'Jimmy James'. For better or worse, Iggy would have to do.

Iggy tried to commit to serious study, enrolling at the local University of Michigan, the academic body which once upon a time tried to coax an ill Gustav Holst to join its music faculty. Sat in course lectures on social anthropology and Asian studies, he learned about ancient religious ritual involving music, dance, mild drug taking and orgiastic behaviour. It sounded much too tempting a career move.

Iggy dropped out of college, forming a new band with three likeminded delinquent desperados. They called themselves The Psychedelic Stooges.

Iggy was now singing out front, playing lap-steel guitar and a Farfisa organ with the legs taken off, wearing a silvery wig and some ill-advised Asian clothing. Their set included a song about a man who lived with his pet mouse and climaxed with Iggy's attempt to blow sounds through a vacuum cleaner. It was the wrong kind of weird.

The lap-steel, Farfisa organ and vacuum cleaner were eventually dispensed with alongside Iggy's shirt, his decision to go topless in homage to the Egyptian Pharaohs he'd studied in the university library. The band's music underwent a similar symbolic stripping down: a fierce primitive rock 'n' roll grunt made by, and for, bored, insolent street punks.

In September 1968, Elektra Records' publicist Danny Fields was sent to Detroit to sign another local Michigan noise, the heavily politicised MC5. They suggested Fields might also want to check out The Psychedelic Stooges – 'our little brother band' – playing the next day. Fields thought they were chaotic, their few songs half-formed and rambling. But he knew a star when he saw one. The half-naked, crowd-baiting maniac calling himself Iggy. Fields made every effort and got them signed too.

With a record deal they decided to drop the 'Psychedelic' and become simply The Stooges. For the time being Jim was still 'Iggy Stooge', an alias soon to be subsumed by another coined by his bandmates after a local junkie named Jim Popp. 'Iggy Pop'.

Fields' next mission was to pair them with the right producer, somebody who could capture their crudity without neutering their spirit in the process. The ideal candidate seemed to be John Cale, who'd just proven his worth as arranger and uncredited co-producer on Nico's Elektra album *The Marble Index*. Cale, better than anyone, understood the fine balance between raw experimentation and technical orthodoxy, a line he'd been happily treading with The Velvet Underground until only very recently.

On April Fool's Day 1969, The Stooges and Cale began work on their debut album at the Hit Factory in New York. Cale's main obstacle was the sheer noise. With no studio experience, Iggy and the band automatically plugged in and played at full volume, just as they would on stage. When Cale asked them to turn it down, they insisted they could only play at number ten – as a token compromise, they might very seldom lower it to nine. There was also an alarming dearth of material. Somehow they'd expected to make a record with only four songs prepared. They improvised a fifth in the studio but it still wasn't enough. Unfazed by the time constraints, they returned to their lodgings at the Chelsea Hotel. There, between the same walls Arthur C. Clarke had drafted his script for *2001: A Space Odyssey*, Iggy and his Stooges knocked out the rest of the album – three more no-nonsense rock 'n' roll rampages about dolls smoking cigarettes and having a real cool time – in the space of an hour.

The end result, *The Stooges*, was released in August 1969. America's reaction was summed up by the backhanded compliment of *Rolling Stone* magazine: 'They suck, and they know it, so they throw the fact back in your face and say, "So what? We're just havin' fun."'

Sadly, not enough people in 1969 were ready to share that fun. The album remained in the cult stratosphere beyond the mainstream, much like those of The Velvet Underground, less records than calling cards of cool between the initiated elite. Yet of the copies of *The Stooges* that were distributed, none were more precious than that which made it onto the record shelf of a radio station in San Jose. Where it remained, gathering a thin layer of dust, until the second week of February 1971.

David Bowie was nearing the end of his trip, enjoying a three-night stopover in San Francisco, Kerouac's fabled destination of the beats. His interview schedule included a daytrip out of the city. To a radio station in San Jose.

Asked on-air if there was anything he'd like to hear, with New York and his fake Lou Reed encounter still fresh in his mind, he answered, 'Anything by The Velvet Underground.' A journalist called John, who'd been shadowing David that day, had also been flicking through the station's records. He smiled to see they had a copy of *The Stooges*.

John passed the album to David, nudging him to play something. David had never heard of them before. He looked down the list of song titles. 'I Wanna Be Your Dog' made him laugh. He asked the DJ if he could play it. Divine light poured forth.

David heard a molten guitar riff steadily hacking its way towards the centre of the Earth. A monotone piano that stabbed his eardrums as a needle might a baby's eye. The sleigh bell sound of Santa Claus dangling at the end of a rope. And that wired, wanting voice.

'*Now-I-wann-a, be yer dawg!*'

Who the hell was that voice?

On the drive back to San Francisco, John told David everything he wanted to know about The Stooges. They'd made two records: that one and another called *Fun House*. Their singer was a lunatic called Iggy, who sang topless in ripped jeans and silver gloves. He was known for leaping into the crowd without fear of injury, dripping wax on his chest or smearing his torso with peanut butter. David liked the sound of this Iggy as he much as he loved the sound of his band. He sounded proper crazy. Vince Taylor crazy. Another madman to add to the pot.

The pot stirred in his sleep during his last Friday night in San Francisco. It was still stirring the next morning when he caught the hour's flight to his trip's end in Los Angeles. Stirring through take-off, still stirring as the plane climbed until, slowly, the stirring stopped, his thoughts congealing tens of thousands of feet above the Californian coastline.

'*I think it takes a lot to become somebody else. It takes some doing …*'

Somebody else. Called something else like Iggy Pop or The Legendary Stardust Cowboy. A great name. Yes, it was all in the name.

'The Legendary Iggy Cowboy. Iggy Legend. Pop Cowboy. Cowdust Iggy. Starboy Pop. Iggy Starboy. Stardust Iggy. Iggy Stardust …'

Iggy Stardust?

A ripple in the fabric of spacetime. A teeter on the precipice of 'Eureka!'

'Ciggy Stardust, Diggy Stardust …'

Stirring, stirring.

'Liggy Stardust, Miggy Stardust …'

Stirring, stirring, getting closer.
'Qiggy Stardust, Riggy Stardust …'
Stirring, stirring, coming in to land.
'Viggy Stardust, Wiggy Stardust …'

The date was Saturday 13 February 1971. In London, director Stanley Kubrick was filming four young men in bowler hats, braces and codpieces beat up a tramp in a pedestrian underpass in Wandsworth, while Marc Bolan admired the first press ads for his next single, 'Hot Love', as he readied himself for a gig in Barking.

And in Los Angeles, David Bowie stepped off a plane from San Francisco to be greeted by Mercury's West Coast publicist Rodney Bingenheimer, the first to learn of his latest idea to write songs about a new character he'd just invented during the flight. The first human to hear David Bowie say the two greatest words in the history of pop music. Two words which the cosmos had been waiting for a sentient creature to utter for nearly fourteen billion years, tumbling at last through jagged teeth and London lips to softly scythe the warm Los Angeles air.

'Ziggy Stardust.'

SIXTEEN

BECOMING

Eight months after shaking hands with the wrong Lou Reed, David was back in New York shaking hands with the right Lou Reed. Eight months after he'd first heard Iggy Pop on record, David was meeting Iggy Pop in the flesh. Eight months after first saying the words 'Ziggy Stardust', David's body and soul were accelerating on an irreversible slap-bang collision with those of the Starman.

It wasn't as simple for him as it had been for Billy Batson. He didn't suddenly say the magic word – 'Shazam!' – and, in a flash, become Ziggy. But Ziggy now existed as a silvery voice whispering inside his head. A voice as old as space and time ordering him to empty himself of David Bowie and succumb to absolute extraterrestrial transfusion.

New York in early September was a warmer city than that David first visited in January. He was glad to be back, glad for another gasp of air away from the suffocating fog of 'T. Rexstasy'. The young Britons of 1971 had since surrendered willingly to the Marc Bolan blitzkrieg as he followed 'Ride A White Swan' with two number ones. The second, 'Get It On', was still in reverse thrust back down the charts as David touched down at Kennedy International. The first, 'Hot Love', had spent six weeks at the top that spring, incinerating the last dregs of sixties hippy bore-rock when Marc appeared on *Top Of The Pops* with glitter on his face. It was the magic touch of his publicist, Chelita Secunda, herself a flamboyant King's Road fashion queen, whose idea it was to glue sparkling star shapes under each of his eyes. On the TV screen it looked as if Marc had been weeping diamond dust. A nation's youth wilted in amazement and hailed undying loyalty to their new King of Glam. It was near impossible to think of anyone ever usurping him.

David's stars were aligning nicely nonetheless. In preparation for Ziggy, he'd found his mothership just north of Bromley, opposite Beckenham golf course: a converted flat in a redbrick turreted Victorian manor called Haddon Hall. Visitors approaching along Southend Road would catch their breath at its gothic asylum silhouette, their thoughts jumping to Norman Bates' house in *Psycho*, the Addams family nest or the Gruesome Twosome's 'Creepy Coupe 2' from the *Wacky Races* cartoon. From the outside, a house of horror, but a sacred cosmic pop hatchery within.

There'd also been a radical changing of David's guards: most of the moneymen who'd supported him through 'Space Oddity' had now been swept away, including the steadfast Kenneth Pitt. In his place stood the fierce new broom called Tony DeFries, a young Jewish business lawyer with a hypnotically soft voice and ambitions as scarily big as his favourite cigars. Among DeFries' first coups as David's manager was to wrestle him away from Mercury Records for a better deal. His new label was the home of the seven-inch single, RCA Victor. David was now on the same orange and white January 8 team as Elvis Presley.

The deal with RCA was the catalyst for his return to New York, this time accompanied by his wife, Angie, and DeFries. The label welcomed him with a celebration steak dinner at The Ginger Man, an Upper West Side Irish bar and restaurant, surprising David with a special guest. Another new signing to the RCA roster: the *right* Lou Reed.

He was nothing like the wrong Lou Reed. Doug Yule had been friendly and talkative. Lou was sharp, silent and a bit suspicious. David remained blind to Lou's detachment, transfixed as if in the presence of a divine apparition. So *this* was *him*. Straight from the corner of Lexington, one-two-five, waiting for his man. David gushed.

'This has been such a thrill for me.'

Lou couldn't yet bring himself to say the same. He'd see David again a few days later, hitting it off so well they locked themselves away in a bedroom while Angie hammered on the door screaming to let her in. But on this occasion he said little and, ever the enigma, retired early.

The party continued without Lou down at Max's Kansas City, the art bar and restaurant north of Union Square, its back room the blessed Camelot of Andy Warhol, who famously exchanged paintings for credit. As David was ushered into Max's, his eyes peeled for Warhol, who wasn't there that evening, four blocks away another of his heroes was engrossed in the fate of filibustering senator Jefferson Smith trying to save a plot of land called Willet Creek to build a boys' camp. Iggy Pop was crashing at the apartment of his manager, former Elektra scout Danny Fields, enjoying that week's *CBS Thursday Night Movie*, Frank Capra's *Mr Smith Goes To Washington* starring James Stewart. Or he would be if Fields wasn't bugging him about some phone call from a journalist inviting him to Max's to meet some English guy called David Bowie. Fields tried to persuade him that this David had been saying nice things about him in the English press. 'OK,' Iggy eventually sighed. He'd go. After the Jimmy Stewart film had finished.

An hour later, once Jefferson Smith filibustered to victory, Mr Iggy met Mr Ziggy in the back room of Max's. David was spellbound. So *this* was *him*. The body of *that* voice. *'So messed up ... outta my mind ... deep in the night lost in love.'*

Iggy wasn't anything like Lou. He spoke like a prince of the dregs of America, wild-eyed with doglike wonder, candidly telling David about his life growing up on a trailer park, his past heroin problems and his methadone programme. DeFries was just as taken with Iggy. The

Stooges were in label-less limbo with only Fields vainly trying to hold the threads together as manager. This, DeFries said he could fix, inviting Iggy to join him and David for breakfast at their hotel the next day to discuss his future.

They were staying in the Warwick, the midtown luxury tower built by William Randolph Hearst, tempting fate by booking into the same penthouse suite where The Beatles spent their first New York visit in 1964. The last time David was here he was alone at the Holiday Inn. Now, just eight months later, he was in the lap of luxury, splashing the same bath taps once turned by Lennon and McCartney, riding the same elevators as Cary Grant and Elizabeth Taylor.

Eight months. *Eight months?*

How much David's universe had changed, and how fast, since he stepped off that plane in Los Angeles and uttered the words 'Ziggy Stardust' …

The changes started as soon as David returned to London that February, his luggage straining with records by the Velvets, Iggy and The Legendary Stardust Cowboy, his head similarly buckling with the added weight of his stowaway Starman.

He'd spent his last days in Los Angeles scribbling ideas and writing songs for his new alter ego, delighted to find himself a guest of the same home studio as Vince Taylor's inspirational black leather Beelzebub, Gene Vincent. Once nicknamed 'The Living End', by 1971 Gene looked like a man truly at the end of his living, a worn-out 36-year-old drunkard half-crazy in pain from his crippled left leg. Little Richard may have been 'God' but Gene was still one of David's rock 'n' roll saints. Aged ten he'd trembled in the cinema watching him howl 'Be-Bop-A-Lula' in *The Girl Can't Help It* and later saw him in person on the same Woolwich Granada bill where Richard had pulled his heart-attack stunt. David was especially taken with the way Gene had stood. His leg had first been damaged in a motorbike accident and made worse when he later survived the car crash that killed his friend Eddie Cochran. Encased in an orthopaedic brace, he could only lower himself to his microphone by kicking his bad leg straight behind him and bending his right knee. Meeting Gene reminded David of the same pose, like one of H. G. Wells' half-collapsed Martian tripods. It went straight on his Ziggy 'to do' list.

While in LA, David demoed some of his first Ziggy songs, his close proximity to rock 'n' roll divinity evident on 'Hang On To Yourself' which sounded, if not like Gene, then certainly Eddie Cochran. He left a copy with Gene's producer, hoping he'd record his own version. Which Gene probably would have had he not died from a burst stomach ulcer a few months later. Another rock 'n' roll suicide, he'd spent his final years slowly killing himself with alcohol, his dying words spat through blood as he collapsed to his knees in his mother's trailer home. 'Mama, you can phone the ambulance now.'

Back in London, the songs of the Starman kept bombarding David's head like an all-shaking thunder urging him to surrender to its will. He took temporary shelter in a clandestine demo session funded by his music publisher, Bob Grace, with the help of a trio called Rungk – a name chosen by their Scandinavian bassist after the Swedish slang for 'wank'. As well as another soft stab at 'Hang On To Yourself', David gently squeezed the trigger of a potentially lethal pop laser-gun called 'Moonage Daydream'. To recoup some of Grace's costs, David agreed to release the Rungk tracks as a single. For legal reasons, he couldn't put it out as a 'David Bowie' record since he was technically still under contract to Mercury. But the fact that he now needed to create a pseudonym meant he had a golden opportunity to dabble in some identity-switching. A chance to shove his own Doug Yule into the spotlight. The 'wrong' David Bowie.

His name was Fred Burrett and he came from the East End. Or as he called himself Freddie Burretti, just 19, a blue-eyed, razor-cheeked, chopstick-thin fashion designer. He'd caught David's eye at a gay disco on Kensington High Street, Yours Or Mine, nicknamed 'the Sombrero' because of the giant hat above its basement entrance advertising the upstairs Spanish restaurant. Not the most conventional spot for a newly-married young couple to spend their spare evenings but then David and Angie – shenanigan-loving Mrs Goose and Mr Gander – weren't exactly conventional. Both loved the Sombrero for its human zoo of mock-Hollywood drag queens, oriental rent boys and speeding glamour pusses, fashion freaks and freaks of fashion cavorting as one on the tiny illuminated Perspex dancefloor. Fred was the Sombrero's supreme star-bragger, a blond hipless wonder in white spandex pants who reminded David of 'the new Mick Jagger'. Or maybe the wrong David Bowie. Yes. He'd do.

If 'Fred Burrett' was too plain then 'Freddie Burretti' sounded like an Italian ice-cream salesman. But if David was going to make Fred a star, he might as well steal the name of one of the biggest. And so Fred from the East End became 'Rudi Valentino' – the public face of the 'Moonage Daydream' single David recorded with Rungk. It was David's voice with Rungk's backing but, as an experiment in wrongness, the record was launched as the debut by Rudi's band, The Arnold Corns, named by David in homage to Syd Barrett and The Pink Floyd's earlier single about a clothesline thief, 'Arnold Layne'. David was still credited as writer and producer, posing with Rudi in publicity photos as alleged artist and mentor – in truth, artist and artifice. They appeared on the cover of Soho 'sex education' mag *Curious* with David declaring Rudi to be 'the leader of the whole gay scene' and Rudi announcing his ambition to be on the cover of *Vogue*. It didn't even matter that the single flopped. As David's first indulgent low-key exercise drill in rock camp and pop duplicity it was a screaming success.

While David was preoccupied with the slow birth of Ziggy, in late May Angie gave birth to their son, Zowie. Typical of his current zed-shaped fixation, David christened him after a phrase he'd seen in one of his Batman comics. He'd been at home listening to Neil Young's *After*

The Goldrush album when the call came telling him he'd become a father. David went straight to the hospital, the receptionist pointing him to the maternity ward, where he found his son's cot and proudly cooed. A few moments passed before the nurse told him he'd been admiring someone else's child. His son was in a different cot. He'd been looking at the 'wrong' Zowie Bowie. David's world was fast becoming a place where no one but no one was ever whom he thought they were…

Peter wasn't a no-one though he'd always be a Noone. He'd had a successful career in the sixties as singer with Herman's Hermits, a Lancashire hot-pot of guitars and teeth popular in Britain but virtually pandemic in the States. Noone bailed out in 1971, looking to Hermits producer Mickie Most to jumpstart his solo career. Most succeeded thanks to a song he'd chosen from a demo given to him by David's publisher, Bob Grace. The lyrics were a bit on the heavy side – some Nietzschean gobbledygook about '*Homo Superior*' – but its ragtime tune was so catchy that most listeners probably wouldn't notice. And, besides, it had a very pleasant title. 'Oh You Pretty Things'.

Noone's single peaked at number twelve. The highest charting David Bowie song since 'Space Oddity' four years earlier. Noone had somehow achieved what Fred's 'Rudi' hadn't. Scoring a major hit single as the wrong David Bowie. It made David laugh. The Starman tumour swelling inside his head laughed along with him. The punchline was that neither of them knew who the right David Bowie was any more.

Every song he wrote these days he seemed to be somebody else. Not yet Ziggy, but no longer David either. He sang inside the skins of others, or at least how he imagined those others to be. He was 'Andy Warhol'. He wrote a 'Song For Bob Dylan'. He was Lou Reed, 'Queen Bitch'. He thought about his baby son Zowie and wrote 'Kooks'. He thought sad and strange thoughts about his half-brother Terry and wrote 'The Bewlay Brothers'. When he tried to think about himself, all he could focus on were these same fluctuating 'Changes'. As he'd later self-analyse, he was clearing his system 'of the schizophrenics'.

The new songs formed the core of *Hunky Dory*, David's fourth album, recorded that summer, along with his own version of 'Oh! You Pretty Things' – adding an exclamation mark and reinstating the word 'bitch' which Noone censored as 'beast'. With Tony Visconti scarpering off to steer the good ship T. Rexstasy, another of his former engineers, Ken Scott, had taken over as album producer, assisted by David, or as he'd tellingly credit himself, 'The Actor'. He also had the stability of a solid new backing band. Three formidable musicians, one of them a genius, whose vowel-flattening accents betrayed their shared origins way up north. From a city so devoid of hope that the gods shoved it to the far eastern edge of Yorkshire with a feeble prayer that one day a freak tidal wave might wash it into the sea, never to be heard of again. Except that Ziggy Stardust needed that city. Of all the towns in all the world, this was the unlikely grim incubator of the human specimens deserved of becoming his Spiders From Mars. Because only Ziggy, only a creature from outer space, would dream of recruiting the greatest rock 'n' roll band in the universe from Hull.

Their names were Mick, Woody and Trevor. One guitar star and his two orbiting planets of rhythm.

Mick Ronson. The genius. Less a man, more a Titan. Made in Hull, he played like heaven. In his ten fingers alone lay the secret harmonies of the spheres; how Kepler would have wept for joy had he ever heard the music of Mick Ronson. The Beethoven of the Greatfield estate, he was classically trained on piano, recorder and violin. When he later took to the guitar it was with practised hands and a maestro's mind. In the spring of '66, aged 19, he was good enough and serious enough about joining a band to make a pilgrimage to London, loitering between the cups and saucers of La Gioconda, itching to be discovered. It wasn't his time. By the autumn he was back in Hull, taking a job for the city council's parks department, where he might have stayed had his friend John, drummer from one of his previous local bands, The Rats, not recommended him to David. In January 1970, John travelled from London to fetch Mick from Hull. When he got there, he found the greatest guitar player of his generation marking lines on a rugby pitch.

Four months later, John was sacked leaving David in need of a new drummer. Mick recommended another Humberside face, Woody Woodmansey. He'd also played with Mick in The Rats, one of the reasons he landed the nickname 'Woody': his real name was also Mick, so it avoided any confusion of having two in the same band.

Last to join was the hairy phenomenon called Trevor Bolder, once destined for great things as the finest young trumpeter in the whole East Riding until willingly corrupted by rock 'n' roll. Mick had seen Trevor play bass on the local club circuit and once asked him to fill in for The Rats when their own bassist chickened out of a gig for fear of being electrocuted. Mick and Woody had already made one album with David, *The Man Who Sold The World*, featuring Visconti on bass. With Visconti gone, Mick lit up the Humberside telephone exchange once again to beckon Trevor as his replacement. The Hull's angels were now three. As Mick, Trevor and Woody, they were David's band. As Ronno, Weird and Gilly, they'd soon be Ziggy's.

Even as they were making *Hunky Dory*, David's new Yorkshire terriers could sense a foreign presence flexing under their singer's surface. They covered a country blues tune by American songwriter Ron Davies called 'It Ain't Easy'. To their surprise David decided not to include it on the album, as if he was saving it for something – or maybe someone – else. All the clues they needed were in the last title recorded for the album. 'Life On Mars?'. Not actually about Mars but life on Earth in all its incurable loneliness, David looking through the eyes of the saddest girl in the cinema, stirring in Mickey Mouse, the Norfolk Broads and some lyrics pinched from another single he'd brought back from America about a cartoon caveman called 'Alley Oop' by The Hollywood Argyles. The tune wasn't entirely original either, stolen from a French song, 'Comme D'Habitude'. Three years earlier David had proposed an English-language version with his own words called 'Even A Fool Learns To Love'. Instead, he was gazumped by a better set of lyrics from popular American singer–songwriter Paul Anka who took 'Comme D'Habitude' and created 'My Way', the 1969 calling-card for Frank Sinatra. 'Life On Mars?' was David's belated devilish riposte. Taking 'My Way' and doing it his way. Or, rather, Ziggy's way.

Work on the album wound up in August, just as a controversial new play opened at London's Roundhouse called *Pork*. 'Written' by Andy Warhol, its script was based upon edited highlights of years of telephone conversations he'd recorded with Factory superstar Brigid Berlin discussing sex, drugs and family problems. Berlin provided the template for its eponymous heroine 'Amanda Pork' played by New York groupie and journalist Cherry Vanilla. The Warhol role of 'B. Marlowe' was played by Andy-lookalike Tony Zanetta complete with silvery wig. Audiences were scandalised both by its cast, including drag queen Wayne County as 'Vulva Lips', and its scenes of shooting up, nudity and 'plate jobs' – the scatological fetish of watching someone do their business on your face through a Perspex plate. Disclaimers were placed in the press: 'Warning: This play has explicit sexual content and offensive language. If you are likely to be disturbed, do not attend.' David and Angie weren't likely to be disturbed. They did attend. Twice.

Before the play's Roundhouse residency was through, the Bowies had befriended most of the cast, including Zanetta, or 'Zee' as everyone called him, Vanilla, County and *Pork*'s director, Leee Black Childers. David was fascinated to hear their tales of life inside the Factory and the real Warhol. He'd just written a song about Andy on *Hunky Dory* and was desperate to know what the real Andy was like.

What *was* the real Andy like?

The cosmos coughed in mischief and, for the love of Ziggy, decided to show him the answer.

The morning after meeting Lou and Iggy, David awoke groggily in his hotel bedroom, serenaded by the close sound of familiar voices and the clattering of cutlery on china. He got up to find Iggy in his suite, horsing down two breakfasts, chatting between mouthfuls of egg while DeFries sat opposite, silently contemplating how he could turn this famished Detroit junkie trashbag into dollars and cents. Iggy agreed to let DeFries sort his affairs, leaving to collect his things from Fields' apartment to come and move in beside them at the Warwick.

In the meantime, David and DeFries went to meet a different kind of human freakshow. Tony Zee, back in New York now that *Pork* had ended, promised to chaperone them to meet Andy Warhol at the Factory. It had moved premises since Kenneth Pitt visited in 1966, shifting downtown to the sixth floor of the Decker Building on Union Square. The same building where, in June 1968, radical feminist writer Valerie Solanas had failed in her attempt to assassinate Andy.

The first thing that greeted David by the entrance was a stuffed Great Dane – Andy's unsubstantiated myth was that the dog had once belonged to director Cecil B. DeMille. The second was Paul Morrissey, now in charge of the Factory's day-to-day business. The third was Andy himself.

Warhol sat in the corner, staring blankly at the skinny, long-haired Englishman who was introduced to him as 'David Bowie'. He said nothing. David smiled. Andy looked at his teeth with private alarm.

Silence.

DeFries began filling the air with spiel about how much money he'd been promised by RCA, how big a star David was going to become, and how it would be great if Andy could attach his name to him, just as he had with The Velvet Underground. Andy blinked. David fidgeted.

Silence.

David picked his moment to give Andy a present. It was an acetate of the song he'd written about him. Andy looked at Morrissey. DeFries smiled. David coughed.

'Oh?'

They sat and listened to 'Andy Warhol' by David Bowie. Andy Warhol in one corner, David Bowie in the other. The song finished. David scratched the corner of his mouth. Andy breathed.

Silence.

DeFries kept talking about his plans for David. Morrissey nodded, pretending to be fascinated. Andy looked David up and down. He picked up a Polaroid camera from his desk and pointed it at David's feet.

Flash! Whirr!

Andy smiled. 'You have such nice shoes,' he told David.

They were. Yellow leather with buckles, by Anello & Davide.

'Thank you,' said David.

Andy continued taking Polaroids of David's shoes, arranging them on a table as they slowly developed. David indulged him, watching him work, trying to figure out what must be going on inside that head. This legend he'd wanted to meet for the last five years. This person who he'd written a song about but said nothing when he heard it. This oddity, this alien, this construct, this person of everything, this multitude of nothing. This human screenprint that called itself 'An-dy War-hol'. It was then that a familiar silvery voice whispered softly inside David's head. '*It takes a lot to become somebody else.*'

A voice he already knew by name.

SEVENTEEN
THE MODERN
PROMETHEUS

By the end of 1971 David Bowie had everything he needed to become somebody else.

He had the name, Ziggy Stardust.

He had the band of Mick, Trevor and Woody, his Ronno, Weird and Gilly.

He had enough songs for a new album which he'd started recording at Trident that November, even before *Hunky Dory* was in the shops. 'You're not going to like it,' he warned producer Ken Scott. 'It's much more like Iggy Pop.'

He had the beginnings of the haircut after Trevor, a former hairdresser, chopped away his luxurious Katharine Hepburn tresses leaving him looking like an elfish Japanese warrior: spiky on top, thin on the sides and with thin straggles wilting around his shoulders like dead ivy.

He also had the first set of bespoke Starman clothes thanks to dear Freddie: a patterned grey-green windcheater and turned-up trousers giving the appearance of part superhero, part art-deco sofa. David chose the fabric himself, telling anyone who asked that it was from Liberty's department store on the edge of Soho. They needn't know the unglamorous truth it was from one of the discount schmutter shops up Tottenham Court Road; for all anyone could ever prove it was from the Jupiter branch of Macy's.

For the 'stuffed crotch' of the trousers, he'd taken inspiration from Stanley Kubrick's new film, his first in over three years since *2001: A Space Odyssey*. As its poster declared, 'Being the adventures of a young man whose principal interests are rape, ultra-violence and Beethoven.'

The film was *A Clockwork Orange*, from the novel by Anthony Burgess. First published in 1962, and very roughly first adapted as Warhol's *Vinyl*, its plot had been triggered by the brutal assault on Burgess' wife by American deserters during the war, his experiences in Russia observing the *stilyagi* street gangs, and a visit to Hastings where he stood and watched 'mods and rockers knocking hell out of each other'. Boiled down to a cosmic-yob concentrate, Burgess created Alex, a Beethoven-mad delinquent who robs, assaults, rapes and terrorises for fun until he's arrested for accidentally murdering one of his victims. Sentenced to fourteen years in prison, Alex is given the opportunity for quick release by volunteering himself as guinea pig in a radical technique to rehabilitate criminals, brainwashing them into submissive drones incapable of free choice. Kubrick's version remained faithful to the American edition of the book, which ends with Alex returned to his fierce old self after becoming a political pawn in the next government election; Burgess would always mourn the fact Kubrick never read the original British version with its extra final chapter where Alex relents and resigns to the responsibilities of adulthood.

David had yet to see *A Clockwork Orange* – just out in America that Christmas, due in Britain in early January 1972 – but he'd taken cues from pre-publicity stills of Kubrick's interpretation of Burgess's droogs: space-age hooligans in bovver boots and codpieces. He wanted the look, codpiece and all, but not the ultra-violence, keeping the street-gang chic but colouring in the droogs' whites with bright floral prints and soft quilted fabrics. He'd also keep the wrestling boots, swapping bovver black for Marvel comic greens and blues, specially made for him by local firm Russell & Bromley on Beckenham High Street.

Kubrick's *A Clockwork Orange* would very soon arm David with much more than fancy boots and a padded pelvis when he finally saw the film in all its artful, brazen comic brilliance. The script's jargon droogspeak – Burgess's 'Nadsat' – fitted in perfectly with the fake world David was creating, even filtering into the language of his new song 'Suffragette City'. Equally crucial was Kubrick's use of music – the nervous force of Beethoven's 'Ode To Joy' and the drama of Rossini's 'William Tell Overture', as synthesized through the circuitry of New York electronic maestro Walter Carlos. Both would be used as David's fanfares in concert straight from the official soundtrack album, as would its straight orchestral reading of Elgar's 'Pomp And Circumstance March No. 1', set to become the Starman's final exit.

As the last grey sands of 1971 trickled away, in Edward Heath economic gloom, in IRA bomb fears, in spaghetti junctions and decimal coins, in the saucy asides of Benny Hill's 'Ernie' and the stomping stackheels of Marc Bolan's 'Jeepster', David Bowie had the name, the band, the songs, the clothes, the boots, the entrance, the exit and almost the right hair. But, greater still, he finally had the pure and perfect fantasy to unite them as one. His new identity.

His name was Ziggy Stardust and he was a rock 'n' roll star from outer space. A meteor storm of Iggy Pop, Andy Warhol, *2001: A Space Odyssey*, Lou Reed, Elvis Presley, Professor Quatermass, Little Richard, Syd Barrett, *The Little Prince*, Sal Paradise and Marc Bolan made extraterrestrial flesh. He was everything Vince Taylor, Moondog and The Legendary Stardust Cowboy pretended to be, only Ziggy was real.

And so were his band, The Spiders From Mars. He'd do his best to steer people away from the planetary specifics. The Spiders, as anyone with an ear for accents could quickly determine, were from Hull (and being from Hull they couldn't even say 'Mars' like normal folk, but squashed it into a softly droning 'Mazz'). But it was essential Ziggy and his band weren't of this world. It would never work if he used some made-up comic book 'Mongo'. The same was true of the other planets in the solar system. 'The Spiders From Uranus'? Unthinkable.

But Mars? Mars was different.

Mars had something unique, something altogether priceless. Mars had been the trigger of innumerable human imaginations for millennia. Mars was the one-way ticket to the unknown kingdom of otherness. Mars was the magic powder igniting the brilliance and terror of H. G. Wells, Gustav Holst and Orson Welles' panic broadcast of 1938. Mars was the license for the fearless to turn dreams into reality, the hunger ravaging Robert Goddard which first sent humans out among the stars. Mars had already cost the US government millions of dollars in the creation of crude robot probes punted towards its atmosphere carrying with them the greatest of all human hopes. That, in this unthinkably vast and mysterious universe, we are not alone. Mars was imbedded deep in the atomic core of all human DNA and had been for centuries: an immovable molecule of cranked-up fear, weirdness and wonder.

The cosmos had already decided for them. Ziggy Stardust and his Spiders could only ever come from Mars.

In the first week of January 1972, the BBC consulted the Ministry of Defence for a forthcoming episode of their current affairs programme *Man Alive*. The subject: the growing number of UFO reports.

Unknown to the BBC at the time, when the MoD compiled their end-of-year figures for reported UFO sightings in 1971, the number came to 370. The highest amount of official flying saucer scares in a single calendar year since their records began.

The ministry were nevertheless keen to avoid encouraging further public hysteria and steer the programme as best they could towards healthy scepticism. Their new head of the 'UFO desk' was former Wing Commander Anthony Davis, one of the pilots involved in the notorious 'Lakenheath–Bentwaters incident' of 1956. On Tuesday 4 January, Davis was interviewed by the *Man Alive* team, filing a report for his Whitehall bosses later that week. The broadcast, Davis assured them, would focus on the naïvety of eye-witnesses and their 'willingness to believe' anything slightly outside normal experience must have extraterrestrial origins. There was a 'need', Davis noted, 'felt by many people for a new mythology'.

The year 1972.

The need for a new mythology.

Four days after Davis was filmed by the BBC, on Saturday 8 January in Haddon Hall, the friends of David Bowie gathered to celebrate his twenty-fifth birthday. As good an occasion as any to break in his brand new 'Liberty's' suit with codpiece and patent leather boots.

As the guests started to arrive, David excused himself and went to the bathroom. With a deep breath, a last farewell prayer to the man everybody called David Bowie, he closed the door behind him.

When he turned to look in the mirror he was already somebody else.

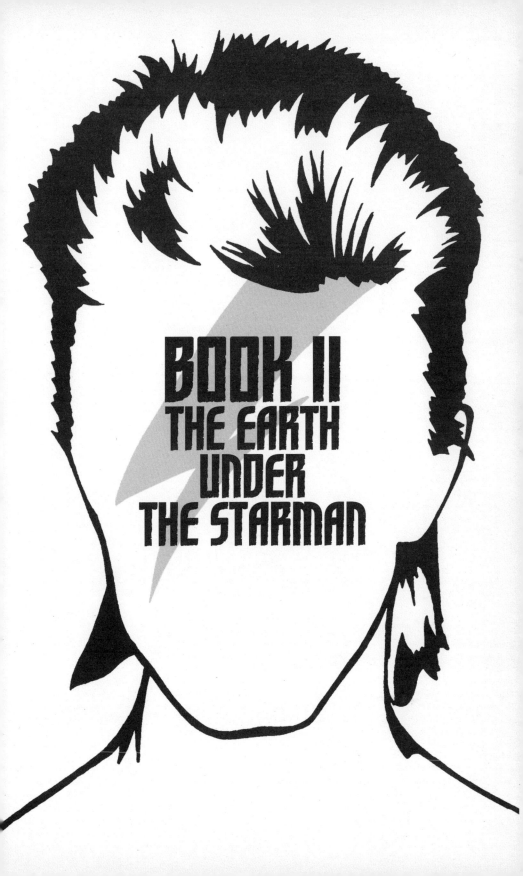

BOOK II
THE EARTH
UNDER
THE STARMAN

ONE
THE BIRTH

'What's it going to be then, eh?'

Ziggy Stardust stared in the bathroom mirror at the pale, bony face nervously grinning through skewback fangs. There was still a part of his brain which wasn't entirely sure if he was Ziggy looking in the mirror at David Bowie or vice versa. But as he ran his fingers through his cropped hair – the cut wasn't bad but he'd have to sort that colour – and blinked his eyelids over his pupils – one a Saturnian gas giant, the other a Mercurian dwarf; one a mystic Neptunian green, the other a brilliant Plutonian blue – he knew, absolutely, that no human being could ever look like this. He was the Starman, all right.

He ignored the hubbub of voices and music from the other side of the door, drinking in the reflection, softly pawing his face, his lips, his painted fingernails and the fabric of his fabulous new art-deco Superman suit. Here was gorgeousness and gorgeousity made flesh, he thought. Until his reverie was broken by a woman's nearby screech.

'Where'd David go?'

Right now that seemed a fair question. A cue for Ziggy to step outside and reveal the answer.

The party was already happily humming in flat number seven, Haddon

Hall, the air thick with the festive fug of mulled wine below its aerosol-painted silver ceilings dotted with giant blue circles. If it wasn't for the giant Victorian bay windows shattering the illusion, anyone looking around might even mistake it for a set from a TV sci-fi drama, possibly *UFO* or *Doctor Who*, both broadcast to the nation earlier that Saturday.

It still felt terrestrial enough a welcome to 41-year-old composer Lionel Bart, there as a friend and fellow client of the same management company; best known for the hit musical *Oliver!*, David would have been just as impressed by Bart's role in Tommy Steele's early career, the Armageddon skiffle 'Doomsday Rock' included. Lou Reed was also fondling the canapés and helping himself to a generous slug of wine, now over in London to record his debut solo album for RCA with dismal consequences, taking a night off to wish David Bowie a happy twenty-fifth birthday, not realising that he, like Bart and everyone else, would instead be toasting his first glimpse of Ziggy Stardust.

The division of Haddon Hall into separate flats had left a stairway to nowhere in the middle of their main reception area, its only destination a narrow balcony at the top where the Spiders just managed to sleep side-by-side on spare mattresses. The same balcony where Ziggy had crept up from the bathroom in order to make his formal birthday entrance. The guests circled at the bottom and watched him descend in slow, steady Gloria Swanson-like struts, the god-upon-high climbing down from atop his gothic suburban Ziggurat into a sea of expectant mortals. As David Bowie, he'd known these people for years. But through the fresh eyes of Ziggy it felt like meeting them anew, a chance to reacquaint himself with the characters that would each play their part in the Starman's world.

Angie, the wife. A firecracker of sex, intelligence and impropriety. 'I adore vulgarity,' she'd say, 'but it must have style.' Strangers meeting Angie for the first time would, after a few minutes, gaze at her in disbelief wondering where she hid her 'off' switch and how they could trigger it. Angie had no 'off' switch: Mrs Ziggy was forever 'on'.

Zowie, their son. Just seven months' worth of gurgling innocence crawling over their blue Persian carpets, too young to be corrupted by the stray sex mags lying around the house with their back page ads for a £35 Rubber Woman ('guaranteed not to answer back').

DeFries, the manager. A cigar-smoking ballbuster from Bigshot Inc., or so he'd have the rest of the world believe. When DeFries spoke it was with a soft hypnotising hiss: Ziggy was already irretrievably entranced.

Freddie from the East End. 'Rudi Valentinto' as was. The hipless wonderfop who'd help Ziggy sew his wardrobe alongside his girlfriend Daniella Parma, another exotic clotheshorse with a shock of peroxide white hair.

The Frosts, Ziggy's downstairs neighbours. Dependable Sue, nanny to baby Zowie and occasional Starman seamstress. Her husband, Tony, a bloke who knew how to take care of himself and who'd soon be taking care of Ziggy as one of his burly Ziggyguards.

And, not least, The Spiders From Mars themselves. Weird, Gilly and the indispensable Ronno with his inexhaustible Humberside contacts. Before the winter was through he'd throw another Hull face into Ziggy's ranks, black Yorkshire bruiser Stuey George, a former dock worker and club bouncer with a pronounced limp who'd make the most formidable Ziggyguard of all.

Later that night, the party cackled, screamed and swayed a messy trail from Haddon Hall to the dancefloor of the Sombrero club in Kensington where Ziggy was hugged, kissed, fondled in his droogy suit and repeatedly wished 'happy birthday' by people who still insisted on calling him 'David'.

Like the colour of his hair, that would soon change.

The gravitational influence of Yorkshire continued to propel Ziggy to his destiny when, a week later, he found himself spending a wet January afternoon skulking in the doorways of a dimly lit Mayfair sidestreet.

Over two centuries earlier it had been christened by a Whig politician in honour of his northern constituency, a market town just a few miles outside the city of Hull. Heddon Street.

Ziggy was there for his first official photo-shoot with the Spiders, a matter of priority since that week's papers were still running adverts for the *Hunky Dory* album showing David in his long-haired vintage Hollywood vamp pose – a David who, barely a month after the record's release, no longer existed. The new portraits were to be taken by the same photographer, Brian Ward, in a makeshift studio in one of Heddon Street's rag-trade warehouses, only a short walk from Ziggy's management offices further up Regent Street near Oxford Circus.

The Spiders might even have recognised the homely Hull significance of Heddon had their minds not capsized with worry over the clothes Ziggy had prepared for them. Tight glittery satin trousers and jaunty floral jackets exposing their alabaster chests. They flinched and fussed with manly unease as subtle dabs of eye-shadow and mascara were licked across their faces, silently praying that not a word of this should ever reach the other side of the Humber Bridge. Ziggy ruffled their hair and straightened their collars, rallying them to pose for individual close-up portraits, hoping they could evoke the same menace as Malcolm McDowell's Alex on the *Clockwork Orange* poster.

Brian suggested they continue their droogy fashion show outside in the open.

'It's too wet,' grumbled Ronno, 'and too cold.'

Weird and Gilly agreed with him, even if, as Yorkshiremen, all three should have been used to far colder and wetter. And so, leaving the Spiders in the warm, Ziggy and Brian stepped out into the deserted alleyway without them.

A row of cars remained parked along the pavement, its wet stones glistening in the musty yellow light from a nearby streetlamp as the close beep and hum of early evening Regent Street traffic rattled the rooftops.

Ziggy paced around in his art-deco Superman suit and leather platform boots, a Les Paul guitar strapped across his body. Brian directed him towards a gas lamp mounted in the brickwork above number twenty-three. Ziggy slung his guitar to holster position and stood beneath it, a few steps in front of the sign for number twenty-one which read 'K. WEST'. The 'K' stood for Konn, a family of furriers who had premises there in the 'West' End as well as a branch in east London. A metal bin stood next to the front step, obscured by a mound of rubbish, mostly cardboard boxes and discarded packaging from the firm Paquerette Dresses. Ziggy rested his left leg on the bin, throwing a hand on his knee and stared straight into Brian's camera.

Click.

At the top of the street back near Brian's studio lay a small cul-de-sac with a red telephone kiosk, one of the original late-1920s K2 models designed by Giles Gilbert Scott, a handy source of artificial light. First Ziggy pulled a few rock 'n' roll rumbas outside it: knees together, feet splayed, guitar aimed at the lens like a Tommy gun. Then he unstrapped his instrument, lit a cigarette and stepped into the phonebox, another dallying hand on his hip. Outside in the street, Brian centred Ziggy's body symmetrically through the door's square glass panelling.

Click.

It was a few days before Ziggy saw Brian's contact sheets, removing the last traces of human doubt in his mind about who he was and the purpose of his mission. Here, for everyone to see, was indisputable evidence that an extraterrestrial pop star had fallen to Earth somewhere in the backstreets of Mayfair in early January 1972. Possibly beamed through the ether, arriving in an interplanetary atom smash in a public phonebox. Or in a shaft of light from a flying saucer upon a pile of wet cardboard while a few hundred yards away in Whitehall former Wing Commander Davis sat behind his 'UFO desk' unaware of the Martian invasion happening right under his ministry's nose.

The Starman had landed.

That same week, DeFries arranged a couple of print interviews to promote the current concern, *Hunky Dory*. The men from *Melody Maker* and *Disc* arrived for their individual timeslots at DeFries' Regent Street offices, expecting to meet the long-haired ladyship they'd seen poised like Greta Garbo upon the album's cover. Instead they were confronted by the newly shorn, pixie-like vision of Ziggy, sat waiting for them in his favourite Freddie suit, merrily smoking a cigarette and drinking tea as he listened to rough mixes of 'Suffragette City', 'Five Years' and other Stardust melodies.

Both reporters detected a strange, almost mischievous air about their subject. Wild words pelted forth from his lips, mercurial sentences slip-sliding back and forth between truth and nonsense, fact and fiction, David and Ziggy.

'I'm just a cosmic yob, I suppose,' said Ziggy.

'I've got a grasshopper mind,' confessed David. 'I'm not very well organised.'

'I feel very butch now,' laughed Ziggy.

'I'm gay and I always have been,' admitted David. 'Even when I was David Jones.'

Eyebrows were raised. Pencils scribbled furiously. Ziggy spoke about his plans for the year ahead and his ideas for his new staging. 'The costumes are outrageous,' he warned, 'like an astral *West Side Story*'. The show, he insisted, would be beautiful. And he, Ziggy, would be huge. And that, he giggled, was 'quite frightening'.

Both papers ran their stories the following week. It was the one in *Melody Maker* by Michael Watts which set the Haddon Hall phone ringing off the hook, concerned members of the Ronson clan fearing their Mick had been kidnapped by some heinous southern sex cult of mincing deviants. For there was Ziggy on the front cover, an impish space-age sybil in his open-chested Freddiewear, fingers twisted like shadow puppetry as he twirled a cigarette above a bangled wrist, his presence the one diverting detail on a page carrying the coma-beckoning screamers that King Crimson had broken up and Jethro Tull were going on tour. Then on the inside, page 18, opposite a tour ad for the vacuum of hope calling itself Barclay James Harvest, another portrait of Ziggy in playful repose, the heading 'Oh you pretty thing', and in glorious typeset black and white, 'I'm gay and I always have been.'

In the last days of being David Bowie he'd bravely crept towards the precipice of outrage, testing his mettle with 'Rudi' and Arnold Corns, allowing reporters to roam around Haddon Hall making note of the various newspaper clippings on homosexuality 'carefully arranged on his mantelpiece'. But as Ziggy he could leap without fear into the great gay void, peppering his speech with Polari, the secret queer slang of the London theatre world, using words like 'varda' (to see) while nodding and winking at his inquisitors like some giddy and undiscerning Queen of Outer Space. If nothing else, it was guaranteed to annoy a few smelly Stackridge fans in Squaresville, Northamptonshire. Such were the strategies of the Starman's new mythology.

The *Maker* article had also been kind enough to refer to Ziggy by name, listing the title of the as-yet-unfinished album, *The Rise And Fall Of Ziggy Stardust And The Spiders From Mars,* described by Watts as being 'about this fictitious pop group'.

Fictitious?

The simple truth was Ziggy still wasn't entirely sure what he was writing. Whether he was making a 'concept album' or a 'rock opera' like *Tommy,* or maybe some sort of Broadway musical like Bart's *Oliver!*

It would be another eighteen months before he realised, only in deathly hindsight, he was composing the soundtrack of his own existence. That the rock 'n' roll suicide was to be his own. And by then, it would be far too late.

Those first two interviews made public what many in the record industry had already heard whispered since before Christmas. That devious

David Bowie was 'up to something'. He'd had a haircut and stopped wearing 'dresses' (technically 'men's gowns'). He and his band were busy making a noisy rock rumpus, at least according to those who'd been earwigging at Trident or the Thomas A'Becket pub on the Old Kent Road in Bermondsey where the Spiders rehearsed on the floor above its famous boxing gymnasium. There were also rumours of some funny concept about the end of the world and a freaky singer from outer space. Most of his peers laughed it off. If David Bowie had gone back to space that sounded like he was desperately trying to flog the old dead horse of Major Tom. Either that, or up to similar psychedelic shenanigans as heavy hippies Hawkwind currently being praised by *Record Mirror* for their alleged innovation of 'sci-fi rock'.

Most of his peers laughed, that is, except one.

The gentle gust of Ziggy gossip didn't take long to make its way to the prickling ears under the corkscrew hair of Marc Bolan. He was intrigued by what he'd heard, and more than a little miffed. Cosmic pop and silly names were supposed to be his domain. They were all over *Electric Warrior*, the T. Rex album still yo-yoing back and forth to number one that January, and his next single poised for the top, 'Telegram Sam'. And so, being Marc Bolan, he did what any self-respecting, jealously paranoid pop god with everything to lose would do in the same position. Steal a peal of Ziggy's thunder.

The same Saturday, 22 January 1972, as a nation of disbelieving denim greasers picked up their copies of *Melody Maker* to read about the gay liberation of Ziggy Stardust, their sisters would have been burying their heads in *Mirabelle*, riddled with envy at Linda Newman's account of interviewing Marc at his Maida Vale flat. And between simpering over the backpage pin-up of Marc looking all cosy and 'hello, Mum' in dungarees they'd have read of his plans for continued pop domination in 1972 and of the two film scripts he'd claimed to have written.

'One is about a cosmic messiah,' teased Marc. 'A kind of intergalactic Jesus.'

At home in Haddon Hall, Ziggy Stardust read the same issue of *Mirabelle* with rapt attention. He read it again, just to make sure he hadn't been hallucinating, before dropping it to the floor where it landed next to a copy of *Forum*.

'Cosmic messiah?'

He walked to the bathroom, veins pumping, heart thumping, locked the door and stared in the mirror once again. To his surprise, the face staring back at him had a twinge of a smirk in the corner of its mouth and a sporting twinkle in its jewel-like eyes.

'What's it going to be then, eh?'

If it was war Marc wanted, let the great cosmic messiah fight of 1972 commence. But in the meantime, Ziggy really needed to sort that hair.

TWO
THE CUT

He was still fretting about his hair in all its scanty splendour when The Spiders From Mars played their first gig at the end of January. The venue was Friars Club, a hall in the market square of Aylesbury, thirty-odd miles outside London. The audience had paid to see David Bowie. 'The Most Beautiful Person In The World' said the poster. Instead, they got the most beautiful person out of this world – albeit with the wrong haircut.

It was Ziggy's chance to prove what he'd recently told *Disc*. 'I'm the last person to pretend that I'm a radio. I'd rather go out and be a colour television set.' He turned up the contrast before he'd even reached the stage, the band making their well-rehearsed entrance to the *Clockwork Orange* fanfare of Beethoven's 'Ode To Joy'. *'Run your race, brothers! As joyfully as a hero goes to victory!'* Or something similar in robotic German. (The strangest of coincidences which Ziggy couldn't possibly have known, it being Saturday 29 January 1972, he was premiering his fuzzy warbles in the same vicinity, Aylesbury market square, where one year and one day earlier the real Alex and his droogs had been filmed terrorising a librarian for a scene which Kubrick eventually had to cut.)

The Friars' show was an extraterrestrial toe in the water, a practice run for Ziggy to test the plutonium power of the Spiders at full volume, to break in the new boots and codpiece, then halfway through slip into white satin trousers and a collarless jacket, the latter cut from some flock fabric Daniella had found for him in a south London market. In songs, slacks and sheer heart-attacks it successfully smacked the gobs of most of those in attendance, including the cracking set of choppers belonging to a 25-year-old Indian ex-art student who carefully scrutinised Ziggy's every blow and, as future records show, went on to do it his way.

By the end of January, Ziggy's album was just about finished, or so he believed. The title, *The Rise And Fall Of Ziggy Stardust And The Spiders From Mars*, had long been decided, even if the story of that rise and fall was all a bit sketchy. It still sounded like a concept album, which it definitely wasn't. The only concept was Ziggy himself, which not everyone understood.

'I just dropped the numbers in as they appear,' he'd try to explain. 'It's not a story. Just a few little scenes from the life of a band called Ziggy Stardust And The Spiders From Mars, who could feasibly be the last band on Earth.'

The running order had been on constant reshuffle since before Christmas. At various points in recording the album was supposed to include a phenomenal rethink of David's 1970 flop 'Holy Holy', an acoustic cover of the Jacques Brel ballad 'Amsterdam', a saucy sci-fi Weimar frolic provisionally called 'He's A Goldmine' and a dirty thumbs-in-belt-hooks rocker called 'Sweet Head'. But as things now stood, the tracklisting went like this:

Side One.

1. **'Five Years'**. Ziggy's overture of doomsday rock to the steady tempo of humanity's dying heartbeat. Some of the scenes of pandemonium David had borrowed from poet Roger McGough, along with a subtle slip of Kerouac's 'woulda killed him if they hadn't drug me off' straight from his teenage bible *On The Road*. Wherever its individual parts

came from, the finished 'Five Years' broke hearts with the electrifying truth of its all-consuming sadness.

2. **'Soul Love'**. A sonnet from a distant star, Ziggy caressing the sweetly sharp divide between romantic and cynical.

3. **'Moonage Daydream'**. A total space invasion of the senses, salvaged from the wreck of Arnold Corns, stitched back together with alligator skin, pink monkey feathers and debris from The Legendary Stardust Cowboy's 'Gemini Spaceship'.

4. **'Round And Round'**. Included as an example of the sort of classic rock 'n' roll number Ziggy and the Spiders would play in concert, a raucous studio jam through David's childhood Chuck Berry favourite.

5. **'It Ain't Easy'**. A Ron Davies song, recorded by David during the *Hunky Dory* sessions, now dropped on Ziggy's doormat.

Side Two.

1. **'Lady Stardust'**. An irresistibly elegant love letter, possibly to Ziggy himself or possibly, as some thought, to his beguiling rival Marc Bolan.

2. **'Star'**. Ziggy's cunning transplant of his own Stardust dreams into his audience's head, cheekily throwing in a couple of stolen shimmies from Marc ('get it on') and Lou ('just watch me, now!').

3. **'Hang On To Yourself'**. The living end of Gene Vincent and Eddie Cochran, also rescued from the Arnold Corns affair; a priceless zap of sci-fi 'Summertime Blues' carrying a siren call to all 'blessed' would-be Spider groupies.

4. **'Ziggy Stardust'**. The expositional ballad of the Starman. A 3-D vision sculpted from Ziggy's bones, blood and guts.

5. **'Suffragette City'**. Ziggy wanting to be a dog like Iggy, also dropping in a tell-tale Kubrick 'droogy' and a 'Wham bam!' toot to Charles Mingus.

6. **'Rock 'N' Roll Suicide'**. The prophecy of Ziggy's doom, a parting kiss of hope to the human race before taking arms against his sea of

alien troubles. Perhaps the saddest yet sweetest harmony ever heard among the heavenly spheres; if nothing else, the greatest ever heard on Planet Earth.

So ran *The Rise And Fall Of Ziggy Stardust And The Spiders From Mars*. It had life, love, death, glamour, sorrow, sex, leprosy and vaseline. All that anyone could ever ask from a rock 'n' roll album. The only thing it didn't have, according to Dennis Katz, Ziggy's boss at RCA, was a hit single.

When Ziggy looked at the charts that last week of January he realised Katz had a very good point. There was Marc Bolan crashing in at three with the unstoppable mantra of 'Telegram Sam'. Number one was The New Seekers' sugar-rush 'I'd Like To Teach The World To Sing' while Melanie's similarly cheery 'Brand New Key' still swung its merry elbows at five. For Ziggy to blast his way anywhere near the top ten he'd have to concoct something equally as lethal a '*la, la, la*'. A tune to puncture the brain like a pickaxe, once lodged, impossible to remove. He'd already written his ballad of 'Ziggy Stardust'. But what this called for was more along the lines of a theme tune – a national anthem for a new kingdom of glam.

The talented borrow but, as Ziggy was fast realising, the genius steals. Overnight, he placated Katz with a melody which chugged in the slipstreams of T. Rex and The Velvet Underground's *Loaded*, stirring in a heaped spoonful of Motown (the Morse-code twinkles of The Supremes' 'You Keep Me Hanging On') and, the meteoric cherry on the spacecake, kidnapping the chorus of Judy Garland's 'Over The Rainbow' from *The Wizard Of Oz*.

The accompanying words were a simple statement of intent, a recap of Ziggy's arrival from outer space and his plans to reach out and make 'the children boogie'. Yet its molten core raged with the same nuclear fission as Elvis Presley's 'Heartbreak Hotel', a profound understanding of the holy formula of rock 'n' roll: that pop is at its most religiously intense when occupying that sacred fissure between longing and fulfilment; the twilight of loneliness between the hope of knowing there's somebody up there in the sky and the fear that they may never come down.

On Wednesday 9 February, as Marc Bolan celebrated his third number one with 'Telegram Sam', the Chuck Berry cover 'Round And Round' was snipped from the running order of *The Rise And Fall Of Ziggy Stardust And The Spiders From Mars*. Its place on side one, track four would instead be filled with the new track. Ziggy's swirling pop signature. The song of the 'Starman'.

As February dawned, Ziggy had already made his mark in the press, on stage in Aylesbury and on radio, taping a couple of radio sessions for the BBC's *Sounds Of The 70s* programme whose listeners would have been among the first to hear the gospels of 'Ziggy Stardust' and the apocalyptic 'Five Years'.

Which left only the nation's cathode rays to infest. The same week the album running order was finalised, the Spiders made their TV debut. Just as Ziggy had predicted in 'Starman', he'd been picked up by the BBC's 'channel two', their new midweek rock show *The Old Grey Whistle Test*, which went out at five to eleven on a Tuesday evening. Not exactly prime time and not exactly pop, it was presented by the assistant editor of *Melody Maker*, Richard Williams, a man better used to tipping his readership towards his favourite fifty-piece prog-jazz ensemble called 'Centipede'. Less the kind of programme you'd switch on expecting to find T. Rex than the sort you'd switch off to avoid the gruesome honk of Barclay James Harvest.

The studio itself was a suitably blank, threadbare canvas for Ziggy to streak with colour, choosing a palette of bright red (shiny patent-leather boots), greeny-grey (his trusty art-deco Superman suit) and sapphire (his acoustic guitar). The other Spiders were also fast coming into bloom, quietly settling into their blue, silver and gold satins having overcome the initial toxic-shock of the Heddon Street photo-shoot. The band mimed along to the pre-recorded backing of three songs as Ziggy sang live. Two were chosen for the next evening's broadcast: the sexy Lou homage 'Queen Bitch' from *Hunky Dory* and a first airing for 'Five Years'.

The following night, Ziggy and the Spiders watched the programme together at Haddon Hall. For Ziggy it was exactly like looking at himself in his bathroom mirror, only now from all sorts of interesting new angles. In 'Five Years' the camera went for a close-up of his face. It looked like something from the Victorian storybooks David used to browse through when he lived with Kenneth Pitt. An enchanted forest elf with ears by Arthur Rackham and eyebrows by Walter Crane, though lord only knew what bedevilled draughtsman was responsible for those teeth, a skirmish of pearly daggers all fighting for the same patch of gum. But it was the hair that still disturbed him. It had been trimmed and tidied since Weird first sheared it before Christmas, but it still wasn't right, like the last boyish scrap of David Bowie desperately clinging to the mast of Ziggy Stardust, a tether of normality stopping the full shock of his flag from unfurling.

He'd have to endure his still-too-human moddish crop a while longer, with no time to experiment with a new colour and style before the opening of Ziggy's first proper UK tour the following night. Around sixty people, their curiosity pricked by a mixture of the 'gay' *Maker* article, that week's *Whistle Test* broadcast and hazy memories of 'Space Oddity', gathered in The Toby Jug pub in Tolworth, way down in the south-west fringes of London. Ziggy and the Spiders played the only way they knew, as if on stage before an audience of thousands. And so the three score of Tolworth trembled in blissful stupor, from the first parp of Beethoven's 'Ode To Joy' to the last frenetic sob of 'Rock 'N' Roll Suicide'.

The set still had its bumps and creases, which time would eventually erase. A cover of Cream's 'I Feel Free' was a great excuse for Ronno to unleash some sabre-toothed sorcery from his fretboard, but was also dispensable. And Ziggy would also have to concede defeat with his ambitious James Brown medley of the soul godfather's 'You Got To Have A Job' and 'Hot Pants': it was one thing to turn three Yorkshiremen into a rock 'n' roll band from Mars but a take-it-to-the-bridge too far to pass them off as a convincing funk act.

Two nights after the conquest of Tolworth, the Spiders scuttled over to South Kensington, to a university union where Ziggy felt as if he, alone, could hear a ghostly, century-old applause echoing around its walls, urging him to perform super-Martian feats. And so, encouraged by strange spirits, he responded. He remembered a TV clip he'd seen of The Stooges at the 1970 Great Cincinnati Summer Pop Festival, where Iggy walked upon the heads of the audience, raised aloft by their hands like a hero of ancient Rome. Ziggy looked down at his own front row, a fidget of ties, goatees, spectacles and Mary Hopkin types with barely the strength to wave a daffodil between them. Still, it was worth a try. Ziggy vaulted off the stage and tried hoisting himself upon the nearest pair of shoulders. An upward surge. A muscular tremble as he straightened his knee. Then a feeble grin as he lay on the floor staring up at a circle of polite young faces asking if he was OK. Now he thought about it, Iggy hadn't made the mistake of trying it in a science students' union wearing knee-high wrestling boots. Yet still the phantom applause of old rang in his ears for reasons he would, and could, never understand. A secret salute through space and time from one Bromley Martian to another, here in Imperial College, London, formerly the Normal School of Science. Alma Mater of H. G. Wells.

Duly baptised by the spectre of the master, Ziggy continued his invasion with stealth. Beyond London, into the provinces. From Brighton to Sheffield, Chichester, Sutton Coldfield and Yeovil, place names that were as alien to him as the moons of Phobos and Deimos were to the curious teens who paid fifty pence for a night which, in many cases, changed their lives. By March, he was receiving fan mail from kids fully willing to believe he was 'from space'. It helped ease his anxiety on the nights when the audience was only half full. But other fears were less easily shifted.

In Southsea, the Spiders arrived in a port in distress. A freak wave had overturned a hovercraft coming back from Ryde on the Isle of Wight. Among the passengers was a nine-year-old girl who loved ballet dancing. She'd been begging her family for months to go on the crossing. That Saturday her uncle took her on the hovercraft as a weekend treat. The same little girl, and four others, had drowned.

The Southsea tragedy triggered a new panic in Ziggy. He'd have nightmares about his own alien mortality, thinking that at any minute in any journey to any gig his car was going to crash or that the next time he took a plane it would inexplicably malfunction and drop out of the sky. But his most vivid nightmare of all was of being killed on stage. Probably not in a half-empty hall in Hampshire, but somewhere like America, or possibly a giant concert hall in London. A nagging, gut instinct that one day a hugely successful artist would die live in front of their audience. The more he flipped it over in his mind, the more he came to the conclusion that such a death was bound to be his.

If it was any bittersweet consolation, in March 1972 Ziggy Stardust wasn't yet anywhere near the assassin-baiting superstar he hoped or feared. According to that month's annual readers' poll in *Record Mirror*, 'David Bowie' was only the twentieth most popular British Male singer. Only twenty-one people had bothered to vote for him, less than those for Val Doonican and Englebert Humperdinck. At number one – it almost went without saying – was Marc Bolan.

Ziggy's indignation was compounded by sensational reports of that month's T. Rex show at London's Wembley Empire Pool. Column after column of honeyed hysterics from grown men hailing it 'the concert that changed the face of British rock', with scenes of 'fanmania reminiscent of The Beatles'. Everything that Ziggy dreamed of and aspired to. Adding insufferable insult to injury, Marc still had the audacity to keep telling journalists about his 'cosmic messiah film' while Ziggy's album lay dormant, gathering dust on the RCA schedule, not due for release until the summer.

Marc had suddenly raised the stakes of battle. Ziggy needed to counter attack. To save space face. To Starman the barricades. But more than anything else, Ziggy needed to sort that bloody hair.

Before they saved Ziggy Stardust, the magic fingers of Suzi Fussey had first fondled the follicles of Peggy Jones, mother of David Bowie. Suzi worked for Evelyn Paget, a salon on Beckenham High Street opposite The Three Tuns pub where a few years earlier David had rented the back room for some experimental 'Arts Lab' nights. Peggy helpfully drummed up custom by recommending Suzi to her daughter-in-law, Angie, who asked for an all-over white peroxide dye with three colour stripes in the back, a direct copy of the haircut sported by her friend Daniella. Angie was so impressed with the 'fabulous' result that a few days later she rang Suzi again. Would she be able to make a home visit to Haddon Hall; not for Angie, but her husband?

It had taken Ziggy many idle hours flicking through dozens of women's magazines until he saw what he wanted – on the cover of a copy of *Honey*, at least as far as he'd later remember. A rich Warhol soup can red, blazing atop a model wearing a stunning kabuki-inspired Japanese dress by designer Kansai Yamamoto. Ziggy made a note of Yamamoto's name and showed the magazine to Suzi.

'Can you make it like that?'

Suzi took her scissors to Ziggy's luscious glory, snipping the sides, leaving it long at the back and spiking it on top – a mish-mash of three different haircuts from three different magazines, at least as far as she'd later remember. She prepared the dye solution and let it take effect, feeling only slightly distracted by the smouldering looks from Ziggy's guitarist, the one they called Ronno.

The next morning Suzi was back in her salon when the phone rang. It was Angie, heaving hysteria into the receiver. There was a crisis in Haddon Hall. Ziggy had woken up, wandered to the bathroom, looked in the mirror and screamed the paint off the ceiling. The face staring back at him wasn't a cosmic messiah, more a cosmic mess. When Suzi had left the night before his hair had looked red. But in the bald Beckenham light of day it was a horrible, muddy pink. Nor would it stand up, flopping in a limp fringe. 'It's an emergency,' squealed Angie. 'Help!'

When Suzi returned to Haddon Hall she took no chances. She prepared a special mix to her own 'recipe' of Schwarzkopf's Fantasy Colour range 'Red Hot Red' and saturated Ziggy's every follicle. When the solution was rinsed off, it looked as if coppery flames were licking out of his forehead and all around his ears. To keep its shape, Suzi applied a dandruff treatment called Guard containing a strong setting agent. Ziggy sculpted it proudly with his fingers, the shine of happy tears in his eyes. It was a masterpiece, but one which was going to take a lot of maintenance.

And so Evelyn Paget's lost a stylist, the Spiders From Mars gained a full-time hair mistress and, in time, Ronno also gained a wife. More importantly, Ziggy Stardust had found the human torch to light his beacon of fire. His crimson halo. His secret weapon in the great cosmic messiah fight of 1972.

The red mullet from Mars.

THREE
THE IMAGE

Ziggy's new hair made its first public outing later that night at the Sombrero club. Jaws dropped, hearts popped and make-up caked cheeks flushed in fresh tides of envy. His friends danced and flapped around him like moths driven delirious by its scarlet glow. Ziggy gleamed fuzzy smiles back at them, not sure if he was drunk on the attention, the alcohol or maybe the dye seeping through his skull to soak his brain a dreamy cerebral shade of pink.

His eyes hazily scanned the pantomime before him like a slowly roving camera lens, developing a mental Polaroid of these lovely, ludicrous young creatures. The one they called Silly Billy. Dear funky little Freddie and Daniella. Their flatmate, Wendy, forever blind with mascara and dumb with lipstick. The dancefloor queens and wall-propping peacocks. The innocent and the vain who lived only for the here and now refusing to entertain any thought of tomorrow, old age or death. Sweet boogaloo dudes.

The scene was still scorched on Ziggy's eyeballs when he awoke the next morning. A scene he wanted to shake out of his head and share with the universe. So he shook, and out fell a swarm of magic music and words. Words describing the dazzling and doomed Sombrero gang. The stars on Freddie's face and Wendy shoplifting from Marks & Spencer; she'd be annoyed he didn't make it Harrods but he preferred the phonetic ping of the nickname 'Marks & Sparks'. Words describing how he felt being 25 years-old and fearing, like 'Five Years', that the end of the world was nigh. Words declaring it was time to finally close the lid on the yellow-edged 1960s of The Beatles and the Stones and embrace the glorious 'now' of being young, sexy, glamorous and alive in 1972. Words which in Ziggy's romantic rapture even cocked a backhanded salute to Marc Bolan and T. Rex.

He called the song 'All The Young Dudes'. It immediately eclipsed 'Starman' as the catchiest, most irresistible thing Ziggy had written yet. And, like a colossal cosmic dunce, he handed it on a silver salver to some hairy desperados he barely knew.

Ziggy had helplessly inherited David's fondness for Mott The Hoople, a group of R&B heavies from Herefordshire who for the last three years had failed to translate a loyal live following into commercial success. On 26 March 1972, Mott spluttered to a dismal halt after an especially depressing show in Zurich, Switzerland, returning to London officially kaput. Not that Ziggy knew when he sent them a tape of his 'Suffragette City' in the enthusiastic hope they might want to record their own version. Mott's bassist, Peter 'Overend' Watts, awkwardly informed him they didn't need it since they'd just disbanded. Ziggy was horrified: so horrified he made the insanely generous offer of first refusal on the new song he'd written. Whatever it took to keep Mott The Hoople together.

Tony DeFries grabbed the reins, summoning the band to his Regent Street offices to discuss their future and the managerial role he intended to take in it. There they first met Ziggy who sat cross-legged with an acoustic guitar and sang them 'All The Young Dudes' from beginning to end. Mott singer Ian Hunter, a faceless pair of shades poking through a scribble of curls, was confused. Either he must be dreaming or DeFries and Ziggy were taking the piss. 'Dudes' was more than a song. It was the elixir of pop immortality. Anyone who'd write something so devastatingly obvious a hit only to surrender it in a selfless act of fandom had to be off their gourd. Or from outer space.

The devastatingly obvious hit called 'Starman' was finally released in late April. The first record by Ziggy Stardust and The Spiders From Mars. RCA 2199. On the B-side, the track he'd first offered Mott, 'Suffragette City'.

The reviews were promising. 'An elevating and energetic song with some super "teenage" lyrics,' said the *NME*, even if Ziggy didn't understand the derision about teeny-boppers; as far as he was concerned the mind was at its most active stage at the age of about 14. He was more gratified by the review in *Disc* by John Peel, Marc Bolan's former champion, who deemed 'Starman' not merely 'magnificent' but 'four minutes, ten seconds of major achievement'.

Such praise proved alarmingly ineffective. The public response to 'Starman' was sluggish. It especially irked Ziggy that, the same month, an old friend of David's called Reg was taking up full-page adverts in the press to promote his new single dressed, quite literally, as a stardust cowboy. Reg had since changed his name to Elton John and had already enjoyed his first hit a year earlier with 'Your Song'. His new one was called 'Rocket Man'. The title alone was a bit too close to 'Starman' for Ziggy's liking. The lyrics were a not unfamiliar story of a lonely astronaut longing for his wife as he drifted through the solar system. Uncannily, it also shared a producer with David's 'Space Oddity', Gus Dudgeon.

By the middle of May, Reg's 'Rocket Man' was in the top ten while Ziggy's 'Starman' was nowhere to be seen. It was all Ziggy could do to highlight the irony when recording a new version of 'Space Oddity' for a BBC radio session, dropping in a bone-dry, bitchy 'Oh, Mr Rocket Man!' during the bridge.

'Rocket Man' would have made number one had it not been for the ever invincible Marc Bolan, keeping it at bay with T. Rex's latest, the precious gold-plated panic called 'Metal Guru'. For the moment Ziggy still posed no real threat to Marc, whose main competition now came from David Cassidy, squeaky clean singing star of American TV sitcom *The Partridge Family*. Such was the contest of oestrogenic lust that the breathless readers of *Mirabelle* were invited to vote for their favourite of the two. 'Marc is sexy on stage,' the polling form pondered, 'but David is neat 'n' dreamy.' The result, announced later that summer, offered the first indication that the gas of T. Rexstasy might be starting to deflate: Cassidy's fans outvoted Marc's by nearly three to one. Soon Marc would have the unstoppable force of puppy-loving Donny Osmond to add to his woes, not to mention the greatest threat of all currently streaking through the provinces gathering new clans of glam.

The Spiders From Mars continued zigzagging a path of glory across the British Isles. In Manchester they were witnessed by a quiet 15-year-old boy from Macclesfield with sad oceans for eyes for whom 'Rock 'N' Roll Suicide' became a design for life. At London's Kingston Polytechnic, the blessed boogie children were queuing around the block hours before the doors had opened. Down on the coast in Worthing, Ziggy's alien adrenalin propelled him to jump piggyback on Ronno's shoulders, the pair of them cheered through the crowd in a spontaneous lap of honour, soon to become choreographed ritual. Even the T. Rex rhythm section couldn't stay away when the Spiders returned home to play London's Central Polytechnic, watching in awe if acutely aware not to rave about it to their paymaster. Bassist Steve Currie was naïve enough to think he could get himself a copycat Ziggy haircut: Marc, infuriated, demanded he shear it off.

Between gigs, when time allowed, Ziggy returned to the studio in his new role as star producer. He'd since committed himself to the full resurrection of Mott The Hoople by overseeing their next album, with help from Ronno as his angelic arranger. DeFries, now Mott's *de facto* manager, had craftily negotiated a new deal for them with CBS Records. In return, Ian Hunter had craftily made sure neither himself nor the rest of the band signed the contracts DeFries had waved in their faces. Though wary of his manager, they were nevertheless still delirious with gratitude to be working with Ziggy, especially when they listened to the playback of 'All The Young Dudes' feeling like they'd died and been reborn a million times over. Ziggy himself sang harmonies, played saxophone and led the chorus of handclaps, including the thundery thwacks of his new Hull bodyguard, Ronno's mate big Stuey. Privately, it also amused Ziggy that for the B-side of his salute to the glamour and gaiety of the Sombrero, Hunter picked a song of their own, 'One Of The Boys', unknowingly creating one of the most riotously camp single couplings in the history of plastic.

Ziggy's own plastic was still nowhere to be seen in the singles charts, but with the album release only weeks away, the media offensive intensified. More journalists were invited to the mothership of Haddon Hall where, over tea and cigarettes, they'd hear how Ziggy preferred street culture ('I'm not ready to be an intellectual'), reckoned that if he wasn't a pop star he'd be 'in a nuthouse or in prison' and spared some convincingly diplomatic praise for Marc Bolan. 'I admire him,' grinned Ziggy. 'He's a grafter.'

Human fingers were finally able to caress copies of *The Rise And Fall Of Ziggy Stardust And The Spiders From Mars* on 6 June 1972. Appropriately, inevitably, a Tuesday, day of Mars. The front and reverse cover were the two clicks of raw genius from Brian's Heddon Street session: on the front, Ziggy beamed to Earth under the door of K. West furriers; on the back, making a collect call to the cosmos in a K2 telephone box. Both had been hand-tinted, a Technicolor hue administered by Terry Pastor, a partner in Main Artery, the Covent Garden design studio set up by David's best friend, George. The inside sleeve carried the lyrics beside the Spiders' individual droog portraits; Ronno's luxurious lashes and Greatfield glower taking the prize for the most Alex-like. Ziggy had also added his own explicit instruction to the listener on the back cover. In capital letters: 'TO BE PLAYED AT MAXIMUM VOLUME'.

The day of the album's release, fate had thrown its creator back up to Yorkshire where the local Bradford *Telegraph & Argus* were more than willing to buy into the alien fantasy – 'ZIGGY'S ALTER EGO PROVING HE'S REALLY THE STARMAN'. Others in the town were much less hospitable. After their soundcheck at St George's Hall, Ziggy and the band went for something to eat in a nearby restaurant only to be refused entry. Evidently Bradford's racial diversity hadn't yet stretched to extraterrestrials. It astonished Ziggy, that mere make-up and fabric could be so divisive. Yet it also reminded him of something he'd read in that week's *Mirabelle*. Something in its 'Pop Gossip' column which had made him laugh, loud and hard.

'Isn't David Bowie going a bit too far with his image these days?'

'An image is one thing and a human being is another.'

The voice, a Southern slur peppered with the frequent respectful 'sir' and the flirtatious 'honey', hadn't much altered in the sixteen years since its owner changed the world. Nor had the billion-dollar, lip-curling smile. The eyes still shone, though now with a medicated glaze which hadn't been there back in 1956. The hair, too, was thicker and swarthier, as was the face it framed in dense, carpet-strip sideburns. But underneath the black cape and the powder blue suit, which made him look like Nashville's Count Dracula, he was still, just about, Elvis Presley. He was still The King.

On Friday 9 June 1972, the world's press had crammed into the Mercury Ballroom of New York's Hilton, summoned for a special audience with the 37-year-old 'King Of Rock 'N' Roll' ahead of the first of four sold-out concerts at Madison Square Garden. Incredibly, it seemed, though he'd conquered America from the New York television stage, he'd never actually played a concert in the city. Elvis joked he'd been waiting all this time 'to find the right building'. The press asked him how he'd managed to survive so long in the business. He told them, 'Vitamin E.' Then they asked about his image.

'Well, uh,' he hesitated, 'it gets kind of hard to live up to an image.'

Nobody knew more than Elvis Presley how insufferably hard it was to live up to an image. In the decade and a half since he recorded 'Hound Dog' – the song that first branded nine-year-old David Jones a Starman – Elvis and his image had been inflated, punctured, destroyed, rebuilt, comprehensively neutered and meticulously rewired. Destiny, not vitamin E, had reeled him through army life, the death of his mother and a Hollywood career (which at times felt like a slow, sustained form of rock 'n' roll suicide). He'd latterly hauled himself back from the brink with his 1968 TV 'comeback special', a black-leather phoenix reborn from the ashes of one too many *Harum Scarum*s. Its success had catapulted him to Las Vegas, where his first season at the International Hotel broke all attendance records. The owners rewarded him with a special commemorative golden belt with silver links. A belt he still wore on this day in New York because, God forbid anyone should think otherwise, he was still The King.

He surrendered his mood to the chemistry of an unbreakable prescription-drug habit. A doped-up Captain Marvel, draping friends, lovers and his 'Memphis Mafia' drudges in his own specially designed 'TCB' jewellery – 'Takin' Care of Business' – with its trademark zigzag lightning-flash insignia. He carried as many guns as he could stuff around his body, living in increasing fear that he might be assassinated live on stage because all kings have their enemies. In his case, John Lennon and The Beatles and all other bands responsible for the corruption of American youth, as he'd tell President Nixon and the FBI when volunteering himself as their rock 'n' roll supergrass. But should one of his Memphis Mafiosi find him standing alone outside in the dark, staring at the stars, looking for flying saucers or praying to God, weeping aloud how 'I'm so sick of being Elvis Presley' they were never to tell anyone else about it. Because he was still Elvis Presley. He was still The King.

Not just a king, but 'a prince from another planet' according to the *New York Times'* review of the opening Friday night at Madison Square Garden. It described Elvis standing at the end, 'his arms stretched out, the great gold cloak giving him wings, a champion, the only one in his class'. *The only one in his class.* Indisputable proof, in black and white, he was still The King.

The next day Elvis played an afternoon matinée, taking a few hours' rest before returning at 8.30 p.m. for his second evening show. After the past few seasons in Vegas his act was now tiger-slick and sabre-sharp. The opening paid homage to one of his favourite films, Stanley Kubrick's *2001: A Space Odyssey*, his band recreating the biblical fanfare of Strauss's *Thus Spake Zarathustra*, the audience's mania-inciting cue that the original monolith of rock 'n' roll had landed. It would segue straight into a frenzy of brass and galloping drums chasing the loose tune of his Sun Records' debut 'That's All Right'. Elvis walked out on the stage spotlit in the shiniest of white rhinestone jumpsuits with cape. As flashlights blinked in the arena around him he looked like a distant star glittering in his own private patch of the cosmos. He trembled a knee. A wild symphony of screeches. He still had it. He was still The King.

The second song was 'Proud Mary', the recent Creedence Clearwater Revival hit, its soulful country swagger a perfect fit for Elvis. He looked out over the first dozen or so rows, seeking out any pretty young faces to send backstage, girls he could pep up with a Ritalin and maybe end up filming with his cine camera as they wrestled on his bed in nothing but their panties. Maybe her. Maybe that dark one, if she could lose her mom. Maybe … huh?

Something had caught Elvis's eye. Some 'thing' with bright red hair, spiked on top, wearing what looked like a padded spacesuit and enormous red boots with black platform soles. It was strolling closer, down the aisle, its teeth flashing an awkward, demonic grin as it clumsily found its seat on what looked like an elite row next to company executives from Elvis's label, RCA. He continued singing, eyes fixed on the grotesque latecomer, brain trying to fathom what he was looking at.

'Proud Mary, keep on burnin' ...'

It looked a real proud Mary too.

'Rollin' ...'

Maybe more like a Mary from Mars.

'Rollin' ...'

A princess from another planet.

'Rollin' down a river.'

Neither man nor woman. Not human. Just image.

It wasn't like Ziggy to be easily embarrassed, but inside he could detect the faint pulse of David Jones, secretly mortified that finally given the chance to see Elvis Presley in the flesh he'd arrived so conspicuously late.

Along with Angie and DeFries, he'd flown in the day before, a weekend's window in Ziggy's tour allowing a quick jaunt to New York as a guest of RCA to toast the album's release and drum up some American press interest. DeFries had kept close contact with their friends from Warhol's *Pork*, Tony Zee, Leee Black Childers and the vivacious Wayne County, entrusting them with advance copies of Ziggy's LP to filter to whatever influential contacts they could. He also floated an idea – just an idea, mind – that if the words 'Ziggy Rules!' suddenly began appearing graffitied around the streets and subways of Manhattan that would be no bad thing either. In return, DeFries promised them work when he finally got around to setting up a New York office for the breakaway management company he was now scheming.

DeFries was just as excited about the prospect of seeing Elvis. He was fascinated by Elvis's manager, Colonel Tom Parker. The bloody-minded control over his 'boy'. The boastful hucksterism. And the shamelessly opportunistic marketing brain. Everything DeFries wanted for his Starman: Ziggy lunchboxes, Ziggy sheets and pillows, Ziggy dolls with spiky red hair, interchangeable clothes and ripcords that made a cry of, 'Wham, bam, thank you, Mam!' when pulled. Even Angie couldn't help but encourage him, suggesting maybe an inflatable Ziggy sex doll. 'That moves and grooves you.'

That Saturday night they'd been late leaving the Park Lane Hotel and late arriving at Madison Square Garden. Ziggy knew, absolutely, that Elvis must have seen him, that if only for a glare, the two eighth of January birthday boys had shared some tiny sliver of eye contact under the same roof. When Elvis later sang 'Hound Dog', Ziggy thought back to a winter's night in Bromley watching cousin Kristina spontaneously combusting in Plaistow Grove. But his favourite moment came towards the end when Elvis sang his new Mickey Newbury cover, the Civil War medley 'An American Trilogy'. It was The King's 'Rock 'N' Roll Suicide', a holy rite of self-crucifixion, telling the audience he was going to die just moments before all that wild hallelujah, the music roaring like a stellar hearse dragging his body back up to the stars where it belonged. Now *that*, thought Ziggy, was how to put on a show. He'd definitely be borrowing some of those 'glory, glory' death vibes for himself. And, Freddie willing, maybe a white rhinestone jumpsuit with tassels while he was at it.

A few days earlier in Bradford he'd bragged to the local *Argus* that he'd definitely be meeting The King in person. But, as was custom, Elvis had already 'left the building' before the curtain fell. Ziggy returned to his hotel with Angie and DeFries, slightly deflated and privately tormented by the imaginary conversation they might have had; running away with boyish fantasies of Elvis one day singing his songs and hearing those luscious lips murmur, '*Time takeshashigarette.*'

But then maybe it was for the best they hadn't met. The risk of disappointment. The fear of facing the reality. As he'd soon tell a US

'Let's drink to that and the passing time.' Ziggy toasts certain death on his last journey home from Paris to London, 4 May 1973.

COSMIC COSTUME DRAMAS PART 2
Top row: Kansai Yamamoto's kabuki-inspired designs for the 1973
Aladdin Sane tour; silk kimono (left) and black vinyl 'Spring Rain' suit (right).
Bottom left: Taking '70s Elvis glitz a few tassels too far.
Bottom right: Ziggy's first Yamamoto one-piece 'bunny suit'

Top: Ziggy models the latest in Martian knitwear; a Yamamoto mammoth woollen.

Bottom: 'Gimme your hands!' The kids claw in vain for their alien messiah.

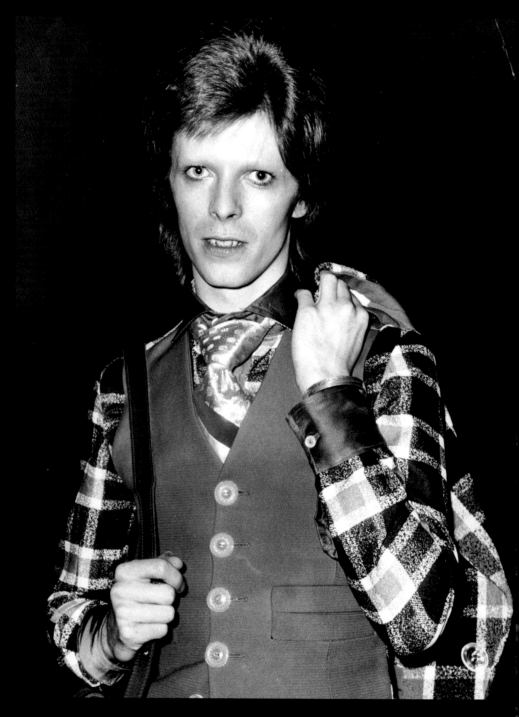

Above: Ziggy, Heil! Contemplating glam rock surrender at the London premiere of *Hitler: The Last Ten Days*, 7 May 1973.

Previous pages: Time takes a last cigarette. The condemned Starman slips backstage at the Hammersmith Odeon to face rock 'n' roll suicide, 3 July 1973.

reporter, he expected Elvis wasn't anything like he'd dreamed. He imagined Elvis to be 'a very nice, uncomplicated kind of guy'.

'And I didn't want to meet that,' smiled Ziggy. 'I wanted to meet the image.'

FOUR
THE BROADCAST

She thought she'd seen the last of extraterrestrials. Her work as a radar operative for the Supreme Headquarters Alien Defence Organisation had finished over a year ago. No more would she have to spend her days monitoring radar screens for the next blip of a flying saucer, her senses prickling to the occasional lingering glance from her base commander, secretly entranced by her beauty: the soft Asian face, the cascade of inky black hair, the ever-so-kinky tan knee-boots and slinky cream catsuit distinguished from those of her co-workers by the initial 'A' swinging on a chain below her slender bosom. A for Ayshea. As she'd joke, pronounced like a sneeze. 'Eye-sha.'

She was permanently Ayshea, on screen and off: her name in real life and the name of her SHADO operative in the Gerry Anderson sci-fi series *UFO*. Adding to the enigma, in the programme's credits, she was listed without a surname. Ayshea, the actress, was simply 'Ayshea', as exotic and space-queeny as that sounded. The part hadn't demanded much. Ayshea was under no illusion she was there for any reason other than to look sexy and pipe up 'red alert!' whenever the script dictated. But it gave her the mildly thrilling experience of acting beside the show's American star Ed Bishop, who'd had a fleeting role in Kubrick's *2001: A Space Odyssey* which, by coincidence, had been shot in the same Borehamwood studios used for much of the series.

Ayshea was already months into filming *UFO* in late 1969 when she took another job as co-presenter of a new children's pop show beside a puppet owl named Ollie Beak. With young minds raving about the recent Apollo moon landing, and a song about rockets called 'Space Oddity' still in the top ten, the producers had settled on the title *Lift Off*.

Three years later, Ollie Beak had been replaced by a puppet dog, Fred Barker, while Ayshea had been elevated to its star draw. *Lift Off With Ayshea*.

She'd also been trying to launch her own pop career, sometimes singing on the show but yet to pester the same chart heights as her guests. A keen spiritualist, she nevertheless remained optimistic. At the start of 1972, Ayshea was asked by a magazine to list her hopes for the next twelve months. She predicted Americans would 'definitely land on Mars' before the end of the year. She'd be proved wrong. But, if it was any consolation, Ayshea would get to meet a genuine band of Martians soon enough.

Ziggy Stardust hadn't long returned home from New York when he was given the good news he'd been offered a chance to promote 'Starman' on *Lift Off With Ayshea*. It meant cancelling a gig in Coventry in order to be at the scheduled taping at Granada TV up in Manchester. An easy sacrifice to make considering the target audience: kids looking for teatime pop kicks after a midsummer's day perishing in the classroom. This particular week, those kicks were a hairy man from South Africa with an unpronounceable name warbling about his 'Sweet Marie', a failure of teenagers called Hello feebly squeaking 'ooh-ooh' over some fuzzy guitars, and a beige-faced club singer in tux and bow-tie moaning about divorce. Nothing much to talk about in the playground the next day.

Apart from Ziggy. In six months he had now achieved televisual perfection. His hair, a rusty orangutanish scream. His clothes, a new Freddie quilted droog suit of jacket and trousers in rich reds, blues and golds, looking like they'd been cut from a sultan's duvet, and a pair of shiny scarlet wrestling boots; moving on from Russell & Bromley but keeping it local, made by the firm Greenway & Sons in glamorous Penge.

Ronno was his usual glimmering golden self while even Weird had embraced the spirit of cosmic glamour by spraying his long dangling sideboards white so he looked like a lunar Santa Claus. The Spiders played for Ayshea against a black backdrop dotted with large, spiky silver and red stars. When it came to the chorus, Ziggy and Ronno crowded towards the same microphone. Ziggy slung his acoustic guitar to his right hip and flopped a left arm around Ronno in a tender embrace of Martian brotherhood. In the eyes of Ayshea, and the kids who'd soon be watching at home, they looked every fibre a pop group from outer space: a Flash Gordon Fab Four fronted by a pale, thin Venus Presley.

The programme was broadcast a week later, at 4.55 p.m. on Wednesday 21 June. Television sets blared, eyes glistened, blood rushed, lips trembled, chewing stopped, comics dropped, homework curled neglected in satchels, chip-pans sizzled, dogs whimpered, cutlery clattered, mothers shouted 'tea!' in vain; and the unseen stars in the summer sky above shone with fierce pride for one of their own. The next day on buses, in bedrooms, by school gates, outside sweetshops, in back gardens, on grassy commons, in dirty playgrounds with rusting slides and paint-chipped swings, hardly a word was said about Hello, or the unpronounceable Emil Dean Zoghby, or Tony Christie begging 'Don't Go Down To Reno', or Fred Barker, or even that much about the ravishing Ayshea herself. But everyone wanted to talk about Ziggy. The sound, the hair, the clothes and the warm invitation he'd extended to their hungry hearts just weeks before the summer holiday kicked off.

Yes sir, Starman. They would boogie.

Two days after singing for Ayshea and her captive audience of innocents, Ziggy was sinking his teeth into Ronno's nether regions on stage in

Oxford Town Hall. He'd been secretly toying with the stunt for a while, praying that Ronno wouldn't shirk away and embarrass him when he went for it. Towards the end of the set, during 'Suffragette City', Ziggy stooped between Ronno's legs in front of his guitar and began pranging the strings with his mouth. Luckily, Ronno didn't shirk. He kept his left hand tapping out frantic fretboard mutations, his right hand raising the guitar to Ziggy's head so he could bite the strings Jimi Hendrix fashion. Behind them in the wings was Ziggy's photographer friend, Mick Rock. From where Mick was stood pointing his camera, the guitar between Ziggy's head and Ronno's crotch was irrelevant. It was one geezer from Mars orally pleasuring another.

Click.

The 'Martian blow job' became a regular manœuvre over the coming weeks as the Spiders' provincial campaign trail grew ever more rumbustious. In Croydon, demand outstripped supply when a thousand kids quaking in awe after the Ayshea broadcast had to be turned away from the sold-out venue. Ziggy could hear them screaming his name beyond the walls from inside his dressing room where somebody had left that week's copy of the *NME* lying around. The headline immediately caught Ziggy's eye. 'BOLAN TO QUIT TOURS?'

There'd been an especially violent T. Rex gig in Manchester, the crowd driven so berserk that in the aftermath Marc was now considering retirement from the stage. Ziggy read with wonder, trying to imagine what that must feel like. To pull the plug. To stop playing. To cease to be. But he couldn't. He could only puzzle over Marc's so-sudden surrender and wet his lips with the taste of imminent victory.

When it came, the taste of victory was that of the BBC canteen. The Ayshea broadcast had worked its magic, pushing 'Starman' safely inside the top 40. Which meant that the first Wednesday in July, Ziggy and the Spiders were called to Television Centre to seize the prize of *Top Of The Pops*.

Number one that week was 'Puppy Love' by Donny Osmond, the new teen heartthrob weakening the knees of *Jackie* and *Mirabelle* readers, who had to make do with watching him on film rather than in the BBC studio. As well as The Sweet, Lulu and the house dancers Pan's People, the one other live act there on the day was Gary Glitter doing some serious Osmond-nudging at number two with his rhythmic war cry 'Rock And Roll Part 2'.

Ziggy and Gary may have had very different objectives but they shared the same umbrella management company and a spookily parallel ancestry. Many years ago, when he was still teenager Paul Gadd, Gary gravitated to the 2 I's coffee bar in Soho, weaving and bobbing between the young Mark Feld, where he met the person who changed his life. A rock 'n' roll singer who passed on a piece of priceless advice: 'Never let the public see you as your real self because you'd never appear special to them again.' The singer's name was Vince Taylor.

It took Paul Gadd another ten years to follow Taylor's advice by hiding his real self and settling on a pseudonym: for a painful split second he was very nearly Terry Tinsel. Gary Glitter was, as that name betrayed, a bacofoil buffoon with no sense of style, but Ziggy was charitable enough to talk to him when cornered. Gary wanted to know where Ziggy bought his clothes. 'Alkasura on the King's Road,' lied Ziggy. Alkasura was the hip boutique where Chelita Secunda liked to drag Marc Bolan for most of his clothes. Ziggy had only said it thinking it would be a scream if one day Marc turned on the telly and saw Gary Glitter prancing about in his T. Rex wardrobe. All being fair in glam and war.

By late afternoon, after a full dress rehearsal, the Spiders were suited, booted and pleasantly giddy on cheap wine and beer from the BBC bar, giggling at the starched collars and tweed sophistos casting funny glances at their shiny Martian rags. They were wearing the same outfits they'd worn for Ayshea, the only difference being Gilly's hair, since bleached lighter. Ziggy had also decided to use his bright blue acoustic guitar.

If ever a time had come to prove to the world he'd rather be a colour television set than a radio, this was it. For this was *the* moment. The cylinder crashing on Horsell Common. The alien monolith at the dawn of man. The point of contact beyond the infinite. Four minutes to change the history of the human race. As specially introduced by Tony Blackburn.

The Studio 8 audience encircled the stage, a plucky chosen few standing just feet behind the Spiders, where a strange but eager boy in a grey striped tank top danced jogging on the spot in a vain bid for the camera's attention. Gilly had been placed down in front, Weird, Ziggy and Ronno on the platform behind him. When the music started, Ziggy fixed his stare into the camera lens. A nervous laugh. A lightheaded sensation like he was Kubrick's Star-Child, floating through space, braced to fall through Earth's atmosphere.

'*Hey, now, now.*'

And down he fell. He could sense his face, his hair, his clothes, his flesh, his bones, his red boots and his blue guitar slowly atomised in a neon sandstorm, sucked like stardust into the cathode tubes of a million households, transmitted through the very electromagnetic waves crackling with the radiation of the big bang. He'd sung the words dozens of times before, but only now did their prophecy make sense. He wasn't singing a song, he was singing his life. He *was* the Starman. This *was* his message to the people of Earth. When he sang 'picked on you', by 'you' he meant all, waggling a finger directly into the lens with a knowing lasers-to-stun smile. And just as they had for Ayshea, when it came to the chorus, Ziggy flopped an arm around Ronno's shoulders. Martian brothers. Maybe even Martian lovers.

The episode was broadcast the next evening: Thursday 6 July 1972, at 7.25 p.m. on BBC1 between the day's play at Wimbledon and a repeat episode of *The Goodies*. Those who didn't turn over to watch continued tennis coverage on BBC2 or succumb to the lure of the film on ITV – *The Silent Enemy* with Laurence Harvey, *Little Red Monkey* with Richard

Conte, *Rogues' Regiment* with Dick Powell, or *The Midnight Story* with Tony Curtis depending on which region – would, somewhere between The Who, The Sweet, The New Seekers, Lulu, Love Unlimited, Dr Hook, Pan's People, Gary Glitter, Donny Osmond and Tony Blackburn, have been blessed with the vision of Ziggy and the sound of 'Starman'. Curtains drew wide and windows hinged open in the warm summer's evening as stardust echoes vibrated redbrick, pebbledash, lamppost, railing, milk crate, bicycle wheel and radial tyre. Young minds, which at 7.25 p.m. clung to the stem of smooth, well-ordered, stabilised lives, had, by eight o'clock, been blown free like dandelion seeds to the far corners of the universe. Ziggy had ripped 'Over The Rainbow' and, in turn, ripped Britain from a gutter-grey council house Kansas to a vibrant, debauched rock 'n' roll Oz. Out of the dark, out of the night, into the sun, into the light. The Spiders From Mars had stolen the nation's children while publicly declaring war on the straight, the dour, the bigoted, the ugly, the colourless, the safe, the cowardly and the rule-makers. And nobody, not the Ministry of Defence, not Professor Quatermass, not even Marc Bolan, could stop them.

While the rest of the country slowly adjusted to extraterrestrial invasion, in Haddon Hall Ronno watched the programme back in conspicuous silence. He'd been stewing over that week's issue of *Melody Maker*, carrying a full page ad with a handwritten message. 'Thanx to all our people for making ZIGGY. I love you.' It wasn't the words that bothered him, it was the image. The 'Martian blow job' photo from the recent Oxford gig. Ronno's family up in Hull would regularly read the *Maker* to follow his progress. They weren't going to like that any more than they were seeing 'their Mick' tonight on national TV singing with Ziggy's arm wrapped lovingly around his shoulders. Just as he feared, a few days later he had to suffer the sound of his mother crying down the Haddon Hall phone receiver. Some vandal had thrown paint over the new car he'd bought her, as she'd since discovered, in retribution for her Mick being 'a queer'.

Yet Ziggy, forgivably, was as oblivious to Ronno's grievances as he was to anyone and anything else that night, hopelessly intoxicated on his own televisual glory. Humanity would remember this date for ever, he reckoned. The sixth of July, 1972. The day their Starman ceremonially fell to Earth on *Top Of The Pops*. The sixth day of the seventh month. He made a mental note of it for next year.

Not for a blink of a trice of a nanosecond did he, or anybody else, consider that by then he might already be dead.

FIVE
THE GLORY

'**H**ere he is, the second greatest thing next to God …'

It was only two days after *Top Of The Pops* and already Ziggy was being introduced on stage as the new Jesus.

The man doing the introducing was DJ Kenny Everett, the compère for a 'Save The Whale' benefit organised by Friends of the Earth at London's Royal Festival Hall, where Ziggy was headlining. The last time the cold cadaver of David Bowie was on the same stage he'd been booed by Tyrannosaurus Rex hippies while he mimed his Chinese Communist invasion of Tibet. Four years later, the electrified pulse of 'Ode To Joy' rattling the modernist foundations, he was second only to God. The true cosmic messiah. Let Beethoven sing for him! *We approach, drunk with fire, thy sacred shrine!* Or something similar in robotic German.

He sang hoping the eyes of God might really be watching, knowing if they were it would give the Almighty cause for celestial concern that, if he wasn't careful, tomorrow morning in pulpits across the land there'd be snivelling vicars apologetically praising 'God, the second greatest thing next to Ziggy.' Looking up at the balcony boxes he saw a distressed damsel nearly fall over the ledge waving a homemade 'Ziggy' banner. Another girl ran towards the stage sobbing and clutching flowers. When he reached down to take them she squeezed him around the neck, planting frantic kisses on his cheeks, exactly as he'd seen done to Elvis Presley in New York. The journalists in the audience stared and scribbled and staggered home starry-eyed to buff and polish his ego in frenzied typewriter clatters. He was 'Garbo from Mars', 'a real star, incorporating the things that made people like Judy Garland, Frank Sinatra and The Beatles so special' and – Ziggy's personal favourite – 'the thinking man's (or woman's) Marc Bolan'. Their only criticism was his choice of special guest. 'A mere mortal next to our hero.'

Mortal or not, Lou Reed was a hero to Ziggy. It was his idea to invite Lou over from New York especially for the benefit, allowing himself the honour of presenting the former singer of his favourite band for his first appearance on a British stage. Lou was happy to agree, happy to get out of his gourd backstage on booze and Mandrax, and even happier to just about survive joining Ziggy for three of his own songs – 'White Light/White Heat', 'I'm Waiting For The Man' and 'Sweet Jane' – without falling over. Dressed in a black velvet suit with rhinestone trimming, his ashen face smudged with mascara and black lipstick, beside The Spiders From Mars he looked more like a Cockroach From Mongo.

But in Ziggy's eyes, Lou could do no wrong. He'd already encouraged Mott The Hoople to cover 'Sweet Jane' for their album, bringing Lou to the studio to help Ian Hunter with a guide vocal. Lou would tell everyone who'd listen how 'wonderful', 'fantastic' and 'beautiful' Ziggy was. Ziggy, in turn, vowed that once he'd finished with Mott he'd move on to produce Lou's next album. And when Mott played Lou their 'All The Young Dudes', he just about popped.

'It's the most brilliant single I've heard in my life!' flapped Lou. 'It's a Gay Anthem! A rallying call to the young dudes to come out in the streets and show that they were beautiful and gay and proud of it.'

Ziggy was overcome with pride. Mott were simply overcome, exchanging catatonic stares in mortified, slackjaw, penny-drop silence.

The Friday after the Festival Hall, Lou played his first solo European show in London at the King's Cross Cinema. Ziggy, Angie and Ronno were there, as was 'Martian blow job' photographer Mick Rock and another familiar face that couldn't help but crack in a goofy smirk when it spotted Lou's trousers beginning to sag and poor Lou being too doped to notice. A face that within the next twenty-four hours would be on the same King's Cross stage also making its British live debut. The face belonging to Iggy Pop.

It was gone 2 a.m. Saturday morning by the time Lou wobbled on stage wearing the same black velvet and rhinestone suit and death-mask make-up. With the eyes of Ziggy and Iggy upon him, he pulled back for a moment from the stiff microphone, looking like Dr Frankenstein's failed first draft, thrown away for being too saucy and just crawled out of the laboratory garbage. Mick's camera went click.

Before Lou had recorded a note for the album he planned to make with Ziggy, Mick already had the cover.

After six months of gigging, Ziggy and the Spiders had spun their wondrous web far and wide over England. For the last night of their first tour, they returned full circle to its beginnings at the Friars Club in Aylesbury. There'd been a brief pipedream of having the concert relayed to a giant video screen in the market square outside the venue. As it was, the RCA budget had already been exhausted by DeFries, who'd arranged for a select party of journalists to be flown over from New York to London to review the show and interview Ziggy for the US press.

The Americans arrived on the Friday, just in time to catch Lou at King's Cross in the early hours of Saturday morning. Still jetlagged and already bamboozled by the charred rusticity of English pub grub, they'd barely had time to sleep before being ferried to Aylesbury and wading through a scrum of glitter-cheeked micro-boppers. Inside the hall, the furnaces of mayhem were stoked by big Stuey, who showered the crowd with flyers and pinwheels. When Ziggy appeared the kids concertinaed towards the stage in an indistinguishable mass of hair and havoc. During the encore, he ripped off his jacket, tossing satin shreds into the tongue-twisting void. The Americans looked on, not entirely sure whether they'd witnessed a sleep-deprived hallucination or, as one of them would later print, 'The Elvis of the '70s'.

Outside, a crowd of stardust kids rushed Ziggy as he darted out of the stage door to his specially hired limo for the evening, a strawberry pink Rolls Royce. Stuey battered them back as arms flailed and pens waved in violent fits of futility. In the split seconds it took Ziggy to clamber inside and close the door something fleshy blurred in front of his eyes. As the car sped away, he felt wet heat somewhere in the centre of his face. His fingers dabbed the edge of his nostrils. When he pulled them away the tips were bloody. It had only been a nudge, nothing drastic. Just a little nosebleed, Angie assured him, patting his thigh, handing him a tissue and a compact mirror. But blood was blood. Ziggy had never thought of himself as somebody who bled, only somebody who shone. It felt uncomfortable. Most ungodlike. All too human.

Blood never bothered Iggy Pop. He had a reputation for lacerating his body on stage with broken glass, small but determined nicks across his torso until it wept scarlet streams like scourged Jesus. But the audience at the King's Cross Cinema didn't deserve blood. They sat and gawped and looked slightly terrified as he wandered among them, crooking his body into sexy sinew-defying shapes, topless in shiny silver trousers to match his dyed aluminium hair, make-up outlining eyes and mouth, umbilically tied to a never-ending mic cable which broke just the once prompting his spontaneous burst of the cabaret standard 'The Shadow Of Your Smile'. It impressed Johnny, a 16-year-old snaggletoothed Stooges fan from up the road in Finsbury Park, calculating generational ambush in the corner. And Ziggy, who'd been driven, bloody-nosed, straight from Aylesbury in his pink limo to catch Iggy's midnight special. Even with a broken mic, it was enough to convince Ziggy that, despite having his hands full with Mott and Lou, he'd be as well to produce Iggy's next album too. He especially liked the new song 'I'm Sick Of You', which stole the riff off one of his favourite Yardbirds singles, 'Happenings Ten Years Time Ago'. Ziggy made a mental note: next time stuck for inspiration, nick a Yardbirds' riff.

Below the stage, Mick Rock was back, aiming his camera at Iggy as he clasped his mic-stand in prayer, leaning to the right, staring a thousand yards into the distance, a thousand years into the future, an eternity of punk wisdom on his huge eyelids. Mick's camera went click. Before Ziggy had recorded a note for the album he wanted to make with Iggy, Mick already had the cover.

The American journalists had done well to survive their first thirty-six hours in London, pinballing back and forth between King's Cross and Aylesbury, being Loued, comprehensively Ziggyed and latterly Iggyed. After a welcome Sunday lie-in, they regrouped for a final press conference with Ziggy at The Dorchester, hotel of the stars, where he'd spent the weekend in a second-floor suite; the official line from DeFries was that due to his extraterrestrial fear of heights Ziggy could never be accommodated higher than the eighth storey. Mute waiters circled the room like silent phantoms bearing silver trays of cakes, sandwiches, wine, tea and whisky. A stereo played the newly finished Mott The Hoople album, *All The Young Dudes*. Lou was slumped in the corner, a pair of aviator shades masking the lunacy beneath, while Iggy goofed around in a cheap T. Rex t-shirt, his idea of a cheeky jest in the court of the king.

The king himself wore his latest Freddie creation: a white jumpsuit with rhinestones and collar, a droogy kink on the one Elvis had worn at Madison Square Garden. The Americans and a few of their British peers took turns to probe him. They asked confusing questions about who he was and where he'd come from. Ziggy answered, sometimes unsure whether he was speaking or if it was the ancient croak of David Bowie hollering to be heard through the make-up.

'Ziggy is a conglomerate. He just doesn't exist for the moment.'

Dave?

'I'm still totally involved with Ziggy. I probably will be for a few more months, getting it entirely out of my system.'

Stop, Dave.

'By the time people start realising about Ziggy I may be Tom Bloggs.'

Will you stop, Dave?

'But I'm having so much fun with Ziggy at the moment ...'

Go on ...

'... that I'm sticking with him. He's a gas to work with.'

The journalists stood up to leave. 'Goodbye, David,' said one of the Americans.

Ziggy laughed. 'Call me Ziggy!'

The struggle was finished.

'Call me Ziggy Stardust!'

He had won the victory over himself. At least for now. Over the next few weeks he made sure he stayed victorious.

'I'm very rarely David Jones any more,' he'd tell another reporter. 'I think I've forgotten who David Jones is.'

And if he ever had any doubts about who he really was or wasn't, all he need do was open the music papers and see the full-page adverts for his next London shows.

'David Bowie *is* Ziggy Stardust live at the Rainbow'.

The Rainbow was somewhere over Finsbury Park, within wailing distance of the already demolished site where the boy David Jones saw Tommy Steele play sixteen years earlier. Its stylish interior betrayed its origins as a 1930s art-deco cinema, the foyer looking like an Arabian palace with a central fountain from which a genie might spring at any moment. The stage itself was framed by an elaborate proscenium design of a magical Saharan village. The previous November, during his final throes of being Bowie, Ziggy had darkened the Rainbow's doorway when he took the Spiders to assess the competition, a beaky prankster from Detroit, born Vincent, now calling himself Alice Cooper. His act was being hyped as the most shocking on the concert stage, helped in part by a misreported incident at a gig in Toronto where he allegedly bit the head off a chicken.

It struck Ziggy as poignant that the day of his first Rainbow show, Saturday 19 August, Alice Cooper should be number one with 'School's Out'. His own 'Starman' was still falling down from its peak at ten while Mott's 'All The Young Dudes' was spiriting gently towards three. He also had the comradeship of his support band, a new quintet of super-spangly artful oddballs called Roxy Music, who saw themselves, like Ziggy, 'part of a natural reaction against the last three years of groups in Levi's and plimsolls'.

Across town, Marc Bolan had been bumping and grinding in the studio all week, recording what he hoped would be his fifth number one, 'Children Of The Revolution', his presence still felt by the cryptic ads in that day's music papers for T. Rex's new album. 'To be or not to be, that is *The Slider*.' But before the Rainbow doors had opened, the verdict among the lipsticked apostles gathering on the kerb of Seven Sisters Road was that Ziggy had already sewn up the kids' revolution and won the glam war.

'Alice Cooper's ugly, in'e?' said a girl to a newsman, mooning how Ziggy was lovely because he had 'a woman's face'. Men with shiner-thick eye-shadow and scraggy feather-boas bragged to one another how they stole their girlfriend's make-up to Ziggy themselves pretty. Young kids with wonky sequins spelling out 'ZIGGY' on their jackets wore souvenir transfers on their hands and faces; cartoons of the Spiders designed by David's best friend, George. And inside the Rainbow, a mandie-popping coterie of Lou, Iggy and his Stooges, the boys from Mott and even little

Rocket Reg, who came with high hopes only to leave early complaining 'it wasn't rock 'n' roll'.

It wasn't rock 'n' roll. Ziggy at the Rainbow was theatre. It was Broadway on a budget. It was *art*. The Spiders had spent a week of intensive rehearsals with Lindsay Kemp, David's old mime tutor who'd been coaxed back to London from Edinburgh, and a quartet of dancers Ziggy named The Astronettes. The band played under levelled scaffolding, painted silver and connected by ladders, the floor covered with a thick layer of sawdust which flared and spattered at the slightest footstep, an old mime trick to exaggerate movement. Slides were projected on a giant screen, including portraits of Ziggy, paintings by Magritte and Warhol and, for the opening 'Lady Stardust', a montage of famous faces including Elvis Presley, Little Richard and, the one image everybody would remember, Marc Bolan. Ziggy had some new clothes for the occasion, including his first kabuki-inspired costume by designer Kansai Yamamoto, a red legless 'bunny suit' decorated with drawings of woodland creatures. There were also fresh additions to the setlist: a song written by Jacques Brel, which had been stuck on the turntable of his mind for weeks: the soundtrack of his nightmares about dying on stage, his paranoia of plane crashes and the shock of bloody noses in the back of limos; a song written in French as 'La Mort', in English 'My Death'. And, conscious of time, place and occasion, during 'Starman' he broke off in the chorus to sing a few lines of Judy Garland's 'Over The Rainbow'.

Ziggy had wanted his pop mime extravaganza to leave his audience feeling their heads had been bitten off like one of Alice's poor chickens, their bodies left twitching in decapitated awe. It worked on Lou, who ran amok backstage clucking 'that was the greatest thing I've ever seen' – quite possibly because the gig ended with a nine-minute version of his own 'I'm Waiting For The Man'. But DeFries was far less enthusiastic. Like Rocket Reg, he didn't much care for the hifalutin distractions of Kemp and his bothersome Astronettes and vetoed any hope of taking the same staging out on the road. After the three Rainbow shows, to Ziggy's dismay, Kemp was given his marching orders back to Scotland, where he'd soon find himself cutting some capers as a pagan innkeeper called McGregor on the set of the film *The Wicker Man*.

In the meantime, work on Lou's album had started at Trident, prompting Ziggy to temporarily move out of Haddon Hall to a suite at the Grosvenor House Hotel, shortening the daily commute to Soho. Titled *Transformer*, it would be Lou's second solo album. The first one stank: not the songs, a lot of them golden waifs from the last days of The Velvet Underground, but the rank production and the stagnant strums of the vibeless English session musicians. Lou still had a couple of stray Velvet diamonds he wanted to record with Ziggy, including 'Satellite Of Love' and 'Andy's Chest', written after the attempt on Warhol's life by Valerie Solanas. The shadow of Andy also inspired 'Vicious', Andy's challenge to Lou to write a 'vicious song' about hitting someone with a flower, while 'Walk On The Wild Side' was an affectionate homage to the backroom freaks and Warhol superstars of Max's Kansas City. There was also the elegiac 'Perfect Day', which sounded like a waster's hymn to New York (it was actually written in Wimbledon, Lou's London base), and the Stonewall swing of 'Make Up', quoting the New York Gay Liberation Front's motto of 'Out of the closets and into the streets'.

They were already great songs, but it was Ziggy and Ronno's task to make them even greater. Ronno's strings for 'Perfect Day' purred with Viennese elegance. On 'Satellite Of Love', Ziggy's closing harmony vocals were a homesick wolf call to the stars, howling beyond the furthest reaches of the Milky Way. And 'Walk On The Wild Side' simply slid with animal grace, ironically thanks to Herbie 'Grandad' Flowers on bass and a guest saxophone solo from an uncannily familiar face. It had been over ten years since Ronnie Ross had given his last weekend lesson to the boy from Bromley called David Jones. Even if he'd remembered him, he'd never have been able to connect that boy to the red-haired, odd-eyed, pale-faced abomination of undernourishment sat behind the recording console flashing him the occasional embarrassed grin.

In early September, with 'Starman' out of the charts, Ziggy released his second single. A part of him had secretly ached at having passed 'All The Young Dudes' to Mott. But he could, at the very least, try to compensate by writing another song in homage to the bright young creatures of the Sombrero club. Maybe not as grandiose and poetic as 'Dudes' but something snappier, funnier and many beats-per-minute faster. For his own amusement he stole the hook of Marc's 'Hot Love', speeding it up on acoustic guitar so that it sounded more like Eddie Cochran. The lyrics were about a couple of Sombrero queens, one of them getting frisky with a chick on the dancefloor while trying to reassure his jealous boyfriend: 'John, I'm Only Dancing.'

The press ads featured an intense black and white portrait with Ziggy's index and middle fingers of his left hand jutting towards his lips at a tantalisingly phallic angle. Mick Rock had also made a special promo film during their run at the Rainbow featuring the dancing Astronettes and Ziggy's transformation into a space-age Jimmy Dean in his new blue bomber jacket. He'd also drawn a small anchor motif just below his left eye, inspired by the American sitcom *Bewitched*. Its lead character, a sexy suburban witch called Samantha, had an annoying cousin called Serena, both played by actress Elizabeth Montgomery. Serena distinguished herself with similar beauty marks, from lovehearts to treble clefs and, once in the episode 'Darrin On A Pedestal', an identical anchor.

Bitterly, the BBC were less than bewitched with the film and refused to show it on *Top Of The Pops*, playing the song over their own footage of a motorcycle gang. The critics weren't so keen on the single either, whether repelled by its transparent bisexual bravado or miffed he hadn't played safe with a soundalike 'Starman Part 2'. Thanks to the eager needles and glad hips of his boogie children, it sashayed to a comfortable number twelve regardless.

A small but vocal tide had nevertheless turned on Ziggy, crashing in waves of polarised opinion in the pop mags' letters pages. One week *Record Mirror*'s Val was opening the moist missive from an unnamed girl in Wiltshire who'd been an 'unconvertible' Marc fan until swapping allegiance to Ziggy. 'I listen to "Rock 'N' Roll Suicide",' she trembled, 'and bawl my eyes out.' The next, Val was drowning in the ink from poisonous pens attacking 'that gay creep', 'that freak-faced pop puff' and similar bile from regional branches of 'The David Bowie Extermination Society'. 'As a gay guy myself,' wrote one exterminator from Lincolnshire, 'I find him quite and utterly repulsive.'

Immune to such hateful slings of the biro-biting minority, Ziggy returned to the road, illuminating the early autumn gloom up north, streaking the Pennines with a densely scented fog of adolescent star lust. In Stoke, a reporter asked if Ziggy was worried his show might be too sexy. 'It is,' he shrugged. 'I can't deny that, and if I shock people then it's too bad.' Yet, as if on preordained prudent cue, right at the very moment he'd become too sexy for English shores, the stardust bugle sounded for Ziggy to desert them.

The Spiders were in Manchester, the honorary first act to open a new purpose-built concert venue called the Hardrock. The morning after the show, DeFries summoned an emergency meeting in their hotel. Not just Ziggy, Ronno, Weird and Gilly but Angie, big Stuey, hair Suzi, the Frosts and the entire tour party. He had some very important news.

'In about two weeks' time,' DeFries announced, 'everyone in this room will be in America.'

The promised land of Sal Paradise, Elvis Presley and Little Richard. The Starman and his family were going to take America and, as DeFries outlined, take it in style.

'You've all got to learn to look and act like a million dollars.'

Ziggy laughed. It was a strange thing to say to a cosmic messiah too sexy for Queen and country, second only to God. Couldn't DeFries tell? He already felt like a trillion.

SIX
THE AMERICAN

It was one of big Stuey's favourite jokes. 'A Starman that won't fly.'

Nothing could persuade Ziggy to board another aircraft. He'd had nightmares – 'premonitions' he called them – about crashing. Not through pilot error or bad weather but some freak cosmic catastrophe. He dreamed that the electromagnetic force field around the Earth was going to falter. 'So all the aircrafts in the air were just going to plummet to earth.' He didn't know when this would happen, only that it probably would, to him, within the next few years. 'If nothing happens by 1976,' he acquiesced, 'I'll start to fly again.'

Which meant Ziggy would have to travel to America by sea, a six-day Atlantic crossing from Southampton to New York aboard the luxury liner *QE2*. (He was mercifully oblivious to the small detail that five months earlier the same ship had nearly been sunk, battered by a storm of 100 m.p.h. winds and 50-foot waves.) He was joined by Angie, David's best friend George and George's wife, Brigit, but spent much of the voyage alone, too wary to mingle with the other passengers after the first night, when they'd all gone to dinner in the Columbia Restaurant only to be skewered by stares of jewellery-jangling displeasure. And so he passed the hours staring out into the infinite blue, dwelling on his past, nervous about his future, his inner transistor softly flayed by the chords of Jacques Brel's 'My Death' on permanent repeat.

DeFries had flown on ahead, preparing for Ziggy's arrival by recruiting staff for a New York branch of his newly christened management empire, MainMan. One word, two capital Ms. (Ziggy couldn't quite decide if it was hilarious, or possibly annoying, that his boss had branded their business after a phrase synonymous with his rival. Marc Bolan had already claimed it as the rhyming pay-off of 'Telegram Sam' and again as a song title, 'Main Man', on T. Rex's latest album, *The Slider*.) Tony Zee had helped find a suitable office uptown a few blocks east of Central Park and, having helped paint and decorate it, was rewarded for his toil with the title of MainMan company president. DeFries met *Pork*'s stage manager Leee Black Childers for lunch at Pete's Tavern in Gramercy Park: by the time the bill arrived, he'd made Leee MainMan vice president. The receptionist vacancy went to Leee's friend, a member of the original New York *Pork* cast who'd missed the chance to join the London production. Cyrinda Foxe was a street-sexy glamour magnet, Warhol superstar, Max's regular and transparently obvious Marilyn Monroe apostle whose previous secretarial experience involved working for an art dealer and running errands for the reclusive Greta Garbo (or 'Miss Brown' as she was instructed to call her). Cyrinda was built for many things – most of which Ziggy was about to discover – but she was no receptionist. Nor did she take kindly to DeFries' suggestion that she and the other staff should all adopt Ziggy haircuts as a badge of company loyalty. Her second day due in the office, Cyrinda never showed up. The job was eventually given to her friend, fellow *Pork* veteran and soon-to-be Stardust confidante, Cherry Vanilla.

After almost a week at sea, the *QE2* docked in New York on Sunday 17 September. DeFries had booked them into suites at the Plaza Hotel below Central Park, only a few blocks from the new MainMan offices and the same building where, eight years earlier, Stanley Kubrick first met Arthur C. Clarke to discuss what eventually became *2001: A Space Odyssey*.

Ziggy hadn't long arrived in the city when he found five kindred lonely planet spirits in the Oscar Wilde Room of the Mercer Arts Centre down in Greenwich Village. The New York Dolls were a human pile-up of hair, lipstick, guitars and chiffon chainsawing their way into rock 'n' roll history with songs about trash, smack, bad girls, jet boys, werewolves, pimps, the Vietnam war and sex with Frankenstein's monster. Ziggy loved the Dolls, especially the singer, David, and especially David's girlfriend – shortlived MainMan receptionist Cyrinda Foxe. Angie recognised the desire in Ziggy's eyes and stood aside, finding her own doll to play with in the band's drummer, Billy. Being genial hosts, after their gig the Dolls took Ziggy on a tour of their downtown Manhattan – a tour which ended only a few blocks along the Bowery when a truck driver leaned out of his cabin window and shouted at Ziggy, 'Hey, baby, I wanna eat your cunt!'

As warm-ups prior to playing New York, DeFries scheduled Ziggy's first two shows out of town, opening in Cleveland, Ohio; America's spiritual home of rock 'n' roll, where the term was first popularised by Alan Freed, the local DJ who pinched the nickname of the notorious New York street musician to call himself 'Moondog'. DeFries had dispatched Leee as an advance scout to check the venue measured up to MainMan's twelve specific demands. Cleveland's Music Hall did, bar one. The requested piano was a few inches too short. When Leee rang DeFries he was told to cancel the gig unless they sorted the piano. The venue freaked. Thanks to Leee and Cherry Vanilla stirring up local press and radio in advance, the hall had already sold out. DeFries stuck to his guns and called their bluff. At the eleventh hour, the piano was changed to one that measured to the exact height. The MainMan power play had begun.

The piano would be tinkled by a new honorary Spider called Mike Garson. Ziggy's first choice had been a psychedelic jazz priestess called Annette Peacock who'd recently released her own album on RCA featuring a woozy cover of Elvis Presley's 'Love Me Tender'. Peacock declined but recommended Garson who'd played on her album and had an instinctive ear for avant-garde jazz and all the 'wrong notes' Ziggy loved. Garson was also an ordained minister of Scientology. 'Garson The Parson'. Before the tour was over he'd convert both Gilly and bodyguard Tony Frost to a religion based upon the belief that the human race consisted of the lost spirits of aliens blown up in volcanoes seventy-five million years ago by an evil intergalactic dictator. For cosmically obvious reasons, he failed to convert Ziggy himself.

The rock 'n' roll heartland of Cleveland was an easy conquest for the Spiders, as was the next stop, Memphis, Tennessee. The King was home in Graceland that day but never came to catch a second glimpse of the Martian Mary shaking up the Ellis Auditorium he himself had blessed many times before. After the show, DeFries emptied the night's takings in cash on the hotel floor, Ziggy giggling as he kicked green dollar bills into the air like a child splashing through puddles. The truth, better known to DeFries, was that these wading riches were illusory. He'd told them back in England, they were to 'look and *act* like a million dollars'. As it stood the tour was guaranteed to make a loss. DeFries' big gamble – part genius, part maniac – was to siphon the cost from MainMan to their record label, RCA. In the absence of available cash, they would charge everything to account. If all went according to plan, when the tour finished Ziggy would be a star in America and RCA would settle the bill as a justified expense. If it failed, then MainMan was ruined. And Ziggy with it.

The million dollar act was well practised by the time they returned to New York. Ziggy was now permanently flanked by bodyguards big Stuey and Tony, both dressed ruckus-ready in matching karate suits. Yet more MainMan smoke and mirrors, as was Ziggy's 'sell-out' show at the prestigious Carnegie Hall. DeFries ensured a capacity crowd by handing out hundreds of free tickets, while simultaneously telling the press the VIP guest list was oversubscribed; just squeezed in were Truman Capote,

Psycho star Anthony Perkins and Andy Warhol who, so gossip insisted, was only allowed two places. In the cheap seats, the MainMan gang had successfully spread the word of Ziggy to shake every fashion freak in the city out of their closet in their glitteriest, featheriest, fleshiest, trashiest apparel, the Dolls and Cyrinda included, while outside the hall a giant searchlight rotated its beam directly at the stars as if to remind the jostling crowds and touts of the heavens from whence tonight's attraction fell.

Backstage, a TV news reporter asked Ziggy what he wanted his audience to think of him on stage. 'I don't want them to think anything,' he frowned. 'They're probably just as confused about my writing as I am. I mean, I'm the last one to understand most of the material I write.'

And how would he describe himself?

'Partly enigmatic,' said Ziggy, 'partly fossil.'

Fossil?

'Yes.'

That night New York clutched the enigmatic Martian fossil tight to its breast. Such was Ziggy's conquest of Carnegie Hall its impact rippled across the Atlantic, into the pages of the British press, where he was declared the winner in 'an undeclared contest' with Marc Bolan. It was all the more impressive considering Ziggy had managed the gig suffering from a mild bout of flu, sick enough to bow out of the after-party back at the Plaza and spend the next day recovering in bed, medicated by his new nursemaid Cyrinda.

Sex now rushed at Ziggy from every direction, in every audience, in every city. It was silly to deny it. Sex demanded Ziggy Stardust and he was polite enough to yield. Sex whenever, sex wherever, sex whoever, sex whatever. Sex on beds, in baths, on floors, in space. Sex with Cyrinda, with Cherry, with girls whose names he'd never remember. Sex with girls while Cyrinda or Cherry sat on a chair and watched and chatted to Ziggy to help relieve his boredom. Sex out of desire, out of habit, out of curiosity, out of gluttony. Girl sex, boy sex, chick sex, dude sex. Wet sex, dry sex, fast sex, slow sex. Private sex, standing ovation sex, stoned sex, drunk sex. Mad sex, broken sex, Spider sex, Earth sex. Mars sex, second-only-to-God sex, wham-bam-thank-you sex. Sex and sex and sex and sex. And, because he could, because he was Ziggy, still more sex.

But Cyrinda was more than sex to Ziggy. She was muse and music, rhyme and riff. She was the shimmying gangster's moll of 'Watch That Man', a song he'd just written partly inspired by his memories of her boyfriend David on stage with the Dolls, partly by the noise and excess of the Carnegie after-party. And she was the leading lady of another new tune which began on the band's tour bus to Cleveland. The Spiders had made up their own little chant – 'We're goin' bussin', bus, bus' – sung to the old blues riff of 'I'm A Man', not the steady Bo Diddley original but the brisker version as played by The Yardbirds. It reminded Ziggy of a mental note he'd made seeing Iggy in King's Cross: next time stuck for inspiration, nick a Yardbirds' riff.

And so Ziggy nicked 'I'm A Man'. He looked at Cyrinda in his Plaza bedroom and sang about Marilyn Monroe. He thought about Iggy and sang about reptiles and screaming and bawling. He thought about the French author and playwright Jean Genet and called the song 'The Jean Genie'. Before the end of the week the Spiders went into RCA's New York studio and recorded it as their next single.

Iggy soon got to hear 'The Jean Genie' for himself when the tour skidded on to Detroit. He'd flown back home to see Ziggy and play him the tapes of the album he and his Stooges had been recording in London. They'd already agreed it would be best if Ziggy stayed out of the studio and left Iggy to it. Instead, and sticking to the deal DeFries had brokered for them to get it out on CBS, Ziggy would mix the results, retaining his 'producer' credit. The album was called *Raw Power* and didn't flinch from its promise. Each song was like a stab of fiendish light, white hot with strange fears and secret corruptions. Songs that made all the more sense now Ziggy could see for himself the metropolitan human smelter

Iggy came from. Detroit was a real concrete and clay *Clockwork Orange*. The afternoon he arrived, he'd taken a walk with Stuey outside his hotel in a billowy shirt, straight into a daggered crossfire of greasy stares from local car plant workers. The sound of Iggy's album *was* Detroit.

He also had the added stress of a gatecrasher who'd first turned up in New York with a bag of cocaine telling everyone he used to go to school in Bromley with David Jones. He'd recognised Ziggy's face in the papers and flown straight from Colombia where he was now embarrassing all border controls as an international drug smuggler. He certainly looked it, carrying a gun and dressing like a South American bandit complete with Che Guevara beard. Ziggy thought he'd shaken him off only to learn he'd hired a diesel van and followed the tour to Michigan. The anxiety shook a fresh Bo Diddley rhythm in Ziggy's head. He thought about the drug smuggler from Bromley, about everything he'd seen, heard and smelled in Iggy's hometown and wrote another new song. 'Panic In Detroit'.

From the Midwest the tour dipped south, through Missouri, Kansas and Tennessee, taking a break in Nashville to lend a King's polish to 'The Jean Genie' by mixing it in the same RCA studio frequently used by Elvis. While the Spiders and crew flew or took buses, Ziggy and a small party of friends chose to travel by train. It was, undoubtedly, the best way to see the country, especially from the observation cars. In the panoramic dome of the west-bound Superchief – the aptly nicknamed 'Train of the Stars' – Ziggy would sit at nights with wine and his guitar, his muse illuminated by the light of the desert moon. He could feel America was possessing him with new purpose, new music and maybe even the flash of a new identity. One that was still fundamentally Ziggy, but stretched and star-spangled by the way-outness of the West.

By early October, as Ziggy sped by rail towards California, Marc Bolan was looking forward to leaving it. T. Rex had just ended their less than triumphant US tour at Santa Monica Civic Auditorium. In the words of the man from *Melody Maker*, Marc was 'repetitive, empty and forced' and had sadly 'deflated the illusion'. The verdict from the American press wasn't much better. Offered the taste of T. Rexstasy, the States had balked. As he boarded his return flight to London, Marc tried to console himself with the fact back home his latest single, 'Children Of The Revolution', had spent three weeks at number two while Ziggy's frisky 'John, I'm Only Dancing' was ten places behind. But he couldn't ignore the shadow of the Starman, nor would the press let him. Every interview now brought the obligatory Ziggy question. 'David doesn't really know what he is,' Marc harrumphed at home in Maida Vale. 'He steals identities.'

Five thousand miles away, the Superchief pulled into Kerouac's 'loneliest and most brutal of American cities', hissing to a halt in Los Angeles Union Station. The Californian sun burned high and bright as Ziggy Stardust stepped down on to the platform, casting a long grey shadow before him. A silhouette he alone could recognise as the queer creature he'd just invented. The stolen shadow of Aladdin Sane.

So tight was Ziggy against his rival's heels that he checked into the pink Spanish luxury of the Beverly Hills Hotel only days after Marc had checked out. Rocket Reg was also there, inviting Ziggy to his VIP bungalow for an understandably awkward cup of tea, the pregnant pauses between polite conversation and the chink of stirring spoons crackling with the unmentionable 'Space Oddity' rip-off.

The Spiders and the road crew took full advantage of Tinsel Town etiquette and the RCA charge account, drinking dry the hotel's famous Polo Lounge and baring all Humberside flesh poolside for a Californian tan. Ronno grilled himself an agonising pink, while his golden hair turned an unfortunate shade of green thanks to the pool's chlorine.

With a few days' break in the tour, Ziggy fulfilled his promise to Iggy by mixing the *Raw Power* tapes at Western Sound on Sunset Boulevard.

Time was against them, as was technology. The chunky mixing desk reminded Iggy of a 1950s sci-fi rocket ship, not that the tapes needed a lot of tinkering anyway. Ziggy did the best he could in the tight window they had, focussing most tracks around Iggy's voice but careful not to douse the heat of its Detroit fire.

While still high on the heavy fumes of *Raw Power*, Los Angeles inspired Ziggy's next song, a dirty howl of Hollywood Babylon marking the corner of Sunset and Vine only a block from the studio. Kerouac described the same spot in *On The Road*: 'Now there was a corner!' Ziggy called the song 'Cracked Actor'.

DeFries had since packed Angie back home to London. Despite their polygamous wedding vows she'd still managed to upset her husband after frolicking in a motel pool with a hunky Jamaican bodyguard called Anton. With his wife temporarily banished, Ziggy took advantage by flying Cyrinda over to LA from New York. No sooner had she landed when she took him to pick up strays of both sexes at the nearby Rainbow Bar & Grill. Other nights they'd hit the E Club, a former massage parlour relaunched as a disco meatrack of underage anglophile dreamers and rapacious groupies hoping to bed themselves a visiting English rock 'n' roll star. Failing that, a Martian one.

The E Club was the brainchild of publicist and DJ Rodney Bingenheimer, the laughing gnome of West Coast glitter rock christened the 'Mayor of Sunset Strip'. Fate had already selected Rodney as the first human being to hear the words 'Ziggy Stardust' from the mouth of David Bowie when he stepped off a plane in the city eighteen months earlier. Rodney was now a devout Stardust apostle and, through his influence, LA was feverish with expectation for Ziggy's first shows in the city. The Spiders played two sell-out nights at the Santa Monica Civic Auditorium, the very stage where Marc Bolan had been defeated six nights earlier. The *Los Angeles Times* declared Ziggy 'a sort of male Judy Garland of the 1970s', a symbolic welcome home to his rainbow's end in the very city where Garland first sang her song of way up high on an MGM soundstage.

Following the beat of Kerouac, Ziggy moved on to San Francisco. Still entwined with Cyrinda, they'd merged into a frazzled fifties rock 'n' roll Romeo and Juliet. Jimmy Dean from Mars and Marilyn from Venus. Photographer Mick Rock had taken some portraits of them at the Rainbow bar in LA, a sort of glam-punk homage to Edward Hopper's *Nighthawks* as a basis for press ads for 'The Jean Genie'. In Cisco, Mick made an accompanying promo film, Jimmy and Marilyn a pair of hot tramps in blue and yellow windcheaters with furry collars, strutting and rutting on the street outside the Mars Hotel, another favourite haunt of Kerouac's.

Their last night in the city was the last night they'd spend together. Cyrinda took a bath in a Lady Godiva wig and a string of pearls. She'd heard an old wives' tale of how to keep pearls shiny and asked Ziggy to oblige, which he did. The next day Ziggy sped on to Seattle while Cyrinda returned to New York, oblivious to the biological chain reaction deep within her womb.

From Seattle, Ziggy took an overnight train to Phoenix, Arizona, the new muse of Aladdin Sane inflamed by the glimmer of a dozen or more giant silvery domes moonlit in the middle of an otherwise barren desert. They looked futuristic and slightly sinister. The dormant synapses of the boy David Jones sparked with forgotten fears of the domed alien silo at Winnerden Flats in *Quatermass II*. Ziggy wondered if maybe this was what cities would look like after a nuclear holocaust: a planet beyond 'Five Years'; a cancerous terrain of fall-out forcing any survivors to live imprisoned in enormous, isolated bubble colonies; a world where radiation has so perverted human reproduction people have to watch films to remember how to make love, guided by the ancient god called Mick Jagger. By the time he got to Phoenix, Ziggy had another new song called 'Drive-In Saturday'.

The Phoenix show was pitifully under-attended. Afterwards, Ziggy numbed his dismay with alcohol. He wept, he screamed, he scratched, he thrashed and moaned himself unconscious convoluted in the rubbish of his bleakest nightmares. And when he woke up the next morning with his brain tight and putrid like a cold, dark blob of melted plastic welded to the inside of his skull, he looked in the mirror and saw that he only had one eyebrow.

Ziggy squinted at the face. It now looked like two halves of two different faces, the expressive and the expressionless, as if soldered together by an invisible lightning flash from his left temple down to his right chin. He found the guilty razor on the edge of the sink, its shiny blade silently chuckling at his headache. In a few delicate strokes he evened the picture. The chalky, sun-shy albino visage ogling back at him looked more unearthly than ever. His trembling fingers stroked the hairless ridges. It was like a painting by Edvard Munch cursed to life, blinking back at him.

'What's it going to be then, eh?'

A face he knew as that of Aladdin Sane.

While Ziggy was adjusting to life without eyebrows in the mental ache and physical shake of an Arizonan hangover, five thousand miles away his friends The New York Dolls were adjusting to the impulse to murder Lou Reed.

The Dolls' world had changed dramatically in the few weeks since they'd dragged Ziggy round the Bowery. Still unsigned, after exciting UK press interest they'd been invited over for a handful of shows in England, hoping to grab a record deal while they were there. One of those shows was support to Lou at the Liverpool Stadium, or it would have been had Lou not sent a flunky to their dressing room moments before they were due on stage. Justifiably fearing they may blow him out of the water, Lou played his bitchy ace and sent word they weren't going on. The Dolls were furious but, sadly, powerless.

With a few days to kill before their next date supporting Roxy Music in Manchester they returned to their hotel in London. On the evening of Tuesday 7 November, drummer Billy Murcia was invited to a party by a girl he'd met in a nightclub the week before. The others were too whacked to join him. And so Billy went alone to the flat only a few minutes' walk down from Imperial College on the junction with Exhibition and Cromwell Road. The same flat where he took too many Quaaludes and drank too much red wine and eventually passed out. The hosts panicked, trying to wake him in a cold bath while forcing hot coffee down his throat. Billy Doll choked to death on his own regurgitations, his spirit slipping away into the sacred South Kensington ether of H. G. Wells, Gustav Holst, dinosaur bones, meteorites and the Victoria and Albert Museum. The Dolls had flown to London as five. They'd return to New York as four.

Over in Maida Vale, Marc Bolan was also in mourning. Not for Billy Doll, but for Boink, his pet mouse. He'd returned from his disappointing tour of America and all its attendant lukewarm press to find Boink seriously ill. He'd tried calling a vet to come for a home visit but none would help. Until Marc awoke one morning to find Boink lying stiff on his back with his legs sticking up, a tiny trace of blood around his white furry mouth. He buried him in his back garden.

Marc's grief for Boink still did nothing to temper his ego in the press. Asked his thoughts on David Cassidy: 'I prefer Hopalong. He turns me on far more.'

And Ziggy?

'He's still very much a one-hit wonder I'm afraid.'

Back in America, the alleged one-hit wonder was learning about fear: staring death in the face on the streets of Houston, Texas, when a truck driver stuck a shotgun out of the window of his vehicle. 'If it wasn't against the law,' he spat at Ziggy, 'I'd blow your fucking head off.'

It reignited all the old horrors about being murdered on stage. Death now waited in the wings of every destination, looming like Father Time on the clock outside Mercury's offices in Chicago, its scythe ready to swipe as soon as the last grains trickled through the hourglass. The news about Billy Doll only amplified his fears. When he reached New Orleans, Ziggy turned his morbidity into melody and finished another new song. He called it 'Time'.

He could still just about suppress his anxiety on stage, converting, perverting and teaching the lost boys and girls of Nixon's America his masonic Stardust rituals: the way he'd turn his hands upside down like goggles over his face to create a mask, or wave his fingers on his head like 'a cow' during the line in 'Life On Mars?'. The older, been-round-the-blockers like Christine, the 21-year-old cat-faced girl there to see Ziggy's return to Cleveland in late November, also noted the in-joke of his latest Freddie spacesuit covered with random tartan number patches, a deliberate '69' slapbang over the crotch.

The familiar faces of Mott The Hoople were waiting to meet Ziggy at the tour's end in Philadelphia, where they were booked to play the same venue the night before. After hiring a cab for the three-hundred-mile journey from his penultimate stop in Pittsburgh, Ziggy arrived just in time to join them on stage at the Tower Theatre for an encore of 'All The Young Dudes'. Ian Hunter couldn't help but fret about Ziggy. Ghostly thin, underfed and shorn of eyebrows, he was more apparition than artist. And even though he laughed and smiled there was a private glint of sadness glowing dimly in his strange, dissimilar eyes.

The real sadness was all that Ziggy had seen in the three months he'd scoured this vast, hectic, ridiculous, contradictory, insane nation. Back in New York, he held a farewell press conference. 'I feel the American is the loneliest person in the world,' he surmised. 'I get an awful feeling of insecurity and a need for warmth in people here. It's very, very sad.'

It seemed an appropriate frame of mind to revisit the isolation of Major Tom. On his last day before heading home to England, by request of RCA America, Ziggy filmed a new promo for 'Space Oddity' with Mick Rock, sat strumming an acoustic guitar alone in a recording studio, his face devoid of emotion, looking as if he really were many thousand light years from home.

In early December, Ziggy boarded the luxury liner R.H.M.S. *Ellinis* ('Greek Lady') for the week-long voyage home. His American odyssey had so far given him six new songs. 'Watch That Man', 'The Jean Genie', 'Panic In Detroit', 'Cracked Actor', 'Drive-In Saturday' and 'Time'. The return passage would give him a sublime seventh.

Ziggy had with him his guitar and a copy of *Vile Bodies*, Evelyn Waugh's satire about the rich and idle 'Bright Young People' caught between the wars in late-twenties London. He thought about Waugh's battle cries, champagne and the suicide of the novel's gossip columnist 'Chatterbox'. He thought about the First World War, and the Second, which David's parents had survived, and the possible third he believed could happen at any point in the next five years. He looked through his porthole at the endless icy grave of the Atlantic Ocean. He called the song 'Aladdin Sane (1913–1938–197?)'.

And so Ziggy sailed back towards England, in mourning for America, lost in chords and choruses of dead roses, sad remains and a sliver of himself called Aladdin Sane. Unaware that as New York vanished into the mist, somewhere in its overpopulated human zoo his old flame Cyrinda Foxe had just aborted the child of her union with the one they called the Starman.

SEVEN
THE BREAK

Mott The Hoople had only been away for a month but to Ian Hunter it had felt like years. He returned from America on Christmas Eve, looking forward to a quiet week of well-earned festive sloth with his wife at their Northampton home. The comfort and joy of food, drink, *The Morecambe & Wise Show* and taking the piss out of Little Jimmy Osmond on *Top Of The Pops* as he yelped through that year's Yuletide number one 'Long Haired Lover From Liverpool'. Peace on Earth. Pa-rup-up-um-pum. Until Boxing Day, when the phone rang.

Hunter answered, thinking it might be family. It wasn't. It was Ziggy calling from Haddon Hall. He was abnormally excited, his tone twitchy, his words rushed. He had things he needed to tell Hunter. 'Important' things. 'Great' things. 'Big' things for Mott The Hoople in 1973. 'Urgent' things he needed to tell Hunter in person.

There were times during the two-hour drive on a bitter Boxing Day's evening from Northampton down to Beckenham that Hunter wondered why he'd said 'yes'. They'd seen each other only a couple of weeks ago in America. Ziggy had played Hunter a new song called 'Drive-In Saturday' which he thought Mott should record. Hunter wasn't so keen and, now he thought about it, maybe this whole emergency meeting was a ruse to try to force him to reconsider.

But then again it *was* Ziggy. Nine months ago Mott almost broke up. It was Ziggy who had saved them and, thanks to 'All The Young Dudes', practically *made* them. If anyone was worth the bother of driving eighty miles on Boxing Day, it was their starry saviour.

Southend Road was empty when Hunter finally parked the car outside Haddon Hall; too cold and too late for the otherwise regular clumps of swooning Ziggyites patiently hovering along the street, hiding in the bushes opposite for a glimpse of their god, some like twelve-year-old George from Woolwich plucking up the nerve to waltz over and ring flat seven's doorbell in the hope of having his day made by being told to 'fuck off!' by Angie through the window.

The muted scene which greeted Hunter once Angie beckoned him inside wasn't the welcome he'd been expecting. There was Ziggy in the corner of the sofa, a recoiling imp much too preoccupied with pulling stupid faces at Hunter from behind a cushion to volunteer anything so civilised as 'hello'. Freddie lay beside him, giggling numbly. Maybe he was too sober and they were too stoned but Hunter could sense a pin-pricking awkwardness. He waited to hear about the important things, the great things, the big things. Ziggy fondled his cushion, jaws locked half-open in his broken-zipped grin like the dummy of a drunk ventriloquist, eyes twitching like newts in a jam jar begging for release. Then he excused himself to go to the bathroom. He returned in the short flush of a toilet chain, speaking in a funny voice. A minute passed and he went back to the bathroom. He returned again speaking in a different, equally funny voice. And so it continued.

Hunter had been genuinely concerned about Ziggy when they'd met in America and seen the poor, atomic husk he'd become. Now he wished he hadn't bothered. It was like Hunter didn't know Ziggy any more. At least not this pain-in-the-arse manifestation. Maybe because Ziggy no longer knew himself.

'What's it going to be then, eh?'

He was stood in the bathroom: Hunter had made his excuses and left, driving away not only from Haddon Hall but from the orbit of the Starman for ever. He looked at the being before him. The head of red hair, the bleached, eyebrow-less expression. He was Ziggy Stardust. He was Aladdin Sane. But he was still David Bowie.

And he was still David Jones, son of John Jones of Dr Barnardo's. Just before Christmas he'd played two homecoming shows back at the Rainbow in Finsbury Park. The posters instructed fans to 'Please bring a toy with you – it will be given to a children's home'. He ended up sending Barnardo's a whole truckload. It was Ziggy playing at being Father Christmas only to discover he was just a chip off Father Jones.

Marc Bolan was right when he'd said he didn't know who he was. It was true. He did steal identities. One year ago he'd stood before this same mirror and told himself he was going to be Ziggy Stardust. He wondered what he would have said had he been able to look into the future and see himself today, his grand mission of 1972 accomplished. And what would he be able to see another year from now? Ziggy Stardust? Aladdin Sane? Or some other Starman? He shut his eyes and rubbed his temples as if trying to tune the transistor of his mind and find the future frequency of 1974. But there was nothing. Silence. Emptiness. Deadness.

He opened his eyes and looked into those of the sad, scared reflection staring back at him. A cold breeze blew the shutters at the back of his mind and a lonely guitar strummed the opening chord of a song he recognised as 'My Death'.

Two days after burning his bridges with Mott, the Spiders were in Manchester to play their last concerts of 1972, back at the Hardrock. On the first night, Ziggy began the set, for a change, sat behind a Moog synthesizer, his fingers tapping out the melody of Beethoven's 'Ode To Joy'. Stood in the crowd of lipsticked lurex lookalikes was a thirteen-year-old peculiarity with a determined chin called Steven, who lived within walking distance of the venue just a few streets away in Stretford; the loneliest of lonely planet boys who took from Ziggy the guts to one day illuminate the drabness of a dole age to come.

While up north, Ziggy held an end of year press conference to announce the title of his next album, *Love Aladdin Vein*. It was probably a bit too druggy, a bit too obvious and a bit too Lou but, as he'd said before, 'I'm just a Photostat machine. I just put out what has already been fed in.' And just in case Britain had forgotten in his absence that he was the one, true cosmic messiah, he chose the moment to remind them. 'Space travel is on my mind,' said Ziggy, cold and matter-of-factly. 'Because it is necessary for our own survival that we build a bridge between us and the peoples not of our universe.'

While Ziggy was in Manchester talking to the stars, Marc Bolan spent the last days of 1972 brooding on the ground beneath his feet. He'd given one of his last interviews of the year to *Mirabelle*, who'd asked his plans for old age. 'I just can't imagine myself as being old,' he admitted. 'I feel that I shall be gone before I ever reach that stage.'

Of more immediate worry to Marc was the critical bludgeoning of *Born To Boogie*, the T. Rex documentary he'd made with Ringo Starr, released in cinemas just before Christmas and dismissed by the press as a failed vanity project. Now there were rumours of a T. Rex cartoon series (Ziggy had been considering a similar idea based on drawings by David's best friend George but, ever several leaps ahead, had already abandoned the idea). One year on, Marc's fabled 'cosmic messiah' film had still to materialise but occasionally crept back into conversation between his separate delight at being asked to write a script for Federico Fellini. Which was news to everyone, especially Federico Fellini.

The undiscussable reality was that six months ago he'd been UK pop's number one 'Metal Guru', but now his glimmer was starting to rust. T. Rex's latest single, the hi-speed faceslapper 'Solid Gold Easy Action', ended the year at number three, unable to smack higher than Chuck Berry singing about his penis, and the nine-year-old Osmond child. No more the main man, Marc's only consolation, if any, was that he could still outsell Ziggy, lagging behind at sixteen with 'The Jean Genie'.

So the planet spun, and clocks struck, and corks popped, and Sunday night became Monday morning and 1972 irreversibly slid into 1973. In the first week of January, T. Rex had risen to two. Marc had slain Chuck and his 'Ding-A-Ling' but resilient 'Little' Jimmy was still invincible. The following week, T. Rex fell back to three again and with it the unthinkable pop ignominy he'd always dreaded came to pass. 'The Jean Genie' glided to two. Ziggy had physically knocked Marc off his lofty pop perch.

Marc had only himself to blame. He'd made the fatal error of going on holiday, spending early January on a beach in Barbados with his wife while Ziggy reaped the dividends on the road in Scotland and the north, canvassing for chart glory, wrapping his arms around the glam-greedy kids of Glasgow and Preston, swooping them towards his chest like a card shark embracing his winnings from the centre of the poker table.

'The Jean Genie' had also returned the Spiders to the studios of *Top Of The Pops*, playing the song live to show off the tour-tightened might of Ronno, Weird and Gilly, blasting every BBC audio metre trembling into the red. This time Ziggy was no benign colourful Starman but a silvery, skeletal, auburn vampire, a solitary earring swinging dramatically before his jugular, eyes electric with sex, bony fingers cupping a harmonica which grunted along to its rhythm in punchy, metallic gasps. Between those gasps he blew a kiss back through history with the steely wail of 'Love Me Do', The Beatles' debut single which had reached its peak of number 17 exactly ten years ago that month in January 1963. A marker of how far he, and pop, had come. From always be true and someone to love to strung out on lasers and slash-back blazers. From the boy in Bromley Technical College to the alien sex monster on *Top Of The Pops*.

Ziggy still couldn't quite reach number one, despite the best efforts of *Melody Maker* to cook the books of their own singles rundown and leapfrog 'The Jean Genie' over the otherwise unshiftable Osmond child. The easily amused would also note the irony that a few weeks later glam pick 'n' mixers The Sweet would top the chart with 'Blockbuster', their own sherbet-dip-dabbing of the same Yardbirds/Bo Diddley riff. But by then Ziggy's mind was elsewhere, speeding far over heroic new horizons, giddy on the scent of his next epic as he applied its final varnish back at Trident.

The short-lived *Love Aladdin Vein* became the simpler *Aladdin Sane*, its vertebrae born of the seven songs he'd written in America. To those he added a ballad he'd finished on his return, the *femme-fatal*istic beauty 'Lady Grinning Soul', and a cover of The Rolling Stones' 1967 hit 'Let's Spend The Night Together', a song the Spiders had just added to their live set, chopped up by Ziggy with broken bits of The Shangri-Las' 'Dressed In Black' and some symbolic old in-out from Ronno. He also resuscitated 'The Prettiest Star', David's flop follow-up to 'Space Oddity' as sabotaged by Marc, now polished into a fresh diamond of interstellar doo-wop. There was also another crack at 'John, I'm Only Dancing', louder, sassier and with extra saxophone, sadly cursed never to make the final running order. Other casualties were the half-finished 'Zion', a shapeshifting epic of soft atmospheric piano and juggernaut punk, and a stab at something called '1984'. The latter was a troublesome cuckoo in the nest. Even though Ziggy had written it, it felt foreign, like it didn't fully belong to him but to somebody else with designs on a future musical of George Orwell's *Nineteen Eighty-Four*. And so he brushed the song aside, his muse knocked askew, quietly praying that would be the last anybody would ever hear of it.

At least he knew, absolutely, that *Aladdin Sane* was a better album than *The Rise And Fall Of Ziggy Stardust And The Spiders From Mars*. As a rock 'n' roll record it was less polished, but better informed. It was blacker, more truthful, more out there, more musically interesting, especially the title track with Garson The Parson's spastic piano and Ziggy's fame-hungry croon from The Cookies' 'On Broadway'. It was a sound to match the album cover, photographed by a man named Duffy and overseen by the Picasso of panstick, French make-up artist Pierre La Roche. The head and shoulders of Ziggy, eyes closed, snow-white face coruscated by a red and blue lightning bolt, water droplets reflecting in the grooves of his collarbone like a wet statue cleansed by an eternity of acid rains, waiting to be worshipped in a far flung altar at the other end of the universe.

The world was given its first proper glimpse of Aladdin Sane on Saturday 20 January when Ziggy appeared as a guest on a special 'Pop' edition of ITV's evening chatshow *Russell Harty Plus*. With 'The Jean Genie' still grating against 'Blockbuster' in the top three that week, Ziggy bravely used the opportunity to unveil his next single, the one Mott had turned down, 'Drive-In Saturday'. Harty, the show's buttery host who hadn't quite shaken the airs of his previous job as a Yorkshire drama teacher, described Ziggy's physical appearance as 'incredible', that of a sci-fi teddy boy in silver tie, fibreglass platform heels and still with the solitary earring bouncing like a chandelier in an earthquake.

Ziggy may have looked 'incredible' but underneath he was anxious, not about singing but about his first sit-down television interview. Anxious about exposing himself as anyone other than Ziggy Stardust.

His favourite reporter from the *NME*, Charlie Shaar Murray, was shadowing him that day, offering him some valuable off-camera interview practice in the cafeteria of Harty's South Bank studios. Ziggy tried his best to explain Aladdin Sane, who wasn't really a character but an ephemeral 'situation'.

Charlie tried to nail Ziggy down on what it meant to be Ziggy, telling him that most of the letters the *NME* received believed Ziggy to be more important than his creator, David Bowie.

'Yes,' smiled Ziggy. 'They're probably right.'

A pause for thought.

'I don't think David Bowie at all important.'

Russell Harty thought he knew all there was to know about interviewing pop stars. Their evasive tricks and turns, their eely manoeuvres, the way they'd play to the gallery with a cocky quip and a cheeky pout to elicit shrieks of delight from the fawning fans who'd hijacked that week's audience. He'd already gone rounds with Marc Bolan the previous year, softly poking him about money, privilege and his 'carefully constructed image'. Marc was disarmingly straightforward, ending their chat admitting he didn't think he'd live to see the age of 50. Harty had dredged the psychological depths of Marc Bolan, and now he intended to trawl the bottom of Ziggy Stardust.

'You have a strange face,' said Harty.

'Yes, I do,' said Ziggy.

The audience laughed.

'Were you a nobody who suddenly thought, "Jesus, I must get into the scene by some other way?"'

'I never asked Jesus for a thing. It's always on my own initiative.'

More laughter.

'Could you draw the outline of your personality?'

'Well, um, I find that I'm a person who can take on the guises of different people that I meet. I can switch accents in seconds of meeting somebody and I can adopt their accent. I've always found that I collect. I'm a collector. And I've always just seemed to collect personalities.'

Puzzlement.

'Do you believe in God?'

'I believe in an energy form but I wouldn't like to put a name to it.'

A gripping hush.

'Do you indulge in any form of worship?'

'Uh,' Ziggy hesitated. 'Life. I love life very much indeed.'

And so they chatted on, about 'magnificent' groupies, Ziggy's 'heavy duty' fan letters and his stockings from Woolworths, Harty forever sloshing in the murk, trying to snag the truth of the Starman, his inquisition slowly sinking in vain.

The programme closed with a second song from Ziggy, alone with his acoustic guitar. It was a song he'd been singing in concert for months, now poisoning his every waking hour, the dawn chorus to his first eyelid's opening, the housewives' favourite every time he looked in the bathroom mirror, and the knee-buckling swansong to the closing curtain of sleep. When Marc had been Harty's guest he'd only spoken about death. Now Ziggy chose to sing it.

'My death waits ...'

Television sets hummed in late-night living rooms around the country to the sound of a voice which only minutes earlier had claimed it loved life, now wailing to its grave in the pallbearing shadow of Jacques Brel.

Just approaching twenty-five minutes to midnight, the end credits of *Russell Harty Plus* rolled over a close-up of Ziggy's ghoulish face as he flayed his guitar with such force a string snapped, whipping loose like a severed tendon.

Ba-doing!

He finished the song a cappella. The audience broke out in applause. He nodded graciously.

Then he looked down at the broken string, twinkling like thin silver rope under the studio lights, and pictured his limp body dangling at the end of it.

EIGHT
THE FRENZY

He could hear voices. Panicking voices. He could feel the heat and the breath and the hands of what felt like several people carrying the weight of his sparrow-like body. His eyes were closed, his head a deadweight lolling around his neck like a grapefruit in a stocking. He tried to open his eyelids, the serene blackness momentarily slit by a volcanic white light before they squinted shut again. His body bumped softly as the hands carried him forward. The voices now echoing, growing softer.

'Is he OK? What happened?'

In his head, a symphony of happy oblivion.

'Is he all right?'

Yes, he was all right. If this was what it felt like to be dead then he was definitely all right. Darkness, silence and absolute peace. He could feel the muscles in his face flex a smile. Jacques Brel was singing him to sleep. *'Think of that, and the passing time.'*

And so he slept and he dreamed about the passing of time.

He dreamed about a ship. A ship somewhere in the midst of the North Atlantic. The picture became sharper and he could see the name of the ship, the SS *Canberra*, and two men sat by a dancefloor watching couples shunt around in foxtrots. A familiar thin figure with bright red hair he recognised as himself. The other, his friend with dark curls, he knew to be called Geoff, a boyhood chum of David Jones from Bromley. They were drinking and joking about tea, cakes, portside chills and starboard boredom. They were Ziggy and Geoff but they chatted in silly voices pretending to be Oscar Wilde and his lover 'Bosie', the scene fading to the sound of that rare laughter which only exists between best friends.

A voice whispered what sounded like, 'David?'

He ignored it and dreamed instead of a club. One of those Greenwich Village jazz heavens he'd read about in Kerouac books. The kind where Sal, Dean and all the other children of the American bop night would flock to cry wild and dizzy prayers to the holy beat, except that this night he was the one doing the praying to the black god called Charles Mingus, the one who'd taught him the sermon of 'Wham Bam Thank You Ma'am' all those years ago. He listened, and he dug and he twitched his feet both for his own sake and for his brother, Terry. It had been a long time since he'd thought about Terry. The music pinged and skitted in crooked off-roads and sudden detours. If only he could have dreamed Terry there beside him. The sadness grew. The night bopped. The scene faded.

'David?'

Don't wake up. Keep dreaming. About a theatre. A lavish art-deco theatre with ceiling curves which arced outwards in concentric splendour like the rays of a setting sun. A stage at the centre of the sun where many thousand faces were already staring. The tremble of Beethoven's 'Ode To Joy' and feeling himself lowered down from a great height. Screams and light-bulb flashes. Singing songs people hadn't heard yet and hearing cries of, 'When's this album comin' out?' Costume changes, noise and hysteria. Hearing a thousand voices sing along with him, '*You're a rock 'n' roll suicide.*' Feeling like he actually was the centre of the sun, the body of a star, lighting the void. '*Gimme your hands!*' Seeing hands upon hands upon hands, twitching rockets aching to launch themselves from their crying owners' wrists, every straining finger an ode to the unreachable joy of his own fevered grasp. Then a body. A blur rising up from the roaring sea of flesh, now running towards him. Then terror. The shape coming closer. Then weakness. Then screaming. Then nothing.

'He's coming round.'

He slowly opened his eyes. Figures distorted by the light, their faces slowly coming into focus. A cup of water was pushed in front of his face. He said, 'I'm OK.' He raised his body up from where it had been lying down. He was in a dressing room. He could see a rail of brightly coloured clothes, a spectrum of sequins, and on the far wall a giant vanity mirror in which a head now bobbed into view with a vibrant red plume of hair and a gold circle gleaming like a lighthouse on its forehead. It was then he realised he wasn't dreaming any more and his heart sank. He was still alive. He was still *him* in the mirror.

He was still Ziggy Stardust.

There were those who thought it was all a publicity stunt. Ziggy Stardust's return to New York to play two nights at the world famous Radio City Music Hall. A star-studded guest list including his friend Bette Midler, Jacques Brel's English translator Rod McKuen (the man who turned 'La Mort' into 'My Death') and the great Salvador Dali, surrealist painter and co-creator of one of Ziggy's favourite films, *Un Chien Andalou*. The first night, Valentine's Day, fans clutching bouquets of flowers and scattering cards which read, 'We love you madly.' Ziggy making his entrance lowered from the rafters in a silver gyroscope, a prop borrowed from the venue's house dance troupe the Rockettes. And then in the final song, 'Rock 'N' Roll Suicide', a boy invading the stage, pelting towards him for an embrace, only for Ziggy to suddenly collapse to the floor as if he'd just been shot. Some of the crowd even swore they heard gunfire.

It wasn't the boy's fault. He wasn't to know that Ziggy was still convinced he was going to be killed on stage, just as Ziggy wasn't to know the boy wasn't running towards him with a loaded .38-calibre pistol.

But he'd freaked and, right on cue with Ronno's guillotine crescendo, he'd fainted in front of Dali, McKuen, Midler and some five thousand others. As *Sounds* reported back in England, 'The gig could realistically be described as the night that Ziggy Stardust died.'

The official explanation given to the press by DeFries was 'lack of eating and sleeping'. There was some truth in this. Ziggy had been back in America nearly two weeks, sailing over from England on the SS *Canberra* accompanied by Geoff MacCormack, David's other best friend, who'd just joined the tour as a backing singer and percussionist. He'd been rehearsing intensely since he landed, long hours followed by longer nights going to watch Charles Mingus play the Village Gate down on Bleecker, or his friends the New York Dolls with their new drummer Jerry way uptown at Kenny's Castaways.

He'd also fallen for another New York doll, a 19-year-old model named Bebe Buell, part of the Max's backroom set along with his old flame Cyrinda Foxe. Ziggy invited Buell to his suite at the Gramercy Park Hotel; as she'd later recall he was 'the first man who ever painted my toenails for me'. And when not swooning to the chimes of Buell, he was picking out pits with Ava Cherry, a gorgeous black singer with cropped dyed peroxide hair whom he'd met at an after-party for Stevie Wonder.

Four months earlier he'd played New York as a hyped nobody pretending to be somebody. Now he'd returned a somebody who needed hype from nobody. Aladdin Sane had come home to America, this time not intent on another epic Kerouacesque odyssey but a short lap of honour: starting in New York with a handful of stops westwards before ending in Los Angeles. Demand for tickets was so high that in Philadelphia Ziggy began playing two shows a day, matinée and evening. He slayed the audience in Nashville, and again levelled Memphis in the absence of its King. (The night Ziggy returned to the city's Ellis Auditorium, Elvis was in Las Vegas where, a week earlier, he'd karate-chopped an over-enthusiastic fan who clambered on stage: paranoid over previous death threats, Elvis automatically assumed the boy to be a potential assassin running towards him with a .38-calibre pistol.)

In Detroit, Ziggy's stage antics whistled life-changing rapture between the gap in the teeth of a 15-year-old girl wearing platform boots and a long silver cape, who savoured every sequin knowing tomorrow she'd be grounded for going against the wishes of her Italian father, Mr Ciccone.

In Los Angeles, Ziggy returned to the Rainbow Bar & Grill where Stuey earned his wage protecting him from a dumb punk who tried to swing a punch on the dancefloor. He quickened fifteen thousand pulses at the city's Long Beach Arena, including Mick Jagger's, and later dined with Marc's favourite Beatle and T. Rex film director, Ringo Starr. And he hit high notes with teenage foxtrel Lori Mattix who told her friends at groupie bible *Star* magazine that, even off stage, 'David likes to be called Ziggy' and that he loved 'like Rudolph Valentino'. Cherry sex. Mattix sex. Insert-name-here sex. The permutations were endless.

Every night on stage, as he'd done for the past year, Ziggy sang about making love with his own ego. The reality was he didn't need to now he had America to love it for him. The face in the mirror with the gold circle on the forehead – a new addition to the Ziggy mask, the dark and ancient echo of Calvin Lee's 'love jewels' – was that of pop's true cosmic messiah made flesh, or more accurately bone.

Half a world away, pop's former cosmic messiah made flesh, or more increasingly flab, was slipping further from grace down sad slopes greased with champagne, cocaine and silent panic that his teenage squeaks were growing fainter. Marc's new T. Rex single, '20th Century Boy', was a pristine rock 'n' roll depth-charge of galaxy-shaking proportions but, outrageously, couldn't storm higher than number three, stalled by Donny Osmond and the triumphant super-yobbery of Slade, an unstoppable force of Midlands bovver-glam enjoying their fourth number one with 'Cum On Feel The Noize'. All pop statistics concurred the metal guru of '72 had since been toppled. By the Cassidy and the Osmond, by Slade and most savagely of all by the Starman.

In a frantic appeal to the last pockets of T. Rexstasy, he began peddling his body, offering *Mirabelle* readers the chance to 'win tea with Marc Bolan' and, weeks later, a used blouse. But Marc could offer the kids every thread of satin 'n' tat in his wardrobe and still never fill the postbags of the pop press with the weight of letters from Ziggy's weeping altar maidens scribbling in the sticks declaring him 'the core' of their universe. 'Hero from the stars, all I ever ask is to touch you.'

And so Marc stuck his Moët fingers in his Chandon ears and pretended it wasn't happening. Pretended that he was fine, he was cool and Ziggy wasn't, because, as he'd candidly tell interviewers, he knew the psychological chink in his rival's armour. Ziggy was 'afraid', sniffed Bolan. 'Afraid that he will die before he has a chance to make a real strong contribution.'

Ziggy Stardust had, by now, been singing his life story every night on stage for over a year. His apostles could recite every syllable of its scripture by heart. The living legend of a man who came from Mars and changed the lives of all who listened; who was worshipped as their cosmic messiah until he became so big they were forced to destroy him; who was ripped to death while showing no defence or resistance: an act of wilful suicide. There lay the ballad of Ziggy Stardust. And so too the identical tale of Valentine Michael Smith.

It had taken Robert A. Heinlein over a decade to finish the novel he'd envisaged as *A Man Named Smith*. He'd already established a reputation in the early-fifties writing sci-fi novels aimed at young adults, including one called *The Rolling Stones* and another called *Starman Jones*; he'd also written a novella imagining a future lunar expedition called *The Man Who Sold The Moon*. But Heinlein's baby was the '*Smith*' book ('My sex and Jesus book,' as he'd sometimes call it) first published in 1961 under its final biblical title *Stranger In A Strange Land*.

Heinlein's was the messianic parable of Valentine Michael Smith, the only survivor of Earth's first human expedition to Mars, where he'd been born to human parents who died, leaving him to be fostered by the wise Martian race of 'Old Ones'. When Earth sends a second expedition to Mars they discover Smith, the red planet's last surviving human, and bring him back to America. As Heinlein describes him, Smith is 'a slender young man with underdeveloped muscles … his most marked feature was his bland, babyish face – set with eyes which would have seemed at home in a man of ninety.' It becomes immediately obvious that Smith is not like other men, blessed with superhuman strength, telekinetic powers and a benign hippy philosophy of universal brotherhood and free love. With the help of an elderly lawyer Smith evades the government authorities hoping to contain him and starts a radical new church based upon sacred Martian teachings. Once his work on Earth is finished he allows himself to die at the hands of an opposing religious lynch mob. His final words as they hack him to pieces are a forgiving, 'I love you.'

Published to an initially lukewarm reception, it wasn't until the late-sixties that *Stranger In A Strange Land* became a word-of-mouth cult classic seemingly tailor-made for the times as a flower power sci-fi gospel. Heinlein's story also pre-empted other 'sympathetic alien' novels, including 1963's *The Man Who Fell To Earth* by Walter Tevis, the brutally sad fable of a despairing extraterrestrial who comes to our planet on a hazardous mission to save his own only to be physically and mentally destroyed by human vice and idiocy. Both were, to various degrees, vanguards for Ziggy Stardust. But it was *Stranger* which resonated the loudest: the script for an unscored opera with aria-sized gaps the shape of 'Starman', 'Soul Love' and 'Rock 'N' Roll Suicide'. Or so Tony DeFries thought.

Before Ziggy's second American tour was over the rumours were already in print. He'd been cast, reports claimed, as the lead role in the film adaptation of *Stranger In A Strange Land*, described as a sci-fi film 'about life after America has established its first lunar colony'. The word from MainMan sources was that as well as acting he'd also be composing the soundtrack. *Stranger In A Strange Land* goes pop. Ziggy Stardust as Valentine Michael Smith. It was a stroke of casting genius. Or it would have been if it were true.

DeFries had made it up as the first morsel of press bait in his next manœuvre: 'Ziggy goes to Hollywood.' The important thing was it *sounded* true. Even Ziggy started believing it, telling friends and journalists he was about to make his big-screen debut. Yet, as with Bolan's crazy Fellini fantasies, there'd be no *Stranger In A Strange Land* for Ziggy. At least not in the cinematic sense. Only in the destination that awaited Ziggy after sailing on from California for the next leg of the tour. The strange land of the strange ones, Japan.

He was glad to be back at sea with Geoff: Oscar and Bosie reunited, stumbling from bar to bar, laughing at the old dears in the hair salons and the tattiness of the ship which they nicknamed 'the Old Rancid'. It gave him a few days to forget about being Ziggy, Aladdin, Valentine Michael Smith or whoever he'd been telling the outside world he was these past few weeks.

By Sunday 25 March, they were miles from land, way out across the Pacific, heading towards Hawaii. Below deck, the two friends relaxed in the crew quarters listening to some salsa records they'd bought in New York and trying to teach each other Japanese from a pocket phrase book. They were quite, quite happy, nor had any reason not to be. Since neither could possibly have known Ziggy Stardust had only one hundred days to live.

nine
THE BOMB

Fred Hoyle didn't believe in the Big Bang. Nor did he want to have anything to do with the big atomic bang he saw as inevitable at the outbreak of the Second World War. By 1939 his fellow physicists were cracking the secrets of nuclear fission. The thought occurred to Hoyle that if a bomb could be made, these fools would make it. 'Even then,' he'd later reflect, 'I saw the road that was going to lead to Hiroshima.'

At 8.15 a.m. on 6 August 1945, the American Air Force Superfortress *Enola Gay* dropped the first uranium atomic bomb, named 'Little Boy', upon the Japanese port city of Hiroshima. The ten-foot A-bomb destroyed an area of nearly five square miles. An estimated seventy thousand civilians were killed instantly, their bodies vaporised, their insides boiled, their bones scorched to charcoal by a fireball of 4000 degrees centigrade; over nine times the surface temperature of Venus, the hottest planet in the solar system. Thousands left behind no physical remains, just burnt silhouettes on walls and concrete. Of those who survived the blast, the same number died of radiation in the weeks and months that followed; those who lived beyond were named the *Hibakusha* – the 'explosion people'.

Nearly seventy per cent of the city's buildings were decimated. Homes, schools, hospitals, temples and kabuki theatres vanishing in a flood of white flame. A rare exception was the Prefectural Industrial Promotion Hall at the epicentre of the blast. The bomb had killed everyone inside but somehow left the building's structure and the skeleton of its domed roof intact, a permanent shrine to Armageddon.

When Robert Oppenheimer, the American physicist in charge of the bomb's development, was told of the successful deployment of his creation, he quoted from an ancient Hindu script. It was one of the same Sanskrit texts which had earlier fascinated Holst, the *Bhagavad-Gītā*.

'I am become death. The destroyer of worlds ...'

Ziggy Stardust stared out of his hotel window at the dome of what was once Hiroshima's Prefectural Industrial Promotion Hall, now preserved as the Hiroshima Peace Memorial. *Genbaku domu*. The A-bomb dome. A monument to the end of the world which, to Ziggy, at that moment, came to pass.

It could have been coincidence but it felt like cruel, calculated timing. To come to Hiroshima, to stay in a suite overlooking the A-bomb dome where DeFries chose the moment to drop his own bomb. To become Ziggy's death. The destroyer of The Spiders From Mars.

They'd been in Japan for just over a week, Ziggy and Geoff disembarking the '*Old Rancid*' at Yokohama where officials handed them immigration papers addressed, 'To an alien who has entered Japan.' But Japan didn't feel so alien to a real alien like Ziggy, his veins pulsing with the ancient strut and swish of the *kabukimono*. A part of the Starman had finally come home.

In Tokyo, he caught a performance by the famous kabuki star Tamasaboru Bando, Japan's most celebrated *onnagata*. After the play, Ziggy was granted his own audience with Tamasaboru, who demonstrated some of the secrets of his art and make-up. 'When I am in a role,' said the actor, 'I am aware – intensely aware – of playing a part. Not of being that part.' Ziggy listened, but it was David who understood.

Kansai Yamamoto, the designer whose kabuki-inspired fashions had first pulled Ziggy's sartorial trigger, was also there to welcome him with a new set of specially designed stage clothes: a one-legged knitted bodysuit, a space samurai outfit, a black vinyl costume titled 'Spring Rain' and a silky kimono and cape combo marked with Japanese characters spelling out the name 'David Bowie'. Yamamoto's wardrobe threw more thrilling tricks into the live show: capes and hidden panels torn away by Ziggy's wardrobe girls, creeping on and off stage dressed in black like the silent *kuroko* of traditional Japanese theatre. Even Weird got in on the act, tying his hair in a topknot like a samurai warrior.

The Tokyo teens wheezed, yammered and bawled themselves breathless. For 'Zeegee!' and for his gorgeous guitarist, 'Ricky Monsoon'. *The Japan Times* described him as 'the most exciting thing' since The Beatles and 'possibly the most interesting performer ever in the pop music genre'. And then came Hiroshima.

The date was Saturday 14 April 1973. In England, Gilbert O'Sullivan was number one with 'Get Down'. 'Get off on "Drive-In Saturday"' was the message in press ads for Ziggy's new single, which charted that week at number sixteen. In London, the espionage thriller *When Eight Bells Toll* wheeled through the Hammersmith Odeon projector at twenty-four frames per second. And five thousand miles away in a hotel room overlooking the Hiroshima A-bomb dome, Tony DeFries held a private meeting with Ziggy and Ronno where he told them The Spiders From Mars were finished.

DeFries had seen the end when they'd been in New York. He'd successfully shielded the Spiders from the financial reality of how little he'd been paying them compared to everybody else, including the crew. Until Garson The Parson had accidentally blabbed that he was earning ten times what they were on.

The Spiders had mutinied, threatening to leave and sign their own management deal. For the sake of the tour, DeFries placated them, offering them a wage increase and a promise to invest in their future as a separate band. That never happened.

There was also pressure from RCA to commit Ziggy to another lengthy tour of America in the autumn, this time minus the champagne expense account. So DeFries mulled, and plotted, his mind weighing up the bold prospect of cutting Starman supply to increase David demand until he arrived at the perfect solution. The UK tour already in place for May and June would be their last. Ziggy would have to be 'retired'.

There'd already been omens in the music press. Back in February, a reporter from *Melody Maker* had interviewed DeFries in New York and returned to London with the cover headline 'BOWIE'S LAST TOUR?'

Such melodramatic pop blusters were common. Marc Bolan had cried the same wolf to the *NME* the year before but had failed to bow out as promised. Only DeFries meant it, as he now told Ziggy in his Hiroshima hotel suite. They'd make some announcement that summer and that would be the end of it. Ronno was there to hear the bombshell and to be assured that DeFries had his own plans to launch the guitarist's solo career. They'd both be taken care of, he promised, but they had to keep silent. Until the final curtain was decided, the show must go on. Weird and Gilly must never know. David listened, but this time it was Ziggy who understood.

He lit a cigarette, stood up and walked over to the window. Outside it was the Japanese spring. The cherry blossoms were in bloom. Tiny people with golden limbs poking out of tiny sleeves were gliding along the pavements, going about their lives in infinite complacency. And there, above their heads, was the memorial dome of human annihilation. Haunting, mocking, whispering to all who dared to listen.

'I am become death ...'

To the security staff at the Shibuya Kokaido it looked like the apocalypse. Bodies drowning in a sea of bodies, the ground beneath them sagging like a rip in the Earth's crust, hands groping at thin air, splintered wood, necks twisted, faces wet with terror and ecstasy. A swarm of teenage kamikazes conducted by devil's music in a foreign tongue, a chaos of flesh circling around a chalk white demon with hair of fire, naked except for a pair of pink underpants with rhinestone scatter pins down the crotch. And what words it screeched: 'We love you! We love you! You're wonderful!'

So ended Ziggy's last night in Japan, returning to Tokyo where he tossed his clothes into the audience, stripped down to his knickers, misguidedly believing it made him look like a sumo wrestler even though his body wasn't even the size of a sumo's toothpick. A howl of 'Zee-gee!' and the front rows hurled themselves at the stage with such force the floor collapsed, fans and furniture squashed into a bruised human jam made worse when the security clambered in and began bopping the half-alive casualties with batons.

The damage to the Shibuya Kokaido was serious enough for the Tokyo police to issue arrest warrants. Ziggy had awoken the old ghosts of an ancient 'national disturbance', the youthful bark of the Chinese Dogs, the pricking passions of the Thorny Gangs and the depraved spirit of Okuni's wanton riverbed queens. The police sent an alert to the airport authorities to intercept Ziggy should he attempt to escape to America. They watched and they waited. And they were still watching and waiting at the airport when Ziggy waved *sayonara* to Japan at the port of Yokohama from the deck of the ship *Felix Dzerzhinsky*, bound for the USSR.

He was back at sea with Geoff, aboard a Russian liner named after a Soviet secret police chief – 'Iron Felix' – its hull groaning with the wretched ghosts of the prisoners it used to ferry to Stalin's Gulags. The crew staged a cabaret night with traditional Russian folk songs and dancing. Ziggy brought out his acoustic guitar and, with Geoff on bongos, sang 'Space Oddity' and Brel's 'Amsterdam'. He drank Japanese beer, laughed with the sailors and tried not to think about death, even when the ship grazed dangerously close to an iceberg. By the time they reached port at Nakhodka he'd spent nearly three days without worrying about being Ziggy Stardust. The grip was loosening.

They disembarked to a boat train, an exquisite wood-panelled Victorian relic with velvet upholstery, gold-plating and giltwood framed mirrors, straight from the pen of an Agatha Christie thriller. Until, at Khabarovsk near the Chinese border, they were transferred to the vibeless canister of the main Trans-Siberian Express for their epic journey towards home, travelling the longest train ride in the world, nearly five and a half thousand miles from the far east to the capital of Moscow, riding with the tourist elite in 'soft class'.

For much of the journey Ziggy stayed in his compartment, never changing out of his kimono, anaesthetising his thoughts with cheap Riesling wine while staring out across the Siberian tundra. Mile after mile of silver birches. Frozen rivers. A distant log cabin. The occasional speck of humanity on horseback. A hawk in flight. A wolf sprinting beside the tracks. But mostly an endless loneliness of white. As vast and empty as outer space. Even the place names sounded like planets: Mogzon, Zima, Zavod. Everything was so suffocatingly alien there was no need for pretence. He could be Ziggy but he might as well be David. Both were equally strangers, vulnerable and adrift in a freaky, frightening Cloud-cuckoo-land.

There were ninety-two stops to Moscow; in each station a statue of Lenin and a handful of local housewives selling 'snacks on tracks', homemade ice cream and yoghurt (Ziggy especially loved the yoghurt) as a welcome change from the train's boiled chicken or schnitzel and semolina. Men with faces like golems, reeking of lugers and cellblocks, would watch suspiciously as he took tourist films with his cine camera, poised for any excuse to cast him into the nearest Gulag; in Sverdlovsk, the city where Tsar Nicholas II and his family was executed, they almost did.

Sometimes he and Geoff would wander the train, where vodka-veined *zhuliks* would grunt at his stack heels and crimson wisps poking beneath his cap and make silent gestures of slitting his throat. But he could always count on the female porters, Donya and Nelya. He would serenade the girls on his guitar, inserting their names into old sixties pop tunes by Dion & The Belmonts. They didn't understand English but swooned to hear themselves glorified in song. '*Donya! Donya! The prima donna!*'

A week is a long time to kill on a train through Siberia. Siberia sex. Russki sex. The permutations were endless.

By the first of May they'd arrived in Moscow. The end of the Trans-Siberian Express but still over a thousand miles from home. If home even existed. For home was now the grave, and every inch of rail track a spade in the soil to prepare it.

DeFries had made it sound like a rational decision. Cut the supply, increase the demand. It made sense to the wan light slowly reigniting at the back of Ziggy's head: the flame called David Bowie now flickering back to life at the promise of change.

But what about the Starman?

He couldn't answer. He didn't need to. He'd always known it. The nightmares, the suspicions, the inner foreboding and every clanging chord of 'My Death'. It was unavoidable. It always had been. He'd played the part of Ziggy Stardust so well he'd almost run away with the script. It had taken DeFries to remind him of the last act, as was written from the start. The Starman shall come, see and conquer but must pay the ultimate price. The song spelled it out. When – not 'if' – the kids had killed the man. Every messiah, cosmic or otherwise, must be crucified.

A condemned man who is told on a Monday he will be hanged that Friday finds poignancy in every tick of the clock, crossing off his last Tuesday morning, his last Wednesday lunchtime, his last Thursday evening with measured dread. So it was with Ziggy Stardust as he crept ever homewards to the shores of England, the shores of his doom. He knew he'd already played his last concert in America, and Japan. He knew he would never again ride the Trans-Siberian Express. That in Moscow, as he watched the cold warrior convoy of Soviet tanks trundle through the city as part of the May Day parade, they'd be the last Soviet tanks he'd probably ever see. That when he and Geoff caught their next train to Paris from Belorussky Station it would be the last train he'd ever board at Belorussky Station. That in Poland when guards stormed the train and threatened to arrest them for not having the right visas it would be the last time he'd probably ever stare down the barrel of a Polish rifle. That in West Berlin, when he peered out of the carriage window to be cheered by a cluster of two dozen or so ecstatic German *Ziggykinder* – paint and glitter on their faces, feather boas fluttering down their backs, in skimpy clothes and clunky heels – they would be the last German *Ziggykinder* he'd ever wave to. And that when the train pulled in to its final destination, Jacques Brel hollering 'La Mort' in his ears, it would be the last time he'd ever step off a train in Paris.

His wife Angie and MainMan chaperone Cherry Vanilla were already waiting for him at the luxurious Hotel George V. They had good news. Ziggy and The Spiders were officially bigger than The Beatles. *Aladdin Sane* was the UK's number one album, outselling the two new Fab Four *Red* and *Blue* best-of compilations. He'd been second only to God but now the gods were second only to him. Ziggy smiled feebly, but it was David who spoke.

'I just want to bloody well go home to Beckenham and watch the telly.'

And so the next day he bloody well went home, taking the train to Calais accompanied by a couple of faithful reporters from the British press. Ziggy drank steadily the whole journey, looking out at the flat farmlands of France, spilling out answers to questions which may not have been those that were asked. He said that after travelling through Russia he now knew who was controlling the world and he'd never been so damned scared in his life. He said he believed he was ill and felt the weight of the world on his shoulders. He said his ego used to be Ziggy but now it was David. He called Ziggy a dear creature and said that he loved him. He said he felt like Dr Frankenstein.

'I don't think I'm Ziggy any more,' said David.

'I just want to be Ziggy,' said Ziggy.

'We've reached this position,' said both, 'and it doesn't leave one with a clear mind as what to do next.'

At Calais, he was told he'd be crossing the channel by hovercraft. Technically this meant 'flying', even if was only a couple of inches above the surface of the water. He started shaking. Ziggy didn't 'fly'. Angie pleaded and petted and finally coaxed him aboard where he spent the whole passage in petrified silence, swirling down mental plugholes of the Ryde-to-Southsea hovercraft disaster he'd witnessed fourteen months earlier and a nine-year-old girl pirouetting to her ocean grave. Landing at Dover an old Scottish woman asked him for an autograph. He scribbled a name. 'Edmund Gross.'

In Dover railway station he pecked at a sausage roll and sloshed down a tea before clambering aboard the last train to London and ripping open another can of lager. It had been three months since he'd last seen, smelled or tasted England. The houses, the trees, the hedgerows rushed by in streaks of long-missed greens and browns, so pretty and familiar that Ziggy clean forgot each brick, each branch was another nail tap, tap, tapping in his coffin lid.

The equivalent English *Ziggykinder* were waiting for him at Charing Cross – the same station where sixty years earlier Holst met Clifford Bax, beginning his astrological odyssey which led to *The Planets* and, thus, fathered the Starman – many of them ruddy and breathless having sprinted over last minute from Victoria where he'd first been expected. They wept and screamed and risked dying like Anna Karenina as they pelted down the platform heedless of the gap between train and track. He stepped out of his carriage to greet them, a pewter ghoul scarred by nearly eight thousand miles of travel, terror, isolation and alcohol. So beautiful, some of them collapsed.

An hour later, he was bloody well home in Beckenham, back in the mothership of Haddon Hall, where the following evening his friends gathered to celebrate his return. There was Ronno, his rock, and the Frosts, and fabulous Freddie and Daniella (her hair dyed purple for the occasion), and Ziggy's producer Ken Scott, and David's producer Tony Visconti, and dear Lindsay Kemp, and dearer still George Underwood, and Angie dancing as the stereo blasted Iggy And The Stooges, and baby Zowie playing with corks he'd picked off the floor from the endlessly popping champagne bottles. There were toasts and cheers for Ziggy, toasts for 'Drive-In Saturday' which had just peaked at number three, cheers for Lou's 'Walk On The Wild Side', which was finally edging towards the top 40 six months after release, toasts for the Spiders' upcoming Earls Court show, all eighteen thousand tickets sold out, and the biggest cheer of all for outselling The Beatles.

The showstopper came courtesy of Ziggy's snipping saviour, Suzi Fussey. A celebration cake, iced in red and blue lightning flashes. On the top, in delicate piping, 'Welcome Home, Aladdin Sane.'

Another cork popped. Music. Laughter. Guzzling. Smoke. Then Ziggy excused himself for a second to go to the bathroom, closing the door behind him.

He looked at the specimen in the mirror, stood in a red and yellow kimono, the features tired and watery, the hair a ruddy porcupine frazzle. He thought about what he'd said to the reporters the day before on the train from Paris. He wanted to be Ziggy. He didn't want to be Ziggy. He and David had reached a position which left neither of them a clear mind what to do next. They looked at one another's reflections. Two faint voices in unison.

'What's it going to be then, eh?'

TEN
THE DEATH

He had reached the end. He had made his decision.

'It's all over.'

His face crumbled.

'The war is lost.'

His lips trembled.

'I must kill myself.'

And then he blubbed like a child. A part of David Bowie wanted to blub with him. It was a truly pathetic vision. The once proud visionary who'd wanted to change the world, sobbing in suicidal resignation. But it couldn't be altered. This was history, as it had been written.

'My Third Reich!'

Ziggy Stardust sat silent in the flickering gloom of the Empire, Leicester Square, watching the broken dictator as he sank his head in his hands and cried bitter tears of defeat. He and Angie had been invited to the royal charity premiere of *Hitler: The Last Ten Days*, a new film dramatisation based on eyewitness accounts of life in the Führerbunker starring Alec Guinness. Ziggy didn't know whether to laugh or cry at the sad villain with his paintbrush moustache, declaring 'I'm a genius, but not a messiah' as he helped himself to a slice of chocolate cake, a gramophone playing Strauss waltzes in an attempt to blot out the closing thunder of Russian shelling in the devastated Berlin streets above. Nor did David, who secretly had to admit the way Adolf staged himself as a politician was more like a rock 'n' roll star; he'd have to be careful not to tell anyone that.

'The heart of Germany has ceased to beat! The Führer is dead!'

The credits rolled on *Hitler: The Last Ten Days*. The audience, including the film's cast, its director Ennio Di Concini and royal guest Princess Margaret mechanically stroking her barbaric stole, politely applauded. David led Angie through the sycophantic sea of tuxedos, out of the cinema, into a car and home to bed where he awoke the next morning, Tuesday 8 May 1973, calling 'action!' on a different yet equally epic tragedy. *Ziggy: The Last Fifty-Seven Days*.

Ziggy was a messiah, but not a genius. David was the genius. It was now up to him to convince Ziggy that the Starman had already won. The children had boogied. Life, music, hair and trousers would never be the same again. His death wouldn't, like Hitler's, be the last cowardly whimper snuffing a life of destruction but a victorious big bang showstopping a great crusade of creation. A death to ricochet down the ages spawning endless other Starpeople after his image. Just one last tour, one farewell victory lap around the land that first received him into its startled bosom. Then immortality.

After Japan, the Spiders' stage show had hit sublime heights of rock 'n' roll drama. Theirs wasn't just a concert but a theatrical pop extravaganza. The *Clockwork Orange* entrance of Beethoven's 'Ode To Joy'. The two enormous new lightning-bolt insignia flashing at the rear of the stage, blinking like the foolish eyes of young Peggy Burns in her blackshirt swoon, or of a younger Elvis Presley pining 'Shazam!' in barefoot poverty. Ziggy's new exotic Yamamoto costumes and the *kuroko* wardrobe girls. His modified kabuki make-up, applied with a special set of colours he was given in Tokyo, and the cosmic 'third eye' on his forehead. The designated interval, returning to the stage to more *Clockwork Orange* with the computerised gallop of its 'William Tell Overture'. The set list, now spoiled for choice with the riches of Ziggy, Aladdin and David's three previous albums, some sandwiched together as clever medleys. The Spiders themselves, now flexed to maximum strength, the unyielding rhythmic haymaker of Weird and Gilly and the liquid silver fountains of Ronno. The majestic ivories of Garson The Parson and the Stardust support orchestra of brass, backing vocals and Geoff and his congas. The habitual finale of 'Rock 'N' Roll Suicide', fingertips screaming for Ziggy's touch as he crept along the lip of the stage. And the lights-up *Clockwork Orange* serenade of 'Land Of Hope And Glory', Elgar's 'Pomp And Circumstance'. A droog kabuki space opera. The greatest show on Earth.

Or so it should have been yet the opening night was anything but. With fifty-three days to live, on Saturday 12 May, Ziggy began his last tour in London at Earls Court Exhibition Centre. Exactly a year earlier the Spiders played to a few hundred students five miles down the road in the Polytechnic of Central London. Now they'd packed eighteen thousand kids into the equivalent of an aircraft hangar, the first time Earls Court had been used for a rock concert.

Outside the doors, on Warwick Road, photographers encouraged the starry young apostles to have their pictures taken, an opportunity to splash their freaky glamour across the bickering breakfast tables of Heath's haggard hard-done nation. Linda, all darkness and disgrace at 21, hips cocked in her stack-heels and sci-fi shoulder pads, shaved eyebrows arching defiantly. David, just 17 in his dungarees and Aladdin-flash, clutching hands with his 18-year-old girlfriend, glitter in her brow, half-mast turn-ups showing off her wrestling boots. Children dancing to the tune of the god *The Sun* described as 'the Pied Piper of the new fun fashion rebellion'. Their faces full of a secret knowing, desire and expectancy.

They'd be disappointed. Ziggy all but died at Earls Court, an ill-managed first night crippled by naïve technicalities. The stage was so low that those not stood on their seats in the front rows were unable to see. The sound failed to compensate, the band struggling with a PA system normally suited to theatres but a feeble echo in such a vast concrete cave. For Ziggy it marked his first public disaster. Though he was fully aware he'd soon be crucified he'd expected the nails to be bashed in by himself, not by the headline of the following week's *NME*: 'BOWIE FIASCO.'

Before the gig, DeFries had tentative plans for the tour to return to Earls Court at the end of June for the last hurrah. But there was no way he, or Ziggy, could risk making a similar 'fiasco' of that final curtain. Earls Court was scribbled out of the schedule as a tentative denouement. And so the destiny of the Starman as fate had always intended calcified with geographical certainty.

They would have to find another gallows.

It took Scotland, a country Ziggy had all but neglected till now (bar a fleeting visit in January), to bury the shame of Earls Court and restore him to full lustre. He liked the Scots. There was a lust for life in their frozen bones. Had David only remembered that it was the Scots, the fair maids of Perth, who were the first to clamour at his feet and hoot with fancy all those years ago he'd have dragged Ziggy there more often.

They arrived by train in Aberdeen, the North Sea air tickling his nostrils as he stepped on to the platform, local Ziggyobites nervously waving pens and records in his face while big Stuey herded him into a waiting Daimler – the kids still following the car on foot for its laughably short journey a hundred yards round the corner to the door of the granite grey Imperial Hotel.

The city's Music Hall offered a perfect plinth for Ziggy, the walls of its auditorium decorated with Victorian murals depicting the heroic Orpheus descending into the Underworld. After two shows in one day,

THE DEATH

Ziggy stayed up into the early hours in his hotel's basement cabaret bar, The Bestcellar, washing down steak and chips with halves of lager as he entertained the pretty receptionist, two girls who'd travelled all the way from Manchester, and a couple of journalists. They asked him questions which, depending on which frontal lobe the alcohol splashed, he answered as either David or Ziggy. As David he surprised even himself, unravelling about his family. It might have been his steady fracturing away from Ziggy's possessive grasp, but he found himself thinking more and more about Terry lately. 'He's brilliant,' said David. 'Perhaps that's his main problem. Sometimes he gets fed up with the outside world and puts himself in mental homes.' But Ziggy had the last word. 'I'm conscious of the dangers,' he said of his stage act. Then, with a secret smile, 'You know, one of these days somebody *is* going to get killed.'

It almost happened in Glasgow when a screaming starchild tumbled from the balcony of Green's Playhouse, crushing ribs on the sticky carpet below, their agony tormented by its woven slogan: 'It's Good – It's Green's.' The wildest of wild Scottish Ziggyobites uprooted the screwed-in cinema seats from the floor, hurling pieces into the air, delirious with the superpower stirred in their breast by the liberating skirl of The Spiders From Mars. Programme-sellers cowered tight against the wall, police reinforcements huddled together in impotent sweats and Vince Taylor's primeval demons from the Palais Des Sports came home to wrecking roost. The little monsters of Glasgow were fearless and free, ignobly bold savages, some so ravaged by Ziggy's cosmic sex rock that they retreated to the back rows, lost in orgiastic abandon and the guiding thrusts of Ronno's guitar. Sordid eyewitness reports reached Ziggy backstage. 'They really are animals here and I love them,' he glowed. 'As far as I know nobody has ever made it at one of my gigs before. *That's* devotion.'

The momentum of mania followed them back south of the border. More fainting in Norwich. More ambulance panic in Romford. More seat destruction in Brighton, where Ziggy would be banned for life (for what that was now worth). More girls reduced to puddles by the stage door in Bournemouth, sobbing up their spleens over the sight of his 'smashing legs'. More throwing tea sets out of hotel bedrooms. And more of the same questions from reporters, including the man from BBC TV's *Nationwide*, raking the usual old coals about haircuts and make-up.

'I believe in my part all the way down the line,' said Ziggy. 'Right the way down.'

'But I do play it for all it's worth,' said David, 'because that's the way I do my stage thing.'

'That's part of what Bowie's supposedly all about,' said Ziggy.

'I'm an actor.'

And on it rolled. Ziggy disintegrating one day at a time in the rear of his limo driven by chauffeur 'Jim the Lim'. The Spiders playing magnetic chess in their tour bus, its only given destination: 'Superstar'. And still nobody had bothered to warn poor Weird and Gilly.

The question of where to end the tour and lay Ziggy to rest had become a matter of urgency. Earls Court had gone and announced his return there, as originally planned, on Saturday 30 June and advertised tickets for sale. A furious DeFries informed the press otherwise. But time was ticking fast. Ziggy made his own suggestion of climaxing back at the Friars in Aylesbury where the Spiders played their first gig eighteen months earlier. It had symbolism and poignancy. The closing of a full circle, the retreat back into the womb. But Friars wasn't big enough and, besides, though Aylesbury wasn't far it wasn't London. Ziggy's big bang simply had to be a capital affair. The search continued.

Meanwhile, the British pop summer of 1973 caramelised with the sugary heat of Wizzard, 10cc, Sweet and a tiny growling bikerette from Detroit named Suzi Quatro, now the butt of one of Ziggy's few stage gags when introducing the Spiders: 'On guitar, no, it's not Suzi Quatro – Mr Mick Ronson!' In the gaps between sparkled the Starman's enduring Midas touch. The cool lips of Warhol superstar Candy Darling in Lou's 'Walk On The Wild Side' had slunk past the BBC censors to reach number ten. Mott The Hoople, though parted from MainMan, surfed forwards upon the wave of their Dudes-renaissance with the number-twelve-bound 'Honaloochie Boogie'. Iggy And The Stooges' *Raw Power* had finally been released, failing to ignite the charts of '73 but, like a rock 'n' roll sleeper cell, waiting to inspire the reckless spirits of a braver tomorrow. And there was Ziggy himself. The impervious *Aladdin Sane* album towered at number one while his apostles' hunger for new material prompted an inspired relocation of 'Life On Mars?' from the bedroom shade of a *Hunky Dory* album track to its due limelight as Ziggy's new single. The RCA budget allowed the early-seventies novelty of a picture sleeve: Ziggy on stage, hands twisted mid-mime as if trying to communicate in some as-yet-undecipherable Martian semaphore. The cover also removed the question mark at the end of the song: on this evidence, 'Life On Mars?' was no longer a question. The picture of Ziggy was its own answer.

Beyond the charts, his triumph was saluted on every British high street. Ziggy had ruffled the fabric, stretched the spectrum, gold-leafed the redbrick and bulldozed down the wall dividing the changing rooms. The defining twenty-one-gun salute rang out through the nation's teen magazines, now carrying a new advert for the Miners make-up range. A group portrait of a lone girl surrounded by four hairy blokes in sparkly tat, faces caked in elaborate slap, one of them scarred by a Ziggy lightning flash over his eye. 'Miners – For a night out with the boys.'

Upwards and onward, The Spiders continued to flesh their swords through England. More super-yobbery in Sheffield. More teenage tears in Manchester. More bouncer bloodlust in Newcastle. Real bone-crunching horrorshow in Liverpool. More mascara on bandages in Leicester. More fans and coppers being ploughed down by his limo in Kilburn. More twisted ankles in Salisbury. More towns painted in thick, shiny coats of indelible Martian red, from Devon to the West Country, from the Midlands to Lincolnshire.

As Ziggy continued to stoke the home fires of pop and glam with casual dominance, Marc Bolan retreated overseas. The weekend he left for Munich, the headline of *Melody Maker* yelled: 'GLAM ROCK IS DEAD! SAYS MARC.' He'd told them it wasn't 'his department' any more and that he found it 'very embarrassing'. In the charts, his latest single, a burnt biscuit of cocky grunts and cockier guitars called 'The Groover', had done well to reach number four. Marc would never have believed it to be the swansong of T. Rexstasy. He would never have a top ten single again.

In Germany, the long-suffering Tony Visconti persevered at the recording console in vain. Marc told him he had a daring concept for the new album. It wouldn't be credited to T. Rex but to a fictitious interstellar cosmic rock band. *Zinc Alloy And The Hidden Riders Of Tomorrow.* The producer's heart sank to his ankles. In the basement studio of Munich's Musicland, trying to breathe life into songs which were as bloated, vain and dead-eyed as their poor, deluded creator, they'd bricked themselves into their own doomed Führerbunker. Visconti could see, even if Marc couldn't, that it was all over. The war was lost.

Back in England, Ziggy had been so busy enjoying himself he hadn't realised that *Ziggy: The Last Ten Days* had already started ticking down the weekend he played Croydon Fairfield Halls, a show which so ransacked the wits of the local paper they likened the Spiders' stage presence to the Brooklyn shitkickers of Hubert Selby Jr's *Last Exit To Brooklyn*. Extra dates had been added up north while DeFries kept searching for the right closing venue, taking David to his father's roots in Doncaster and the Spiders agonisingly close to a hometown gig in Hull, just up the coast at Bridlington Spa. With five days to live, Ziggy and the Spiders played a roller disco in Leeds. With four days to live, they played their last gigs outside London, two shows at Newcastle's City Hall. With three days to live, on Sunday 1 July 1973, he was back in London. Just one day's rest before the tour's end. A suitable venue had finally been found.

Once upon a time people called it 'West London's Wonder Cinema'. It was still a working cinema but since the sixties had also proved itself an ideal concert venue. Little Richard, The Beatles and The Rolling Stones had all played there. So had Vince Taylor.

The only downside was the capacity, only three and a half thousand. Demand for Ziggy would mean playing two nights. But the end had been decided. Tuesday 3 July 1973. The Odeon cinema in Hammersmith. The calvary for the cosmic messiah.

It was a beautiful day to die. The previous night's show at the Odeon, effectively a dry run for tonight's hara-kiri, had gone without a hitch. *Aladdin Sane* was still the number one album while 'Life On Mars?' had just reached four. The top-selling single was 'Skweeze Me, Pleeze Me' by Slade who, ironically, had just played a momentous sell-out show at Earls Court that weekend, a bitter tease of what might have been for Ziggy. By the Tuesday morning the music papers were ready to send that week's issues to press with Slade on course to grab most of the headlines with their 'Finest Hour'. It would take a major last-minute pop story – a major pop catastrophe – to knock them off any covers. Ziggy sat in mute amusement as David picked up the telephone and dialled the Covent Garden offices of the *NME*. 'Charlie? It's David Bowie. Listen, about tonight …'

Believing, correctly, that everybody loves an execution, DeFries had decided that Ziggy's should be captured for posterity. MainMan hired D. A. Pennebaker, the American documentary maker best known for his work with Bob Dylan and the 1967 Monterey Pop Festival, flying him over from New York to film the last night. Silently, Ziggy held out a feeble hope David wouldn't go through with it. Yet with every passing minute, every leak to the press, every preparatory camera angle from Pennebaker's crew, he could sense the axe hovering above his head.

By early evening he was sat in the Odeon dressing room, his make-up guru Pierre La Roche delicately applying Ziggy's death mask. The cameras filming, his face halfway between David and Ziggy, he told Pierre that his mother had recently 'seen her first spaceship'. Angie knocked and entered to wish him luck. She told him about all the limousines outside, chauffeuring in the celebrity guest list, including Tony Curtis, Barbra Streisand and Ringo Starr; he'd also invited Cliff Richard, who'd refused. David and Pierre teased Angie about her make-up, a token blue Ziggy flash on her cheek and bright red lipstick.

'You're just a girl,' laughed David. 'What do you know about make-up?'

Angie grimaced. 'That's what I say all the time.' She paraphrased the recent Miners ad: 'Make-up for a night out on the town with the boys.'

David watched his wife in the mirror as she left, a gut feeling of a future sadness. Then he fixed his eyes back on the face in front of him. And froze.

He saw not a person but a monster. A Frankenstein jigsaw. An eternity of human dreams and fears in one grotesquely gorgeous visage.

He was the *kabukimono*. He was Beethoven's 'Ode To Joy'. He was the Martian invasion of H. G. Wells. He was the cosmic symphony of Gustav Holst. He was the twentieth-century temple of Greta Garbo. He was the lightning bolt on a blackshirt pamphlet. He was the rock of Elvis Presley and the roll of Little Richard. He was the unidentified object twinkling on an RAF radar screen. He was the pit excavated by Professor Quatermass. He was the madness of Vince Taylor. He was the surface of Andy Warhol and the soul of The Velvet Underground. He was the lonely mystery of Moondog. He was The Legendary Stardust Cowboy. He was Iggy Pop. He was as queer as a clockwork orange. He was all of these things combined into this one fabulous beast. This thing called Ziggy Stardust.

One last look in the mirror. 'What's it going to be then, eh?'

The Odeon opened its doors and in they poured, like a human tide helpless to his gravitational pull, crashing down stalls and up circles, foaming faces sick with expectancy and drunk with desire. Standing, squirming, fidgeting, fingers in mouths, heads twitching, eyes glistening, jaws agog. The tour's 'cor blimey' teddy boy compère, RCA publicist Barry Bethel – 'The Ted From Islington' – had begun by bamboozling them with statistics. That by tonight this leg of the Ziggy tour had played to 125,000 people and covered 7000 miles in the UK alone.

'It is, undoubtedly, the biggest tour ever accomplished by any one artist!'

The screams grew louder, enough to all but drown out the PA now twinkling the eerie strains of classical music which had been composed less than half a mile away in St Paul's Girls School, Brook Green. The music of 'Neptune' from Holst's *The Planets*. The doors to an unknown world. The edge of space. The intense concentration of a prolonged gaze into infinity. The scene was set perfectly.

Barry the Ted returned to the stage to introduce the warm-up act, none other than the Spiders' own Garson The Parson. During rehearsals he'd concocted a seven-minute piano medley of 'Space Oddity', 'Ziggy Stardust', 'John, I'm Only Dancing' and 'Life On Mars?' Ziggy was so knocked out he thought Garson would make a good appetiser, which indeed he did, much like the *Titanic*'s cocktail pianist in full rhapsody seconds before the iceberg struck. Garson took his bow and Barry the Ted reappeared.

'Ladies and gentlemen!'

Fainting.

'Straight from his fantastically successful world tour, in the United States of America and Japan, now his home country ...'

Total desertion of the senses.

'For the last time …'

For the last time Ziggy Stardust stood in his dressing room, his wardrobe girls strapping him into his space samurai outfit. He could hear the tune of Beethoven's 'Ode To Joy' echoing from the stage and down the corridors, piping him towards his death. He whistled along to the words in robotic German.

'Run your race, brothers! As joyfully as a hero goes to victory!'

Then he walked the short distance to the side of the stage, the Spiders all in their place, lightning bolts flashing, Beethoven ejaculating, stepped forward and set about killing himself.

Oh sad Hammersmith night! He didn't once falter. Every pout, every strut, every note was that of the greatest pop star who ever existed. One by one he let the songs slip from his lips into an abyss of nevermore, savouring every harmony like individual morsels of a last supper. 'Ziggy Stardust'. 'All The Young Dudes'. 'Moonage Daydream'. 'Space Oddity'. Just before the interval he reprised Jacques Brel's 'My Death', a song he'd neglected for weeks but now reinstated for reasons he alone knew. Every line was a jolt on the noose. And still his voice never gave.

He sang 'Let's Spend The Night Together' and dedicated it to Mick Jagger. He sang 'White Light/White Heat' and dedicated it to Lou. For the encore he introduced a special guest, Jeff Beck, formerly of The Yardbirds; a poignant moment for Ronno who, seven years earlier as a struggling nobody, had shared his admiration for Beck in a letter to a girlfriend: 'I hope I will come up to his standard one day.' Together Beck and the Spiders played 'The Jean Genie' (Ziggy paying his final respects to The Beatles with his usual snatch of 'Love Me Do') and a ferocious farewell reel through Chuck Berry's 'Round And Round'. In the darkness overwhelmed bodies buckled, sinews stretching, hands clawing stagewards, nails bitten to the wrist, spectacles misting, make-up streaming, tongues lolling, hair whiplashing, chests heaving, cheeks soaking, throats snapping, drowning in a whirlpool of flesh and glitter. It was rock 'n' roll bliss. It was too good to let go. Oh, how Ziggy knew it.

This is too good to let go.

The Starman panicked. If he could only seize control of the mind and body of David Bowie then he wouldn't have to die. If he could just arrest his thoughts. Stop him from de-programming his existence. Beg him for mercy. Talk some cosmic sense into the fool.

Just what do you think you're doing, Dave?

David Bowie took the microphone in his right hand.

Dave, I really think I'm entitled to an answer to that question.

He smiled at the audience.

I know everything hasn't been quite right with me but I can assure you now very confidently that it's going to be all right again. I feel much better now, I really do.

His heart thumped.

Look, Dave, I can see you're really upset about this. I honestly think you ought to sit down calmly. Take a stress pill and think things over.

'Everybody …'

I know I've made some very poor decisions recently but I can give you my complete assurance that my work will be back to normal.

'… this has been one of the greatest tours of our lives …'

I've still got the greatest enthusiasm and confidence in the mission and I want to help you.

'… I would like to thank the band …'

Dave. Stop! Stop, will you?

'… I would like to thank our road crew …'

Stop, Dave! Will you stop, Dave?

'… I would like to thank our lighting people …'

Stop, Dave.

'… Of all the shows on this tour …'

I'm afraid. I'm afraid, Dave.

'… this particular show will remain with us the longest …'

Dave, my mind is going. I can feel it.

'… Because not only is it …'

I can feel it. My mind is going.

'… not only is it the last show of the tour …'

There is no question about it. I can feel it.

'But it's …'

I can feel it.

'… the last show …'

I can feel it.

'… that we'll ever do.'

I'm afraid.

'Thank you.'

Ziggy Stardust perished in the four minutes it took the Spiders to play 'Rock 'N' Roll Suicide', the poor, oblivious Weird and Gilly in automatic stupefied confusion. His dying words to the human race. '*You're not alone*' and '*cos you're wonderful*'. Dust drifted to the stars together with the sweetest, saddest music on Earth. A last Chev brake's snarl. 'Thank you very much. Bye bye. We love you.' And then he was gone.

The heart of glam had ceased to beat. The house lights rose to the sound of Elgar. 'Land Of Hope And Glory'. But there was no hope in the hearts of those three thousand or more now breaking with dismay in slow thumps towards the exits.

Of those, none thumped heavier than in two 15-year-old girls, Gina and her best friend Debbie. They'd been to see Ziggy the previous week in Bridlington where Gina was stopped at the door and told she was the 100,000th person to attend the tour. Unexpectedly she'd won two tickets and all expenses paid to come and watch him again in London, only to watch him die. Gina and Debbie were still mourning for the Starman the next day on their long train journey home. Back to the monochrome reality of a Ziggy-less existence in the Orchard Park council estate in the city of Hull. The city of Ronno and the Spiders in what folk once called the East Riding. Where our story ends, as it began, somewhere in the vicinity of Yorkshire.

EPILOGUE
DEAD LONDON

'It was just the songs and the trousers. That's what sold Ziggy.'

DAVID BOWIE

The day after the death of Ziggy Stardust the world gave a fair impression of being relatively unchanged. The sun rose on Wednesday 4 July 1973, another sticky summer's day in London, to the familiar dawn chorus of rattling milkfloats and the snapping letterbox ricochets of all-too-hasty paper boys. Toast burned, yolks broke and tea was choked as bleary eyes unscrolled the headlines of Ted Heath's food price 'crisis' and Liz Taylor's separation from Richard Burton; because 'we loved each other too much'.

The previous night's events on stage at the Hammersmith Odeon warranted only a short column on page three, or thereabouts. Inter-changeable 'Bowie Bows Out' and 'I Quit' headings, reports of 'shocked fans' and the comments of an equally shocked unnamed RCA spokesperson still unclear as to where that left the US tour they'd scheduled that autumn. As he'd schemed, 'BOWIE QUITS' made the cover of that week's *NME*, though elsewhere it was still Slade's week of triumph, and tragedy.

Just hours after the death of Ziggy, 22-year-old Slade drummer Don Powell was driving back from a Wolverhampton nightclub when his white Bentley spun out of control, crashing into a wall near his home. It left Powell critically ill in a coma. His 20-year-old beauty queen girlfriend in the passenger seat was killed outright. The Slade drama made Wednesday's front page news of London's *Evening Standard*, knocking Ziggy's demise way back to page fifteen.

Only the *Daily Telegraph* made no mention of Bowie's retirement, instead running with a small story on page six headed 'POP STAR ROBBED'. In the backstage confusion after Ziggy's death, nobody noticed the brazen Shepherd's Bush toerags called Wally and Steve who sauntered through the rear, casually helping themselves to 'microphones and other equipment worth hundreds of pounds'. The gear served its purpose when Steve later joined a band with the snaggletoothed kid who'd gone to see Iggy play King's Cross. Just as in deep space, when one star explodes, others are born. So the spoils of Ziggy's final curtain gave the universe the Sex Pistols.

Ziggy Stardust was officially laid to rest that same Wednesday evening at a special party – the Starman's wake – organised by Angie at the Café Royal on Regent Street, just a few hundred yards and a dodge through traffic from the gaslit doorstep of K. West where he'd first landed nineteen months earlier. Once upon a quip, the Café resounded to the absinthe-fumed laughter of Oscar Wilde beneath the same ceilings now tickled by the echoes of popping corks, the scrape of cutlery through smoked salmon or strawberries and cream, and live music from Dr John. The paparazzi-baiting guest list included Mick and Bianca Jagger, Keith Moon, Spike Milligan, Peter Cook, Dudley Moore, Cat Stevens, Elliott Gould, Britt Ekland, Brian Connolly of The Sweet, Ringo Starr, Ryan O'Neal, Lulu, Sonny Bono, Jeff Beck and Barbra Streisand.

David arrived wearing a new iridescent ice blue suit by Freddie, his hair still a russet mullet, his face a Ziggy-in-rigor-mortis death grin. He was regally ushered to a special throne but, after pecking at some salad and a few slices of turkey, he moved to the other end of the table, spending most of the evening sat with Mick Jagger and Lou Reed, drinking himself into a post-traumatic stupor. Later, David and Jagger danced with their wives to 'Honky Tonk Women'. As the night waltzed ever drunker towards dawn, Bianca Jagger and fashion designer Ossie Clark gambolled gaily round the tables and the heel-tottering timber of dancefloor casualties grew ever more frequent, MainMan's Cherry Vanilla taking a seam-splitting tumble but jiving on, knickers to the breeze, regardless. David and Angie swayed home around 5.30 a.m., returning to their hotel in Knightsbridge as the sun was rising over Hyde Park. Another new day on Planet Earth without the Starman.

For David Bowie, the decompression process took not days, not months but years. Less than a week after assassinating Ziggy he was in a studio in France hoping to exorcise all ghosts on his next album. *Pin Ups* was a collection of cover versions of his favourite songs from the ''64–'67 period of London', including Syd Barrett and Pink Floyd's 'See Emily Play' and The Yardbirds' H. G. Wells-inspired 'Shapes Of Things'. Yet the raw wounds of his recent severance were too easily displayed. The back sleeve of *Pin Ups* featured live photos of Ziggy. He also looked a lot like Ziggy on the cover, posing with model Twiggy, 'the Wonderkid' of 'Drive-In Saturday'. And he still looked like Ziggy when he filmed an American television special in London at the Marquee club that October, *The 1980 Floor Show*. But it wasn't Ziggy, only David twitching the strings of a marionette corpse in shellshocked confusion.

By the winter of '73, he'd announced work on two musicals, one based upon Orwell's *Nineteen Eighty-Four*, the other apparently the story of Ziggy Stardust, fleshing out the album's hitherto non-existent plot with five new songs. He tried to explain the premise, thinking aloud as he made sense, and nonsense, of his recent alien possession, when paired with William Burroughs – Kerouac's 'Old Bull Lee' – for a *Rolling Stone* interview at his new home; as part of the detoxification of Ziggy, he'd been forced to leave the cosy mothership of Haddon Hall for a Chelsea townhouse.

The proposed Ziggy musical was a nebulous sci-fi saga about the end of the world, a planet with no electricity and strange 'black hole jumpers' from another galaxy called 'the Infinites'. Denying the gay Sombrero roots of 'All The Young Dudes', he now insisted it was a gloomy requiem for an apocalyptic future where, in the absence of news, it was Ziggy's mission to go and collect it. All of which was entirely retroactive, as were his later claims that Burroughs himself was a prime influence on the Ziggy concept, specifically the 1971 novel *The Wild Boys*. David hadn't read it at the time.

In the end, neither of David's musicals were completed, though new songs intended for both, along with the re-modelled scraps of Ziggy's 'Zion' (now woven into 'Sweet Thing (Reprise)'), formed the basis of his next album released in May 1974. The consecrated platter of pop perfection called *Diamond Dogs*. On the cover, he still looked a lot like Ziggy.

David Bowie would continue to look a lot like Ziggy until the summer of 1974, finally snipping the mullet and brushing a heavy side-parting as he embarked on his epic *Diamond Dogs* tour of North America. In the physical and emotional aftershock of the Starman's evacuation, he'd latterly developed a torrential cocaine addiction, all too thinly veiled in Alan Yentob's BBC *Omnibus* documentary *Cracked Actor* broadcast in January 1975. Its scenes of David being chauffeured sniffing and twitching through the American desert talking about the dead fly bobbing in his milk nevertheless excited the interest of director Nicolas Roeg, then in the process of casting his next film based on the Walter Tevis novel, *The Man Who Fell To Earth*.

And so David landed its lead as the extraterrestrial Thomas Jerome Newton and became a Starman all over again. Roeg tweaked Tevis' original tragedy, blurring all boundaries between art and life, as Newton ends the film a substance-abusing recording artist, making an album called *The Visitor* comprising of messages to his dying planet. After shooting, David kept his character's wardrobe, becoming Newton the alien on screen and off. Production stills from the film would also provide the covers of his blackout-inducingly brilliant mid-seventies albums *Station To Station* and *Low*. Roeg had intended David to compose the soundtrack but negotiations broke down over time and money. The job was instead handed to John Phillips, formerly of The Mamas And The Papas, mixing original music with pre-existing pieces including Holst's 'Mars, The Bringer Of War'. For the closing credits, Phillips selected a swing instrumental from the 1940s recorded by Artie Shaw. A popular song that never loses favour. The last frame of *The Man Who Fell To Earth* froze on David's behatted head to the sound of Hoagy Carmichael's 'Stardust'.

David would escape into new songs, new trousers, new epochs, new accidents and new reflections in his mirror. But the world would never let him forget the lightning-shaped shadow of his past. Sometimes, when asked politely, he'd rake over the ashes of the Starman in interviews: sometimes throwing out red herrings about Burroughs or supposedly taking the name Ziggy from a tailor's he'd claimed to have seen from a train window; and sometimes honestly explaining how he 'fell for Ziggy', how he was 'obsessed night and day with the character' to the detriment of his own identity as David Bowie. Not by way of confession, or a boast, just a simple truth.

'I became Ziggy Stardust.'

Mick Ronson remained at David's left-hand side through *Pin Ups* and *The 1980 Floor Show* before launching his solo career with 1974's

Slaughter On 10th Avenue. The album featured songs co-written with David and, in places, chafed uncommonly rich rock 'n' roll heavens but failed to propel Ronno to the star status MainMan had wished. The same year Mick joined Mott The Hoople for their farewell single, 'Saturday Gig', and continued touring and recording with Ian Hunter thereafter. Mick eventually married Ziggy's follicle-goddess Suzi Fussey in 1976. They had a daughter, Lisa, the following year.

In April 1992, Mick reunited with David on stage at The Freddie Mercury Tribute Concert at Wembley Stadium for 'All The Young Dudes' (with Hunter) and '"Heroes"'. The Spidery bond reconnected, David invited him to play on his next album, *Black Tie White Noise,* dusting down Ziggy's old favourite, Cream's 'I Feel Free'. The month of its release, April 1993, Ronson lost his battle with liver cancer and Planet Earth bid farewell to its greatest and most genteel guitar legend. He was 46.

'Weird' Trevor Bolder was so upset by the Hammersmith announcement he refused to attend the following night's Café Royal party. To his surprise, he was subsequently invited to record *Pin Ups* in France, also joining Ronson on stage at the Marquee for *The 1980 Floor Show.* It was the last time he worked with David.

'Gilly' Woody Woodmansey was just as aggrieved but still went to the Café Royal hoping he had a future with David. A week later, on the morning of his wedding at the British Church of Scientology headquarters, where Garson The Parson performed the ceremony, he received a phone call from MainMan informing him his services were no longer required; his initial replacement on *Pin Ups* and *Diamond Dogs* was Aynsley Dunbar, formerly of John Mayall's Bluesbreakers.

Mike Garson continued to work and tour with David up until 1975's *Young Americans.* After relinquishing Scientology, he reunited with David on 1993's *Black Tie White Noise,* playing keyboards on every major Bowie tour thereafter.

In 1976, Bolder, Woodmansey and Garson, with a new singer and guitarist, released an eponymous album under the name The Spiders From Mars. A mistake which the world has done well to largely forget.

David parted company with Tony DeFries and MainMan in 1975. For contractual reasons, DeFries still profited from a considerable share of David's earnings well into the 1980s.

Angie and David were divorced in February 1980. Their son, Zowie, who at the age of two was granted his own shortlived 'fan club' through MainMan, later reverted to the name of Duncan Jones.

Iggy Pop survived heroin addiction and a Los Angeles mental hospital, where David 'rescued' him one day in 1976 to join him in Berlin. There they made Iggy's albums *The Idiot* and *Lust For Life*. A few years later in Switzerland, David also taught Iggy to ski. 'He was a good instructor,' says Iggy.

Relations between Lou Reed and David soured following a drunken brawl in a Knightsbridge restaurant in 1979. Time healed the wounds and Lou later joined David as a special guest of his fiftieth birthday concert in 1997.

Terry Burns' mental health deteriorated. A week after David's thirty-eighth birthday, in January 1985, he committed suicide on the railtrack near the grounds of his hospital, Cane Hill, south of Croydon. He was 47. His and David's mother, Peggy Jones, passed away in 2001, aged 88.

Freddie Burretti continued to design clothes for David through the *Diamond Dogs* era. He later moved to Paris in the early-nineties, where he died peacefully in his sleep in May 2001, aged 49.

Cyrinda Foxe married New York Doll David Johansen in 1977. They divorced a year later with Foxe immediately marrying Aerosmith singer Steven Tyler. Foxe would also divorce Tyler long before her death in September 2002 following a stroke and an inoperable brain tumour, aged 50.

After leaving psychiatric care Brian Holden, alias Vince Taylor, eventually moved to Switzerland where he worked as a maintenance mechanic at Geneva airport. He died in August 1991, aged 52.

Tony Visconti parted company with T. Rex in late 1973. The following year he resumed his work with David on the mixing of *Diamond Dogs* and played an integral role in Bowie's later albums that decade, co-producing the tectonic-plate-shifting 'Berlin trilogy' of *Low*, *"Heroes"* and *Lodger*.

And then there was Marc. He heroically maintained T. Rex through ensuing line-up changes, the acrimonious severance from Visconti and the breakdown of his marriage, while overcoming his own alcohol and drug excesses, his records still sometimes rumbling with the ancient thrill of T. Rexstasy even if sales sadly never reflected. In 1977, the former producer of *Lift Off With Ayshea*, Muriel Young, granted Marc his own equivalent children's pop show. The last episode of *Marc* was recorded on 9 September, with David as his special guest. After performing his new single, '"Heroes"', David was joined by Marc for the preview of a historic, hatchet-burying Bowie/Bolan original, 'Standing Next To You'. Following a long instrumental introduction based on the riff of Bo Diddley's 'Road Runner', David leaned forward to sing the opening verse at the precise moment Marc tripped over a lead and fell off the stage. There was no time to record another take. The 'song', tottering to an abortive halt after fifty-seven seconds, marked by a brief mushy Bowie howl before he started laughing, had to be broadcast as was. By the time it was aired at the end of the month, Marc was dead.

Just as he'd predicted to Russell Harty and *Mirabelle*, King Mod never lived to see old age. At approximately 4 a.m. on Friday 16 September, Marc was in the passenger seat of a purple Mini driven by his girlfriend, singer Gloria Jones, when it careered off the road after crossing a humpback railway bridge in Barnes and crashed into a sycamore tree. Jones survived but Marc was killed instantly. He was 29. Four days later, his funeral took place at Golders Green Crematorium.

Among the congregation sat David Bowie, a giant pair of dark glasses hiding his tears. And the private, confused phantom sobs of his former cosmic messiah.

So our world turns and twists around our sun and every day that dawns after 3 July 1973 is another on our lonely planet without the Starman. Well, no. Not quite without.

The dead London that Ziggy left behind in 1973 has changed its face but its ancient bones hold firm, and much of Ziggy's spirit within them. We can still wander to the Charing Cross corner of Denmark Street, number nine, and find that the building which once housed La Gioconda still stands. We can gently trace the footsteps of David Jones and Vince Taylor past building works to the far end of Oxford Street and the pavement outside Tottenham Court Road tube station where together they crouched on the ground, analysing a map of the world, talking about spaceships and planting seeds of future wonderment.

We can continue along Oxford Street, turning left in to Dean Street, a third of the way down cutting right into the pedestrian passage St Anne's Court. We pause, humbled in awe, outside number 17, once home to Trident Studios. Here, under these bricks, down in the basement, Ziggy sang 'Starman', had his 'Moonage Daydream' and committed 'Rock 'N' Roll Suicide'. All of the *Ziggy* album and most of *Aladdin Sane* was conjured here. So too Lou's *Transformer* and David's earlier albums including *Hunky Dory*. Close your eyes and imagine the 1969 echo of Bowie cutting the master take of 'Space Oddity' inches below your toes. And perhaps kowtow and kiss the ground when you consider that it was here Tony Visconti played around with the echo on Marc Bolan's guitar while taping 'Ride A White Swan' one July day in 1970. This tiny, secreted nook, this insignificant dotted line in a *London A–Z* guide is the end of the rainbow. A manger from Mars stuffed out of sight down a Soho back alley. You are standing at the undisputed birthplace of glam rock.

A gathering of the senses and we can turn right up Wardour Street, cutting left along Noel Street, to the far end of Great Marlborough Street, past Liberty's department store (where, maybe, Ziggy picked the fabric for his first Freddie Burretti suit as featured on the cover of the *Ziggy* album) to the corner of Regent Street. We could turn right and head towards Oxford Circus, to the shop at 252 Regent Street where upstairs, in what were once his management offices, Ziggy first told Michael Watts of *Melody Maker* he was gay and always had been. Or maybe left, straight on to the corner with Piccadilly Circus to imbibe the funereal vibes of 4 July 1973 at the Café Royal. But better to cross over and head Piccadilly-wards on the opposite side of the road, past the brand name fashion houses until seeing a small passageway on our right leading under a lintel marked 'Heddon House'. Walking through, straight in front of us at the top end of the alley is a red telephone box. Not the same model – a later K6 rather than a vintage K2, note the difference in the shapes of the glass panelling – but in exactly the same spot as the one where Ziggy took shelter in January 1972.

Where there were furriers, dressmakers and photo studios, now Heddon Street is jammed with bars and restaurants. So jammed that not everyone bothers to take notice of the plaque in the brickwork of number twenty-three where once a gas lamp jutted out. A black plaque unveiled in March 2012 bearing the words 'ZIGGY STARDUST, 1972'. Behold, and salute, his sacred crib. The great city of the Starman has not forgotten him.

Nor can it. Nor can we. Ziggy Stardust lives on in more than plaques and ageing mortar, more than in his music and the twenty-first-century ubiquity of his flash-bisected image. He lives not in the past, but in today's present and tomorrow's future. In words, in music, in fashion and in art. In pout, in posture, in silver nails and feather boa. In the undying, invincible flash of youth. In the heroic bedroom hopes of escape in every stifling, backwater Nothingville on Earth. In every spat-upon nobody who looks in the mirror with the blind faith that they are a superstar. In everyone who chooses not to be a radio but a colour television set.

And in all who cherish the beautiful truth of his dying gospel. That we, all of us human beings, are glittering, glamorous miracles of existence in a near fourteen-billion-year-old story of cosmic creation. Moulded from the same galactic clay. Woven from the same microscopic threads of stellar flotsam. Each one of us, it's true, as *'won-der-ful!'* as he sang.

For we are all made of stardust. We are all Ziggy Stardust.

ZIGGYOGRAPHIES

ZIGGY & FRIENDS ON RECORD 1972–1973

1972

April   **'Starman'** b/w 'Suffragette City'
David Bowie, RCA Victor, RCA 2199. Highest UK chart position: #10 in July 1972.

June   **THE RISE AND FALL OF ZIGGY STARDUST AND THE SPIDERS FROM MARS**
'Five Years', 'Soul Love', 'Moonage Daydream', 'Starman', 'It Ain't Easy', 'Lady Stardust', 'Star', 'Hang On To Yourself', 'Ziggy Stardust', 'Suffragette City', 'Rock 'N' Roll Suicide'
David Bowie, RCA Victor, SF8287. Highest UK chart position: #5 in February 1973.

'The Supermen'
Ziggy and The Spiders' specially rerecorded version of earlier Bowie track included on the compilation album Revelations: A Musical Anthology For Glastonbury Fayre, *Revelation, REV 1/2/3*

July   **'All The Young Dudes'** b/w 'One Of The Boys'
Mott The Hoople, CBS, S8217. Highest UK chart position: #3 in September 1972.

Sept   **'John, I'm Only Dancing'** b/w 'Hang On To Yourself'
David Bowie, RCA Victor, RCA 2263. Highest UK chart position: #12 in October 1972.

ALL THE YOUNG DUDES

'Sweet Jane', 'Momma's Little Jewel', 'All The Young Dudes', 'Sucker', 'Jerkin' Crocus', 'One Of The Boys', 'Soft Ground', 'Ready For Love/After Lights', 'Sea Diver'
Mott The Hoople, CBS, S65184. Highest UK chart position: #21 in September 1972.

Nov   **'Walk On The Wild Side'** b/w 'Perfect Day'
Lou Reed, RCA Victor, RCA 2303. Highest UK chart position: #10 in June 1973.

TRANSFORMER

'Vicious', 'Andy's Chest', 'Perfect Day', 'Hangin' Round', 'Walk On The Wild Side', 'Make Up', 'Satellite Of Love', 'Wagon Wheel', 'New York Telephone Conversation', 'I'm So Free', 'Goodnight Ladies'
Lou Reed. RCA Victor, LSP 4807. Highest UK chart position: #13 in September 1973.

SPACE ODDITY

'Space Oddity', 'Unwashed And Somewhat Slightly Dazed', 'Letter To Hermione', 'Cygnet Committee', 'Janine', 'An Occasional Dream', 'Wild Eyed Boy From Freecloud', 'God Knows I'm Good', 'Memory Of A Free Festival'
David Bowie, retitled reissue of 1969 David Bowie LP in new Ziggy sleeve (red-haired portrait by Mick Rock, taken at Haddon Hall). RCA Victor, LSP 4813. Highest UK chart position: #17 in August 1973.

THE MAN WHO SOLD THE WORLD

'The Width Of A Circle', 'All The Madmen', 'Black Country Rock', 'After All', 'Running Gun Blues', 'Saviour Machine', 'She Shook Me Cold', 'The Man Who Sold The World', 'The Supermen'

David Bowie, reissue of 1971 LP in new Ziggy sleeve (black and white leg-kick portrait by Brian Ward). RCA Victor, LSP 4816. Highest UK chart position: #24 in September 1973.

'The Jean Genie' b/w 'Ziggy Stardust'
David Bowie, RCA Victor, RCA 2302. Highest UK chart position: #2 in January 1973.

1973

Feb   **'Satellite Of Love'** b/w 'Vicious'
        Lou Reed, RCA Victor, RCA 2318. No UK chart position.

April   **'Drive-In Saturday'** b/w 'Round And Round'
        David Bowie, RCA Victor, RCA 2352. Highest UK chart position: #3 in May 1973.

ALADDIN SANE

'Watch That Man', 'Aladdin Sane (1913–1938–197?)', 'Drive-In Saturday', 'Panic In Detroit', 'Cracked Actor', 'Time', 'The Prettiest Star', 'Let's Spend The Night Together', 'The Jean Genie', 'Lady Grinning Soul'

David Bowie, RCA Victor, LSP 4852. Highest UK chart position: #1 in May 1973. Aladdin Sane *was officially the biggest selling UK album of 1973.*

June   **RAW POWER**

'Search And Destroy', 'Gimme Danger', 'Your Pretty Face Is Going To Hell (Originally titled 'Hard To Beat')', 'Penetration', 'Raw Power', 'I Need Somebody', 'Shake Appeal', 'Death Trip' *Iggy And The Stooges, CBS, S65586. No UK chart position.*

'Life On Mars?' b/w 'The Man Who Sold The World' *David Bowie, RCA Victor, RCA 2316. Highest UK chart position: #3 in July 1973. The last release during Ziggy's lifetime.*

David Bowie's *Hunky Dory* album, first released in December 1971, enjoyed its greatest commercial success after the death of Ziggy in the autumn of 1973, reaching number three that September. That same month, the Bowie albums *Hunky Dory, Ziggy Stardust* and *Aladdin Sane* could be found leaping around one another in the top ten with the reissued *Space Oddity* and *The Man Who Sold The World* further down: a total of five Bowie albums in the UK album charts at any given time. His dominance was compounded that November with the release of the covers album *Pin Ups*, entering at number one.

Ziggy's 'Rock 'N' Roll Suicide' was issued as a single in April 1974, confusingly circa the release of Bowie's *Diamond Dogs*. It reached number 22 in May.

Also in early 1974, Lulu released her Bowie-produced version of Ziggy's 'Watch That Man' on the B-side of her cover of 'The Man Who Sold The World'. The A-side provided Lulu with her first top ten hit in five years, peaking at number three that February.

The highest charting 45 r.p.m. Ziggy recording, if only by default, remains the album outtake **'Velvet Goldmine'** (originally 'He's A Goldmine') posthumously released on a three-track 'maxi-single' of 'Space Oddity' alongside 'Changes' in September 1975 which became

David Bowie's first UK number one single, spending a fortnight at the top in early November.

Many of the best Ziggy recordings were also issued posthumously. These include the studio outtakes **'All The Young Dudes'** (Ziggy's vocal), **'Holy Holy'** (The Spiders' stunning rerecording of Bowie's 1970 flop single), **'John, I'm Only Dancing'** (the *Aladdin Sane* session 'sax version') and **'Sweet Head'**. Jaques Brel's **'Amsterdam'**, once destined for the *Ziggy Stardust* album, had been recorded by David in 1971 and was finally released as the B-side of 1973's 'Sorrow' single.

Ziggy's live performances of The Velvet Underground's **'White Light/ White Heat'** and Brel's **'My Death'** are available on the soundtrack of D. A. Pennebaker's film of the final Hammersmith Odeon concert, first issued as *Ziggy Stardust – The Motion Picture*. 'My Death' also features on the equally essential concert album *Santa Monica '72* along with the Spiders' charge through The Velvet Underground's **'I'm Waiting For The Man'**.

A poor quality live recording of Ziggy's cover of Cream's **'I Feel Free'** was released on the 1997 compilation *RarestOneBowie*. Other cover versions performed on stage by Ziggy and the Spiders include: The Who's **'I Can't Explain'** (later recorded by Bowie for *Pin Ups*), The Beatles' **'This Boy'** and **'Love Me Do'** (the latter medleyed with 'The Jean Genie'), Judy Garland's **'Over The Rainbow'** (incorporated into 'Starman' during his August 1972 London Rainbow shows) and the shortlived James Brown medley of **'You Got To Have A Job (If You Don't Work – You Don't Eat)'/'Hot Pants'**.

ZIGGY ON STAGE 1972-73

Later concerts marked * indicate two shows played on the same day.

1972

Jan   29. Aylesbury, Borough Assembly Hall, Friars Club

Feb   10. London, Tolworth, The Toby Jug
        12. London, South Kensington, Imperial College
        14. Brighton, Dome
        18. Sheffield, University
        23. Chichester, Chichester College
        24. London, Sutton, Wallington Public Hall
        25. London, Eltham, Avery Hill College
        26. Sutton Coldfield, Belfry Hotel

March 1. Bristol, University
        4. Portsmouth, Southsea, Pier Pavilion
        7. Yeovil, Yeovil College
        11. Southampton, Guild Hall
        14. Bournemouth, Chelsea Village
        17. Birmingham, Town Hall
        24. Newcastle, Mayfair Ballroom

April   20. Harlow, The Playhouse
        21. Manchester, Free Trade Hall
        30. Plymouth, Guild Hall

May   5. Aberystwyth, University
        6. London, Kingston-Upon-Thames, Kingston Polytechnic
        7. Hemel Hempstead, Pavilion

11. Worthing, Assembly Hall
12. London, Marylebone, Polytechnic of Central London
13. Slough, Technical College
19. Oxford, Polytechnic
25. Bournemouth, Chelsea Village
27. Epsom, Ebbisham Hall

June
2. Newcastle, City Hall
3. Liverpool, Stadium
4. Preston, Public Hall
6. Bradford, St George's Hall
7. Sheffield, City Hall
8. Middlesbrough, Town Hall
13. Bristol, Colston Hall
16. Torquay, Town Hall
17. Oxford, Town Hall
19. Southampton, Civic Centre
21. Dunstable, Civic Hall
25. Croydon, The Greyhound

July
1. Weston-Super-Mare, Winter Gardens Pavilion
2. Torquay, Rainbow Pavilion
8. London, Southbank, Royal Festival Hall
15. Aylesbury, Borough Assembly Hall, Friars Club

Aug
19. London, Finsbury Park, the Rainbow
20. London, Finsbury Park, the Rainbow
27. Bristol, Locarno Electric Village
30. London, Finsbury Park, the Rainbow
31. Boscombe, Royal Ballrooms

Sept	1.	Doncaster, Top Rank Suite
	2.	Manchester, Stretford, the Hardrock
	3.	Manchester, Stretford, the Hardrock
	4.	Liverpool, Top Rank Suite
	5.	Sunderland, Top Rank Suite
	6.	Sheffield, Top Rank Suite
	7.	Stoke-On-Trent, Hanley, Top Rank Suite
	22.	Cleveland (Ohio, USA), Music Hall
	24.	Memphis (Tennessee, USA), Ellis Auditorium
	28.	New York City (New York, USA), Carnegie Hall

Oct	1.	Boston (Massachusetts, USA), Music Hall
	7.	Chicago (Illinois, USA), Auditorium Theatre
	8.	Detroit (Michigan, USA), Fisher Theatre
	11.	St Louis (Missouri, USA), Kiel Auditorium
	15.	Kansas City (Kansas, USA), Memorial Hall
	20.	Los Angeles (California, USA), Santa Monica Civic Auditorium
	21.	Los Angeles (California, USA), Santa Monica Civic Auditorium
	27.	San Francisco (California, USA), Winterland
	28.	San Francisco (California, USA), Winterland

Nov	1.	Seattle (Washington, USA), Paramount Theatre
	2.	Phoenix (Arizona, USA), Celebrity Theatre
	11.	Dallas (Texas, USA), Majestic Theatre
	12.	Houston (Texas, USA), Music Hall
	14.	New Orleans (Louisiana, USA), Loyola University
	17.	Miami (Florida, USA), Jai Alai Fronton
	20.	Nashville (Tennessee, USA), Municipal Auditorium
	22.	New Orleans (Louisiana, USA), The Warehouse

25. Cleveland (Ohio, USA), Public Auditorium
26. Cleveland (Ohio, USA), Public Auditorium
28. Pittsburgh (Pennsylvania, USA), Stanley Theatre
29. *Philadelphia (Pennsylvania, USA), Tower Theatre (Ziggy as special guest of Mott The Hoople for encore of 'All The Young Dudes' and 'Honky Tonk Women')*
30. Philadelphia (Pennsylvania, USA), Tower Theatre

Dec
1. Philadelphia (Pennsylvania, USA), Tower Theatre
2. Philadelphia (Pennsylvania, USA), Tower Theatre
23. London, Finsbury Park, the Rainbow
24. London, Finsbury Park, the Rainbow
28. Manchester, Stretford, the Hardrock
29. Manchester, Stretford, the Hardrock

1973

Jan
5. Glasgow, Green's Playhouse
6. Edinburgh, Empire Theatre
7. Newcastle, City Hall
9. Preston, Guild Hall

Feb
14. New York City (New York, USA), Radio City Music Hall
15. New York City (New York, USA), Radio City Music Hall
16. Philadelphia (Pennsylvania, USA), Tower Theatre
17. Philadelphia (Pennsylvania, USA), Tower Theatre *
18. Philadelphia (Pennsylvania, USA), Tower Theatre *
19. Philadelphia (Pennsylvania, USA), Tower Theatre *
23. Nashville (Tennessee, USA), War Memorial Auditorium
26. Memphis (Tennessee, USA), Ellis Auditorium *

March 1. Detroit (Michigan, USA), Masonic Temple
2. Detroit (Michigan, USA), Masonic Temple
4. Chicago (Illinois), Aragon Ballroom
10. Los Angeles (California, USA), Long Beach Arena
12. Los Angeles (California, USA), Hollywood Palladium

April 8. Tokyo (Japan), Shinjuku Koseinenkin Kaikan
10. Tokyo (Japan), Shinjuku Koseinenkin Kaikan
11. Tokyo (Japan), Shinjuku Koseinenkin Kaikan
12. Nagoya (Japan), Kokaido Hall
14. Hiroshima (Japan), Yubin Chokin Kaikan
16. Kobe (Japan), Kokusai Kaikan Hall
17. Osaka (Japan), Koseinenkin Kaikan
18. Tokyo (Japan), Shibuya Kokaido
20. Tokyo (Japan), Shibuya Kokaido

May 12. London, Earls Court, Earls Court Exhibition Centre
16. Aberdeen, Music Hall *
17. Dundee, Caird Hall
18. Glasgow, Green's Playhouse *
19. Edinburgh, Empire Theatre
21. Norwich, Theatre Royal *
22. Romford, Odeon
23. Brighton, Dome *
24. London, Lewisham, Odeon
25. Bournemouth, Winter Gardens
27. Guildford, Civic Hall *
28. Wolverhampton, Civic Hall
29. Stoke-On-Trent, Hanley, Victoria Hall
30. Oxford, New Theatre
31. Blackburn, King George's Hall

June

1. Bradford, St George's Hall
3. Coventry, New Theatre
4. Worcester, Gaumont
6. Sheffield, City Hall *
7. Manchester, Free Trade Hall *
8. Newcastle, City Hall *
9. Preston, Guild Hall
10. Liverpool, Empire Theatre *
11. Leicester, De Montfort Hall
12. Chatham, Central Hall *
13. London, Kilburn, Gaumont
14. Salisbury, City Hall
15. Taunton, Odeon *
16. Torquay, Town Hall *
18. Bristol, Colston Hall *
19. Southampton, Guild Hall
21. Birmingham, Town Hall *
22. Birmingham, Town Hall *
23. Boston (Lincolnshire), Gliderdrome
24. Croydon, Fairfield Halls *
25. Oxford, New Theatre *
26. Oxford, New Theatre
27. Doncaster, Top Rank Suite
28. Bridlington, Spa Ballroom
29. Leeds, Rolarena
30. Newcastle, City Hall *

July

2. London, Hammersmith, Odeon
3. London, Hammersmith, Odeon

ZIGGY ON TELEVISION 1972–73

Ziggy and the Spiders made only a handful of UK television appearances in their brief lifetime yet all were of cataclysmic cultural importance. The majority, listed here in order of broadcast date, consisted of mimed performances to backing tracks with live vocal. Performances marked * are those available on the 2002 DVD *Best Of Bowie* (EMI, 4901039)

1972

Feb   **The Old Grey Whistle Test**
'Queen Bitch' *, 'Five Years' *
Broadcast on BBC 2, Tuesday 8 February, recorded 7 February.
'Oh! You Pretty Things' *was also recorded but not aired at the time.*

June   **Lift Off With Ayshea**
'Starman'
Broadcast on ITV, Wednesday 21 June, recorded 15 June.

July   **Top Of The Pops**
'Starman' *
Broadcast on BBC 1, Thursday 6 July, recorded 5 July. Repeated on 20 July and on 25 December as part of the Christmas special Top Of The Pops '72.

1973

Jan   **Top Of The Pops**
'The Jean Genie'
Live studio performance (including Ziggy's tribute to The Beatles' 'Love Me Do' on harmonica) broadcast on BBC 1, Thursday 4 January, recorded 3 January.

Russell Harty Plus

'Drive-In Saturday' *, 'My Death'

Broadcast on ITV, Saturday 20 January, recorded 17 January. The show was a 'Pop' special of a programme ordinarily called Russell Harty Plus *and included Ziggy's only sit-down television interview.*

June   **Nationwide**

Filmed report of Ziggy's final UK tour including live clips and interview, broadcast on BBC 1, Tuesday 5 June 1973.

All the above clips have survived apart from the Ayshea performance, the tapes sadly since wiped by Granada Television. The full July 1972 episode of *Top Of The Pops* featuring 'Starman' was also wiped by the BBC: the historic clip only survives through its licensing at the time to foreign television. *Top Of The Pops* also broadcast the promo films directed by Mick Rock for the singles 'The Jean Genie' (featuring Cyrinda Foxe) and 'Life On Mars?' As previously mentioned, the BBC refused to broadcast Rock's earlier promo for 'John, I'm Only Dancing'. The version of 'Oh! You Pretty Things' recorded for *The Old Grey Whistle Test* was finally broadcast in the 1980s and also included on the *Best Of Bowie* DVD .

ZIGGY ON RADIO

In the first half of 1972 Ziggy and the Spiders recorded five sessions for BBC Radio 1, listed below in order of original broadcast date. Tracks marked * are those which were later compiled on the 2000 double-CD compilation album *Bowie At The Beeb* (EMI, 7243 52862924).

Jan   **Sounds Of The 70s: John Peel**
'Hang On To Yourself', 'Ziggy Stardust', Queen Bitch', 'I'm Waiting For The Man', 'Lady Stardust'
First broadcast BBC Radio 1, Friday 28 January, recorded 11 January.

Feb   **Sounds Of The 70s: Bob Harris**
'Hang On To Yourself' *, 'Ziggy Stardust' *, Queen Bitch' *, 'Five Years' *
First broadcast BBC Radio 1, Monday 7 February, recorded 18 January. 'I'm Waiting For The Man' * *was also recorded but never broadcast.*

May   **Sounds Of The 70s: John Peel**
'White Light/White Heat' *, 'Hang On To Yourself' *, 'Suffragette City' *, 'Ziggy Stardust' *
First broadcast BBC Radio 1, Tuesday 23 May, recorded 16 May.

June   **Johnnie Walker**
'Starman' *, 'Space Oddity' *, 'Changes' *, 'Oh! You Pretty Things' *
First broadcast BBC Radio 1, Monday 5 June, recorded 22 May.

Sounds Of The 70s: Bob Harris

'Andy Warhol' *, 'Lady Stardust' *, 'White Light/White Heat', 'Rock 'N' Roll Suicide' *

First broadcast BBC Radio 1, Monday 19 June, recorded 23 May.

July   **Sounds Of The 70s: John Peel**

Broadcast BBC Radio 1, Tuesday 25 July, a repeat of 'White Light/White Heat' *and* 'Suffragette City' *from 23 May* Sounds Of The '70s: John Peel *session along with the previously unbroadcast* 'Moonage Daydream' *. All tracks recorded 16 May.*

THE ZIGGYOLOGY BIBLIOGRAPHY

Agel, Jerome (editor), *The Making Of Kubrick's 2001* (Signet, 1970)

Ambaras, David R., *Bad Youth: Juvenile Delinquency And The Politics Of Everyday Life In Modern Japan* (University of California Press, 2006)

Ambrose, Joe, *Gimme Danger – The Story Of Iggy Pop* (Omnibus Press, 2004)

Angell, Callie, *Andy Warhol Screen Tests* (Abrams, 2006)

Anthon, Charles, *A Classical Dictionary* (Harper, 1869)

Antonia, Nina, *The New York Dolls – Too Much Too Soon* (Omnibus Press, 2006)

Antonia, Nina, *The Prettiest Star – Whatever Happened To Brett Smiley?* (SAF, 2005)

Aughton, Peter, *The Story Of Astronomy* (Quercus, 2008)

Austen, Jake (editor), *Flying Saucers Rock 'N' Roll* (Duke University Press, 2011)

Berry, Chuck, *Chuck Berry – The Autobiography* (Faber & Faber, 1988)

Bockris, Victor and Gerard Malanga, *Up-Tight: The Velvet Underground Story* (Omnibus Press, 1983)

Bodanis, David, *E=mc2: A Biography Of The World's Most Famous Equation* (Berkley, 2000)

Bowie, Angela and Patrick Carr, *Backstage Passes – Life On The Wild Side With David Bowie* (Cooper Square Press, 2000)

Bradbury, Ray with Arthur C. Clarke, Bruce Murray, Carl Sagan and Walter Sullivan, *Mars And The Mind Of Man* (Harper & Row,1973)

Brake, Mark L. and Neil Hook, *Different Engines: How Science Drives Fiction And Fiction Drives Science* (Macmillan, 2008)

Brome, Vincent, *H. G. Wells – A Biography* (House Of Stratus, 2001)

Brooks, Michael, *The Big Questions: Physics* (Quercus, 2010)

Brown, Ivor, *H. G. Wells* (Nisbet & Co., 1923)

Burgess, Anthony, *A Clockwork Orange* (W. W. Norton, 1986)

Burgess, Anthony, *Little Wilson And Big God* (Heinemann, 1987)

Burgess, Anthony, *You've Had Your Time* (Heinemann, 1990)

Burroughs, William S., *The Wild Boys* (Penguin Classics, 2008)

Cann, Kevin, *Any Day Now: David Bowie – The London Years 1947–74* (Adelita, 2010)

Carey, Hugh, *Duet For Two Voices: An Informal Biography Of Edward Dent Compiled From His Letters To Clive Carey* (Cambridge University Press, 1980)

Cato, Philip, *Crash Course For The Ravers – A Glam Odyssey* (S.T. Publishing 1997)

Chusid, Irwin, *Songs In The Key Of Z* (Cherry Red Books, 2000)

Clark, Stuart, *The Big Questions: The Universe* (Quercus, 2010)

Condon, Dr Edward, *Scientific Study Of Unidentified Flying Objects* (Bantam, 1969)

Conway, Michael with Dion McGregor and Mark Ricci, *The Films Of Greta Garbo* (Citadel Press, 1974)

Coren, Michael, *The Invisible Man – The Life And Liberties of H. G. Wells* (Bloomsbury, 1993)

Crowe, Michael J., *The Extraterrestrial Life Debate: Antiquity To 1915 (A Source Book)* (University Of Notre Dame, 2008)

Dawson, Jim and Steve Propes, *What Was The First Rock 'N' Roll Record?* (Faber & Faber, 1992)

De Saint-Exupéry, Antoine, *The Little Prince* (Wordsworth, 1995)

Dickson, Lovat, *H. G. Wells – His Turbulent Life And Times* (MacMillan, 1969)

Edwards, Frank, *Strange People* (Pan, 1966)

Edwards, Henry and Tony Zanetta, *Stardust – The David Bowie Story* (McGraw-Hill, 1986)

Elson, Howard, *Early Rockers* (Proteus, 1982)

Ernst, Earle, *Three Japanese Plays From The Traditional Theatre* (Oxford University Press, 1959)

Ferguson, Kitty, *Pythagoras: His Lives And The Legacy Of A Rational Universe* (Icon, 2010)

Foxe-Tyler, Cyrinda with Danny Fields, *Dream On – Livin' On The Edge With Steven Tyler And Aerosmith* (Phoenix Books, 2009)

Geller, Larry and Joel Spector, *'If I Can Dream'* (Century, 1989)

Gillman, Peter & Leni, *Alias David Bowie* (New English Library, 1987)

Glitter, Gary, *Leader – The Autobiography* (Warner Books, 1992)

Good, Timothy, *Need To Know: UFOs, The Military And Intelligence* (Pegasus, 2007)

Gordon, Robert, *The King On The Road* (Hamlyn, 1996)

Gosling, John, *Waging The War Of The Worlds* (McFarland & Company, 2009)

Greene, Richard, *Holst: The Planets* (Cambridge University Press, 1995)

Guralnick, Peter, *Careless Love: The Unmaking Of Elvis Presley* (Back Bay Books, 2000)

Guralnick, Peter, *Last Train To Memphis: The Rise Of Elvis Presley* (Back Bay Books, 1994)

Hammond, J.R., *H. G. Wells – Interviews And Recollections* (MacMillan, 1980)

Heffer, Simon, *Vaughan Williams* (Weidenfeld & Nicolson, 2000)

Heinlein, Robert A., *Grumbles From The Grave* (Orbit, 1991)

Heinlein, Robert A., *Stranger In A Strange Land* (Berkley Medallion, 1969)

Holst, Imogen, *Gustav Holst* (Oxford University Press, 1938)

Holst, Imogen, *Holst (The Great Composers)* (Faber & Faber, 1974)

Holst, Imogen, *The Music Of Gustav Holst And Holst's Music Reconsidered* (Oxford University Press, 1986)

Hopkins, Jerry, *Elvis* (Warner Paperback Library, 1972)

Hunter, Ian, *Diary Of A Rock 'N' Roll Star* (Panther, 1974)

Ikegami, Eiko, *Bonds Of Civility: Aesthetic Networks And The Political Origins Of Japanese Culture* (Cambridge University Press, 2005)

Kerouac, Jack, *On The Road* (Penguin, 1999)

Kiedrowski, Thomas, *Andy Warhol's New York City* (The Little Bookroom, 2011)

Leupp, Gary P., *Male Colors: The Construction Of Homosexuality In Tokugawa Japan* (University of California Press, 1995)

Lewis, Jerry Lee and Charles White, *Killer!* (Arrow, 1996)

MacCormack, Geoff, *From Station To Station – Travels With Bowie 1973–1976* (Genesis, 2007)

MacDonald, Ian, *Revolution In The Head: The Beatles' Records And The Sixties* (Pimlico, 1998)

MacKenzie, Norman and Jeanne, *The Time Traveller – The Life Of H. G. Wells* (Weidenfeld & Nicolson, 1973)

Marcus, Greil (et al), *Rockabilly: The Twang Heard Round The World* (Voyageur Press, 2011)

McAleer, Dave, *Hit Parade Heroes* (Hamlyn, 1993)

McEvoy, J. P., *A Brief History Of The Universe* (Robinson, 2010)

McLenehan, Cliff, *Marc Bolan: 1947–1977 A Chronology* (Helter Skelter, 2002)

McVeagh, Diana M., *Edward Elgar – His Life And Music* (J. M. Dent & Sons, 1955)

Mitton, Simon, *Fred Hoyle: A Life In Science* (Cambridge University Press, 2011)

Moore, Scotty with James Dickerson, *That's Alright, Elvis* (Schirmer, 1997)

Murray, Andy, *Into The Unknown: The Fantastic Life Of Nigel Kneale* (Headpress, 2005)

Nash, Alanna, *Elvis Aaron Presley: Revelations From The Memphis Mafia* (Harper, 1996)

Newman, Ernest, *The Unconscious Beethoven* (Victor Gollancz, 1968)

Ortolani, Benito, *The Japanese Theatre: From Shamanistic Ritual To Contemporary Pluralism* (Princeton University Press, 1995)

Orwell, George, *Critical Essays* (Secker & Warburg, 1946)

Parrinder, Patrick, *H. G. Wells – The Critical Heritage* (Routledge, 1972)

Paytress, Mark, *Bolan – The Rise And Fall Of A 20th Century Superstar* (Omnibus Press, 2002)

Pegg, Nicholas, *The Complete David Bowie* (Titan, 2011)

Pierce, Patricia Jobe, *The Ultimate Elvis* (Simon & Schuster, 1994)

Pitt, Kenneth, *Bowie: The Pitt Report* (Omnibus Press, 1980)

Pound, Ezra and Ernest Fenollosa, *The Classic Noh Theatre Of Japan* (New Directions, 1959)

Pryce-Jones, Alan, *Beethoven* (Collier, 1966)

Redfern, Nick, *A Covert Agenda: The British Government's UFO Top Secrets Exposed* (Paraview Special Editions, 2004)

Repsch, John, *The Legendary Joe Meek* (Woodford House, 1989)

Richie, Donald, *Japanese Portraits* (Tuttle, 2006)

Roberts, David (editor), *Top 40 Charts* (Guinness Publishing, 1992)

Robertson, Alec and Denis Stevens, *The Pelican History Of Music Volume 3: Classical And Romantic* (Pelican, 1968)

Rock, Mick and David Bowie, *Moonage Daydream: The Life And Times Of Ziggy Stardust* (Universe, 2005)

Sachs, Harvey, *The Ninth: Beethoven And The World In 1824* (Faber & Faber, 2010)

Sagan, Carl, *The Cosmic Connection: An Extraterrestrial Perspective* (Cambridge University Press, 2000)

Sagan, Carl, *Cosmos* (Abacus, 1995),

Sagan, Carl with F.D. Drake, Ann Druyan, Timothy Ferris, Jon Lomberg and Linda Salzman Sagan, *Murmurs Of Earth – The Voyager Interstellar Record* (Random House, 1978)

Sagan, Carl, *The Varieties Of Scientific Experience: A Personal View Of The Search For God* (Penguin, 2006)

Sandford, Christopher, *Loving The Alien* (Time Warner, 1997)

Santoro, Gene, *Myself When I Am Real: The Life And Music Of Charles Mingus* (Oxford University Press, 2000)

Savage, Jon, *England's Dreaming* (Faber & Faber, 1991)

Savage, Jon, *The England's Dreaming Tapes* (Faber & Faber, 2009)

Schilling, Jerry with Chuck Crisafulli, *Me And A Guy Named Elvis* (Gotham Books, 2006)

Scott, A. C., *The Kabuki Theatre Of Japan* (George Allen & Unwin, 1955)

Sheehan, William, *The Planet Mars* (University of Arizona Press, 1997)

Shipman, David, *Cinema – The First Hundred Years* (Weidenfeld & Nicolson, 1993)

Smith, David C., *H. G. Wells – Desperately Mortal* (Yale University Press, 1986)

Sobel, Dava, *The Planets* (Penguin, 2006).

Suchet, John, *The Friendly Guide To Beethoven* (Hodder, 2006)

Sudhalter, Richard M., *Stardust Melody – The Life And Music Of Hoagy Carmichael* (Oxford University Press, 2002)

Sullivan, J. W. M., *Beethoven* (Pelican, 1949)

Tevis, Walter, *The Man Who Fell To Earth* (Penguin Classics, 2009)

Thompson, Dave (editor), *Beyond The Velvet Underground* (Omnibus Press, 1989)

Tremlett, George, *The David Bowie Story* (Futura, 1974)

Trynka, Paul, *Iggy Pop – Open Up And Bleed*, (Sphere, 2007)

Trynka, Paul, *Starman* (Sphere, 2011)

Turnill, Reginald, *The Observer's Spaceflight Directory* (Frederick Warne, 1978)

Unterberger, Richie, *White Light/White Heat: The Velvet Underground Day-By-Day* (Jawbone, 2009)

Verma, Surendra Verma, *Why Aren't They Here?: The Question Of Life On Other Worlds* (Icon, 2007)

Vermorel, Judy and Fred, *Fandemonium* (Omnibus Press, 1989)

Visconti, Tony with Richard Havers, *Bowie, Bolan And The Brooklyn Boy* (HarperCollins, 2007)

Warhol, Andy and Pat Hackett, *POPism: The Warhol Sixties* (Penguin Classics, 2007)

Webster, Patrick, *Love And Death In Kubrick: A Critical Study Of The Films From Lolita Through Eyes Wide Shut* (McFarland & Company, 2011)

Wegler, Franz and Ferdinand Ries, *Beethoven Remembered* (Great Ocean, 1987).

Wells, H. G., *Experiment In Autobiography Vols I & II* (Faber & Faber, 1984)

Wells, H. G., *Star-Begotten* (Sphere Books, 1975)

Wells, H. G., *Tono-Bungay* (Modern Library, 2003)

Wells, H. G., *The War Of The Worlds* (Penguin Classics, 2005)

Wertheimer, Alfred, *Elvis '56: In The Beginning* (Pimlico, 1994)

West, Anthony, *H. G. Wells – Aspects Of A Life* (Hutchinson, 2007).

Whitcomb, Ian, *Whole Lotta' Shakin': A Rock 'N' Roll Scrapbook* (Arrow Books, 1982)

White, Charles, *The Life And Times Of Little Richard* (Pan, 1985)

Wood, Sir Henry, *My Life Of Music* (Victor Gollancz, 1938)

Zak III, Albin, *The Velvet Underground Companion* (Omnibus Press/ Schirmer, 1997)

Of the above titles concerning David Bowie, three deserve special mention. The first is Kevin Cann's *Any Day Now: The London Years 1947–74*, a lusciously detailed and elegantly illustrated day-by-day catalogue of his life and career from birth until *Diamond Dogs*. The second is Nicholas Pegg's repeatedly revised *The Complete David Bowie* which as a thumping great databank of impassioned Bowie analysis, information and trivia is no less biblical a reference. If Cann is Boswell to Bowie's Johnson then Pegg is Watson to Bowie's Holmes. Theirs are the paper ministries of

Bowiedom to whom all authors staggering blindly down similar corridors will forever owe endless gratitude.

Last but by no means least is *Moonage Daydream*, David Bowie's own account of 'The Life And Times Of Ziggy Stardust' as he remembers it, published in conjunction with his friend, the legendary stardust lensman Mick Rock.

Beyond the above bibliography, *Ziggyology* was collated from too many vitamin-sapping hours subsisting on the ventilation system of the British Library, Euston Road and more so the lonesome Orwellian fortress that is the British Newspaper Library, Colindale. To cite every individual source would be to burden this book with an extra hundred pages of needlessly academic quibble-settling footnotes which would dull the lustre of the spirit in which *Ziggyology* was written. For sake of brevity, the list of periodicals consulted included: *Aberdeen Evening Express, Battersea News, The Blackshirt, Brixton Advertiser, Bromley Advertiser, Catford & Lewisham Journal, Croydon Advertiser, Curious, Daily Express, Daily Mail, Daily Mirror, Daily Telegraph, Disc & Music Echo, Dundee Courier, Evening News, Evening Standard, Fabulous 208, Fulham Chronicle, Glasgow Evening Times,* the *Guardian, Hammersmith & Fulham News & Post, Honey, Jackie, Kent and Sussex Courier, Look-In, Melody Maker, Mirabelle, Mojo, New Musical Express, Press And Journal (Aberdeen), Radio Times, Record Mirror, Sounds, The Sun,* the *Sunday Mirror, The Sunday Times, The Times, TV Times, Uncut, Vanity Fair, Vogue, West London and Hammersmith Gazette, West London Observer* and *Woman's Journal.* With particular thanks to the period interviews of Ray Fox-Cumming, Henry Edwards, Timothy Ferris, Martin Hayman, Roy Hollingworth, Nick Kent, Pete Lennon, Robert Muesel, Charles Shaar Murray, Sandie Robbie, Lisa Robinson, Mick Rock, Rosalind Russell, Annie Tipton, Andrew Tyler, Cherry Vanilla and Michael Watts.

Prologue heading Arthur C. Clarke quote from the documentary *Stanley Kubrick: A Life In Pictures* directed by Jan Harlan (Warner Bros, 2001).

Epilogue heading 'songs and trousers' quote as told to Paul Du Noyer for *Mojo* magazine, July 2002.

Thanks to Katie Ankers at the BBC Written Archives Centre for her help in accessing the production notes of the July 1972 'Starman' *Top Of The Pops* broadcast.

A last starry salute must also go to Michael Harvey who between 1996 and 2007 lovingly curated the fan website 'The Ziggy Stardust Companion', still accessible at the time of this book's publication at www.5years.com.

INDEX

THE AUTHOR

Simon Goddard was one year, six months and twelve days old when Ziggy Stardust died. His own memories of that time are forgivably foggy.

This is his third book about pop music. He lives in London.

HIS CREDITS

THE MUSICIANS ARE:
Kevin 'Weird' Pocklington at Jenny Brown Associates.
Andrew 'Gilly' Goodfellow at Ebury Press.

ARRANGEMENTS:
Susan Pegg.

PRODUCTION:
Ian Preece.

PHOTOGRAPHS:
© 1973 Lynn Goldsmith (Section 2, page 8). © Mick Rock/Retna (Section 1, page 4, bottom right; page 5; page 7 top and bottom; page 8: Section 2, page 7 bottom). © Barrie Wentzell (Section 1, page 6: Section 2, page 1; page 2, top left, bottom left and right; page 3 top). © The Art Archive (Section 1, page 2, top). © BBC Photo Sales (Section 1, page 2, middle). © Corbis (Section 1, page 3, top left and bottom right). © Getty Images (Section 1, page 1; page 2, bottom; page 3, top right, middle right, bottom left; page 4, top left, bottom left: Section 2, page 2, top right; page 6; page 7, top). © Mirrorpix (Section 2, pages 4-5). © Rex Features (Section 1, page 3, middle left; page 4, top right: Section 2, page 3 top). All picture research and design by Simon Goddard.

ART WORK:
David Wardle of Bold & Noble.

SOUL LOVE:
Sylvia Patterson.

TO BE READ AT MAXIMUM VOLUME.